QUICK ESCAPES™
NEW YORK CITY

Praise for previous editions of
Quick Escapes™ from New York City

"Thorough and well-designed . . . this level of detail will make *Quick Escapes [from New York]* a primary source—if not for ideas on destination, then certainly for solid tips on what to do once one gets there."
—*Small Press*

"Many imaginative itineraries for getting away from it all if you live in or are visiting New York City."
—*Booklist* (Chicago, IL)

Help Us Keep This Guide Up to Date

Every effort has been made by the author and editors to make this guide as accurate and useful as possible. However, many things can change after a guide is published—establishments close, phone numbers change, facilities come under new management, etc.

We would love to hear from you concerning your experiences with this guide and how you feel it could be improved and be kept up to date. Though we may not be able to respond to all comments and suggestions, we'll take them to heart, and we'll also make certain to share them with the author. Please send your comments and suggestions to the following address:

The Globe Pequot Press
Reader Response/Editorial Department
P.O. Box 833
Old Saybrook, CT 06475

Or you may e-mail us at:
editorial@globe-pequot.com

Thanks for your input, and happy travels!

QUICK ESCAPES™ SERIES

Quick Escapes™ New York City

Third Edition

31 WEEKEND TRIPS FROM THE BIG APPLE

BY

SUSAN FAREWELL

The Globe Pequot Press

OLD SAYBROOK, CONNECTICUT

Photo credits: Pp. 1, 5, 14, 21, 41, 58: New York State Department of Economic Development; p. 29: Carolyn Mendelker; p. 51: Mary Ellen Kretz; p. 75: Homestead Inn; p. 69: The Fire Island Lighthouse Preservation Society, Inc.; p. 86: Keeler Tavern Museum; pp. 96, 110, 119: Connecticut Economic Development; p. 103: Claire White-Peterson; pp. 71, 131, 178: Jim McElholm, Oxford, Mass.; p. 137: Rhode Island Tourism Division; pp. 143, 147, 167, 186, 197: Kindra Clineff, photos courtesy of Massachusetts Office of Travel & Tourism; p. 139: Rockport Chamber of Commerce; p. 201: Vermont Travel Division; p. 213: photo courtesy of The Captain Lord Mansion; pp. 237, 246: Pennsylvania Department of Commerce; pp. 219, 223: New Jersey Division of Travel and Tourism; p. 228: Mid-Atlantic Center for the Arts; p. 262: Virginia Tourism Corporation.

Cover photo: New England Stock Photo
Cover design by Laura Augustine
Interior design by Nancy Freeborn
Maps by Maryann Dubé

Quick Escapes is a trademark of The Globe Pequot Press.

Library of Congress Cataloging-in-Publication Data
Farewell, Susan.
    Quick escapes from New York City : 31 weekend trips from the Big Apple / by Susan Farewell.
    — 3rd ed.
        p.   cm. — (Quick escapes series)
    Includes index.
    ISBN 0-7627-0397-0
    1. New York Region—Guidebooks.   I. Title.   II. Series.
    F128.18.F25   1999
    917.47'20443—dc21   98-55461
                                                                            CIP

Manufactured in the United States of America
Third Edition/First Printing

For her unconditional love and supportive friendship,
I dedicate this book to my beautiful sister, Joanne.

CONTENTS

The information listed in this guide-
book was confirmed at press time.
We recommend, however, that you
call establishments before traveling to
obtain current information.

ACKNOWLEDGMENTS

I cannot just rattle off a half a dozen or so names of people who helped me with the research of this book. The list would go on and on for pages and include innkeepers, chefs, historians, curators, and tourism officials in all the states I covered. It would also include many of my colleagues and friends who are forever recommending places to visit and a large number of anonymous contributors whom I can only remember as "the blond boy on the bicycle in Nantucket" or the "couple on the ferry to Block Island."

There are several individuals who did, however, make this book actually happen. They include my editor, Laura Strom, who was unflaggingly patient with me, my many friends who accompanied me on trips or provided day-to-day support throughout the writing of it, and my parents, who kept asking, "Have you finished that book yet?"

INTRODUCTION

Have you ever gone away for the weekend without knowing precisely what places to visit (and the easiest way to get there), where to stay, and what to see and do once you have arrived? What should or could have been a little vacation can very often turn into a big disappointment. You find yourself saying things like "There must be some place we could just get a sandwich" or "Well, it cost only $5.00 to get in, not a major loss." Perhaps the most frequently uttered words of all, however, are "Next time." "Next time we'll stay at the inn on the water." "Next time we'll have brunch at that little restaurant in town." "Next time we'll leave enough time to hike to the summit." Unfortunately the "next time" may not happen very soon, if at all. It's hard enough finding the time to get away; the last thing you need is to have regrets.

It is precisely with those concerns in mind that I've compiled the thirty-one quick escapes that follow. They range in length from one to three nights and take you to some well-known and some hardly known destinations in New York State, New Jersey, Connecticut, Massachusetts, Rhode Island, Pennsylvania, Virginia, Washington, D.C., Vermont, and Maine. For those of you who aren't traveling by car, I've included four trips you can make by using public transportation. Keep in mind, however, that several of the Quick Escapes can be done without a car.

Whether you're an out-of-towner visiting the New York area, a newcomer, or a longtime resident, this guide will help you find the places I've been lucky to have discovered or have had pointed out to me over the years both as a child growing up in New York State (on the Connecticut border) and as a travel writer.

Each escape is designed to be a little vacation in itself, offering you a combination platter of things to do and taking in the area's most noteworthy attractions. The itineraries are meant to be used as guides only, so feel free to improvise as you go along. If you see a road that looks compelling, by all means, follow it. Making your own discoveries can be lots of fun. You won't be able to fit in everything I suggest, so choose the things that most appeal to you and, if you have more time, consider combining trips.

In most of the locales, I've suggested restaurants (or great picnic spots) for all meals during your stay. In most cases there are several other eating places worthy of inclusion, some of which are listed under **Other Recommended Restaurants and Lodgings** at the end of the itinerary. Nevertheless there are still others, and to list them all would probably double the length of this book. For a complete list of restaurants and accommodations, contact the tourist offices listed under **For More Information** at the end of each escape.

In the resort areas, be sure to make restaurant reservations. Otherwise, you can wait for hours. If it's a holiday weekend, reservations are a must.

I've avoided listing prices because they change so often and, in the case of hotels, can vary from season to season. The restaurants and accommodations I have included are generally moderately priced or on the splurgey side. My thinking was that you don't need this guide to locate the chain hotels and motels. The places I have selected generally are either full of character or otherwise special in some way, which, in many cases, translates into more money.

It's always a good idea to make lodging reservations as far in advance as possible, especially for shore destinations in summer and ski destinations in winter. Some inns are booked up a year in advance. Many of the island inns (and resort town inns) require a minimum two- or three-night stay for a summer weekend. For destinations all over the area, 99 percent of the time you'll be asked to give an advance deposit with your credit card or to send in a check to guarantee your room. Check-in time is generally between 2:00 and 3:00 in the afternoon; check-out is usually somewhere around noon.

Following each itinerary are lists of additional things to do in the area (from outlet shopping to horseback riding), special annual events, and contact numbers and addresses for more information.

To make your trip go as smoothly as possible, be prepared. Use the following as a checklist before setting out.

GETTING THE CAR READY

Start by making sure that all important car documents are up to date and tucked away in the glove compartment. Be sure to do the following:

- Make sure that all lights are working properly. Walk around the car while someone tests the turn signals, the brake lights, the backup lights, and the emergency flashers.

- Test the horn.
- Check the wiper blades. If they're starting to show signs of wear and tear, replace them.
- Make sure that there is enough windshield-washing solution.
- Inspect the tires for cuts, bulges, or bald patches. Make sure that they have the recommended pressure.
- Check the engine oil level while the engine is off and the vehicle is parked on level ground.
- If you haven't had your car serviced in a while, it's a good idea to do so before any long trip.

Other things to check or have checked:

- Engine-coolant level
- Brake-fluid level
- Power-steering-fluid level
- Automatic-transmission-fluid level
- Battery-electrolyte (water) level
- All belts and hoses

HANDY TAKE-ALONGS

Comfort on the road is important for you and your traveling companions. In addition to dressing comfortably, in loose-fitting layers, consider taking these items along:

- Plastic water bottle that can be refilled along the way and/or a supply of nonalcoholic liquids (in cans, plastic bottles, or a thermos)
- Snacks (preferably dry or nonjuicy fruits, crackers, raw veggies)
- Pillow and blanket for passenger(s)
- Sunglasses
- Reading material for passenger(s)
- Good map or atlas
- Umbrella
- Large box of tissues

- Pocket knife (with corkscrew)
- Camera (with film and extra batteries)
- Binoculars

For auto emergencies be sure to have these items:

- Coins for phone calls
- Flares or reflector triangles
- Jumper cables
- Empty gas can
- Fire extinguisher
- Blanket
- Flashlight (and extra batteries)
- First-aid kit

If you're traveling with children:

- Crayons and coloring books
- Storybooks
- Games (remember that small pieces get lost easily)
- Wipes to clean up messes and sticky hands

If you're traveling with pets:

- Water dish and water supply
- Dry snacks
- Favorite toys

If you're traveling in winter:

- Ice scraper
- Collapsible shovel
- Traction mats
- Sand

QUICK ESCAPES
NEW YORK CITY

SUGGESTED CLOTHING AND FOOTWEAR

What to pack for a trip outside New York City depends entirely on what time of year you go, since the weather varies so dramatically. Nevertheless, there are some items that may come in handy year-round. They include:

- A jacket and tie for men
- At least one dressy outfit for women
- Hiking boots
- A raincoat or poncho
- A robe (especially if you're staying at a bed and breakfast with the bathroom down the hall)
- A sweater (even in summer months)

And don't forget:

- Any prescriptions or medications
- A travel alarm

GETTING IN AND OUT OF THE CITY

Getting caught in rush-hour traffic going out of or coming into Manhattan can put a real damper on a weekend getaway. Do yourself a huge favor and rearrange work schedules or any other responsibilities so you avoid heavy traffic completely. During the warm-weather months (especially in the height of summer), traffic heading out to Long Island, to New Jersey, and to virtually all points north and east of the city, starts getting thick right around lunchtime on Friday afternoons. Same thing late Sunday afternoon returning to the city. Otherwise, the customary rush hours (roughly 7:00 to 10:00 A.M. and from 4:00 to 7:00 P.M.) should be avoided. Also, keep your eyes and ears open for events taking place. Something like the marathon or a presidential visit can keep you stalled in traffic for hours. A good radio station to tune into for these sorts of announcements is WINS (1010 on your AM dial).

As you venture out and discover places along the routes in this guide, feel free to send your findings to my attention at Globe Pequot.

Enjoy!

NEW YORK
ESCAPES

Hudson River Valley I

THE EAST BANK

1 NIGHT

*River estates • Historic houses • Rural countryside • Farms
Shaker Museum Antiques shops • FDR's Home
Culinary Institute of America*

As a major waterway, the Hudson River, which was first explored by Henry Hudson in 1609, is rich with history. Scattered along its banks there are historic riverfront towns and stately old mansions (built by the rich and famous) surrounded by thick woods and spectacular scenery.

You could easily make several trips to the Hudson Valley region and not retrace your steps. For this particular escape we take you north and east of the river through several rural towns and hamlets and then follow the river down along its eastern banks through some of the area's most historically interesting towns. This trip can be combined with the Hudson River Valley II and/or Hudson River Valley III escapes, which follow.

DAY 1

Morning

From Manhattan take the Henry Hudson Parkway north to the Saw Mill River Parkway to the Taconic State Parkway. At Route 44 turn east toward **Millbrook.** Home to many farms, Millbrook and the surrounding hamlets are well known among the horsey set. There are several worthwhile attractions in the Millbrook area including **Wing's Castle** (on Bangall Road, off Route 44;

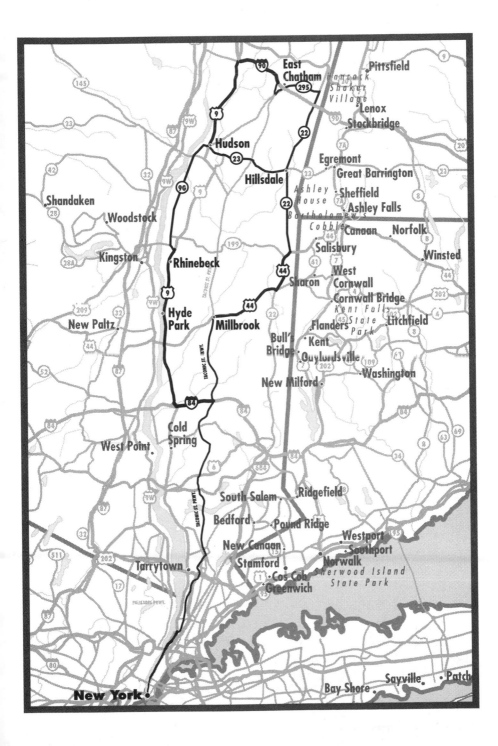

914–677–9085), built by artists Peter and Toni Wing. The castle, which is made from salvaged materials from antique buildings, took them more than twenty-five years to complete. Open May 30 through Christmas, Wednesday through Sunday, 10:00 A.M. to 5:00 P.M. The **Institute of Ecosystem Studies Mary Flagler Cary Arboretum** (on the northern side of Route 44A, 1 mile from the junction with Route 44 to the west and 2 miles from the junction with Route 44 to the east; 914–677–5359) is an ecological research and education center with nature trails, a perennial garden, a fern glen, a greenhouse, and a gift and plant shop. When you reach Route 22 at Millerton, take a left and head north. You'll soon reach **Taconic State Park** and **Copake Falls.** Follow the signs to **Bash Bish Falls** if you want to do a little hiking in an entrancingly beautiful valley that has 50-foot falls as its centerpiece. From the parking lot it's about a mile-long walk.

Afterward return to Route 22 and head north for a couple of miles until you reach Route 23. Turn right and follow signs for the Catamount Ski Area, where you can pause to have lunch.

LUNCH: The **Swiss Hutte,** adjacent to the ski area (518–325–3333), is a good lunch choice. It has everything from chef salad and burgers to filet of sole plus a pretty view of Catamount Mountain.

Afternoon

Continue north on Route 22 to Route 295 and turn left. Follow Route 295 for about 6 miles into East Chatham. Then go right on the Albany Turnpike for about 3 miles to **Old Chatham.** In Old Chatham turn left onto County Route 13 and follow that for about a mile. On the right you'll see the **Shaker Museum,** 149 Shaker Museum Road (518–794–9100), which showcases an unparalleled collection of Shaker furnishings in several farm buildings. Bear in mind that it is closed over the winter months (open from May through late October).

From Old Chatham it's a short drive to **Kinderhook** (follow 9H South), where you'll find three historic houses open to the public. The **James Vanderpoel House,** on Route US 9 (locally known as Broad Street) in the village of Kinderhook (518–758–9265), is a Federal period house that was built around 1820. The **Luykas Van Alen House,** south of town on Route 9H (518–758–9265), was built in 1737 and is now a museum of eighteenth-century Dutch domestic culture. Both are maintained by the Columbia County Historical Society and are open Wednesday through Sunday, from

Lindenwald, Martin Van Buren's retirement home, is open for touring.

Memorial Day to Labor Day. A ticket bought at one house is good for visits to both of them.

Drive south another mile or so and you'll reach **Lindenwald,** which is also known as the **Martin Van Buren National Historic Site,** about 2 miles south of Kinderhook on Route 9H (518–758–9689). This was the retirement home of America's eighth president. The mansion and grounds are open for touring from May to October.

From Lindenwald continue south on Route 9H and then head east on Route 23 to Hillsdale, where you can settle in for the night and a memorable meal.

DINNER: Aubergine, at the junction of Routes 22 and 23, Hillsdale (518–325–3412), has a French-inspired menu with lots of contemporary accents. One of chef-owner David Lawson's signature dishes is Seared Maine Scallop Cakes with sauteed vegetables and a ponzu vinaigrette.

LODGING: You can stay in one of four guestrooms at Aubergine, which is run by Stacy Lawson, wife of the chef at Aubergine's restaurant. Each room is decorated in a French Country style and has its own bathroom.

DAY 2

Morning

BREAKFAST: Croissants, fruit, orange juice, and coffee are served at the inn.

Head west on Route 23 to the former whaling town of **Hudson.** Here you'll find several antiques shops as well as a fine collection of beautifully restored Federal, Greek Revival, and Victorian houses that were built in the eighteenth century. Detailed walking-tour maps are available in most of the shops. There's a firefighting museum in town, the **American Museum of Fire Fighting,** Harry Howard Avenue (518–828–7695), which is filled with antique firefighting equipment including a 1725 fire engine. The museum is open daily year-round.

Head south of town on NY 9G and you'll come to **Olana State Historic Site,** about 5 miles south of Hudson on Route 9G (518–828–0135). This was the home of the nineteenth-century landscape artist Frederic Edwin Church. He built Olana, a five-story Persian-style villa atop a bluff overlooking the Hudson, in the 1870s. There are forty-five-minute tours of the first floor.

Continue south on Route 9G to **Clermont State Historic Site/ Museum** (518–537–4240). Clermont was the home of Robert R. Livingston (and seven generations of his family), one of five men elected to draft the Declaration of Independence. He also was Chancellor of New York and administered the oath of office to George Washington. The house is open for touring May through October, Wednesday through Sunday; the grounds are open year-round for hiking, riding, cross-country skiing, and picnicking.

A little farther south is **Rhinebeck,** which has a museum devoted to vintage aeroplanes, WWI aircraft, and other early craft. The **Old Rhinebeck Aerodrome,** off Route 9 on Stone Church Road (914–758–8610), is open from May 15 to October 31, daily, from 10:00 A.M. to 5:00 P.M. Air shows are on Saturdays and Sundays from mid-June through mid-October.

LUNCH: The Beekman 1766 Tavern at the Beekman Arms hotel, 4 Mill Street, at the junctions of Routes 9 and 308 (914–871–1766), owned by Larry Forgione (of American Place), serves American and continental cuisine prepared by chef Tony Nogales. The hotel itself is said to be the oldest operating hotel in the United States (circa 1700).

Afternoon

After lunch spend a little time checking out the shops in Rhinebeck and then head south again on Route 9. In Staatsburg (between Rhinebeck and Hyde Park), take time out to see **Mills Mansion,** in Mills-Norrie State Park, off Route 9 (914–889–4100). The Beaux Arts estate of Ogden and Ruth Livingston Mills is set on 900 acres. There are hiking trails, guided tours, and beautiful river views. It's open Wednesday through Saturday from 10:00 A.M. to 5:00 P.M. Just before you reach Hyde Park, you'll come to **The Vanderbilt Mansion** (914–229–9115). This fifty-four-room Beaux Arts mansion was designed by McKim, Mead & White for Frederick Vanderbilt. After a tour of the house, be sure to wander around the grounds. The view of the Hudson from here is nonpareil. The house is open 9:00 A.M. to 5:00 P.M. daily from May through October and Thursday through Monday from November through April.

Hyde Park, which is well known as the site of FDR's home, is next on the itinerary. You could easily spend an entire day (or more) here, especially if you're a history buff. Start with the **Home of Franklin D. Roosevelt National Historic Site,** 1 mile south of town on US 9 (914 229 8114). This estate, known as Springwood, was the president's birthplace and lifelong residence. It's open daily 9:00 A.M. to 5:00 P.M. May through October and Thursday through Monday from November through March. Adjacent is the **FDR Museum and Library,** which is filled with memorabilia, letters, documents, and photographs. It's open daily. Two miles east of the estate is the **Eleanor Roosevelt National Historic Site,** which is open daily May through October and on weekends only in March, April, November, and December. For information on all three places, call the number listed above.

Once you've had your fill of presidential history, you can complete your journey with a wonderful meal at The Culinary Institute of America.

DINNER: The Culinary Institute of America, Route 9, Hyde Park (914–471–6608). Be sure to call ahead for reservations at this highly esteemed cooking school. There are four student-staffed restaurants on the 150-acre campus: St. Andrew's Cafe offers contemporary dishes, the Caterina de Medici

Dining Room features regional Italian cuisine, the Escoffier Restaurant serves French cuisine, and the American Bounty Restaurant specializes in American food.

It's about a ninety-minute trip back to New York City from here. Take Route 9 south to 84 east and then pick up the Taconic heading south.

THERE'S MORE

Hiking. Poet's Walk, County Road 103, north of the Rhinecliff-Kingston Bridge, Red Hook; (914) 473–4440. A 120-acre park with trails for hiking and benches scattered about.

Historic Houses. Montgomery Place, River Road, Annandale-on-Hudson; (914) 758–5461. This nineteenth-century estate is set on hundreds of acres overlooking the Hudson River and the Catskill Mountains. There are gardens, a greenhouse, nature trails, and pick-your-own-fruit orchards.

Shopping. Hammertown Barn, Route 199, Pine Plains; (518) 398–7075. Here you'll find nineteenth-century English and American antiques, quilts, woven wool Navajo blankets, birdhouses, handcrafted jewelry, and much more. The barn is 1 mile east of the village of Pine Plains, which is north of Millbrook.

Theater. The Mac-Haydn Theater, Chatham; (518) 392–9292. An excellent summer stock theater.

Vineyards. The Cascade Mountain Winery, Flint Hill Road, Amenia; (914) 373–9021. Tours and tastings offered. There's also a cafe and picnic area. Open year-round, daily, from 10:00 A.M. to 6:00 P.M.

Millbrook Vineyards, Wing Road and Shunpike Road, Millbrook; (914) 677–8383. Tours and tastings. Open year-round, daily, from noon to 5:00 P.M.

SPECIAL EVENTS

May. Rhinebeck Antiques Fair. Held at the Dutchess County Fairgrounds; (914) 758–6186.

June. Crafts at Rhinebeck. A juried show of more than 350 exhibitors. Held at the Dutchess County Fairgrounds; (914) 876–4001.

August. Annual Shaker Museum Antiques Festival, The Shaker Museum, Old Chatham; (518) 794–9100. More than one hundred dealers.

September. Annual Radio Control Jamboree. An air show and other aerial events at the Old Rhinebeck Aerodrome; (914) 229–2371.

October. Crafts at Rhinebeck Fall Festival. More than 200 exhibitors plus harvest-related activities. At the Dutchess County Fairgrounds; (914) 876–4001.

Rhinebeck Antiques Fair. Dealers from all over New England show furniture, folk art, paintings, etc. At the Dutchess County Fairgrounds; (914) 758–6186.

OTHER RECOMMENDED RESTAURANTS AND LODGINGS

Amenia

Cascade Mountain Winery and Restaurant, Flint Hill Road; (914) 373–9021. On weekends only you can get a wonderful Sunday brunch made with ultrafresh ingredients at this winery.

Troutbeck, Leedsville Road; (914) 373–9681. This Twenties-era stone manor house on a Dutchess County estate has a split personality. During the week it's an executive retreat for conferences, and on weekends, it's a romantic country inn. Troutbeck is exquisitely furnished with antiques throughout. Its dining room is a great find, serving contemporary American cuisine.

Old Chatham

The Old Chatham Sheepherding Company Inn, 99 Shaker Museum Road; (518) 794–9774. This is a lovely small inn, with a total of nine rooms in a main house and cottage.

Dover Plains

Old Drovers Inn, Old Post Road (Route 22 near Millbrook); (914) 832–9311. This old inn (it's been welcoming visitors for more than 250 years!) is a member of the elite Relais and Châteaux hotel group. It's full of old-fashioned charm and has a respectable restaurant specializing in innovative American cuisine. There are only four guestrooms, so be sure to make reservations in advance.

Rhinebeck

Foster's Coach House, 9193 Montgomery Street (Route 9); (914) 876–8052. If you're in the mood for a burger, a sandwich, or something else simple and American, you can't go wrong with Foster's.

FOR MORE INFORMATION

Historic Hudson Valley, 150 White Plains Road, Tarrytown, NY 10591; (914) 631–8200, extension 99.

Hudson Valley Tourism, P.O. Box 2840, Salt Point, NY 12578; (800) 232–4782.

Columbia County Tourism, 401 State Street, Hudson, NY 12534; (518) 828–3375.

Dutchess County Tourism Promotion Agency, 532 Albany Post Road, Hyde Park, NY 12538; (914) 229–0033 or (800) 445–3131.

New York Department of Economic Development, Division of Tourism, One Commerce Plaza, Albany, NY 12245; (518) 474–4116 or (800) CALL–NYS.

NEW YORK

Hudson River Valley II

THE LOWER HUDSON

1 NIGHT

Riverside towns and scenery • Woodlands • Hiking
Restaurants • Antiques and crafts shops • Historic houses
Museums • United States Military Academy

Both the east and west banks of the Lower Hudson are liberally sprinkled with historic, contemporary, and natural attractions. To take in the highlights of the area, we suggest driving up the eastern shore, crossing over on I–84, and then returning on the western banks. This trip can be combined with Hudson River Valley I escape and/or Hudson River Valley II escape.

DAY 1

Morning

Head north out of New York on the Henry Hudson Parkway to the Saw Mill River Parkway. Then jog over to US 9 in Hastings, an exit off the Saw Mill River Parkway. Route 9 roughly follows the Hudson shoreline, taking you through a string of historic towns and attractions.

Make your first destination **Tarrytown,** a riverside town that was settled by the Dutch in the mid-1600s and later made famous by the writings of Washington Irving, particularly "The Legend of Sleepy Hollow." There are several noteworthy attractions in the area including **Lyndhurst,** 635 South Broadway (914–631–4481), a Gothic Revival estate that was the former home of financier Jay Gould. It's open for touring Tuesday through Sunday, 10:00

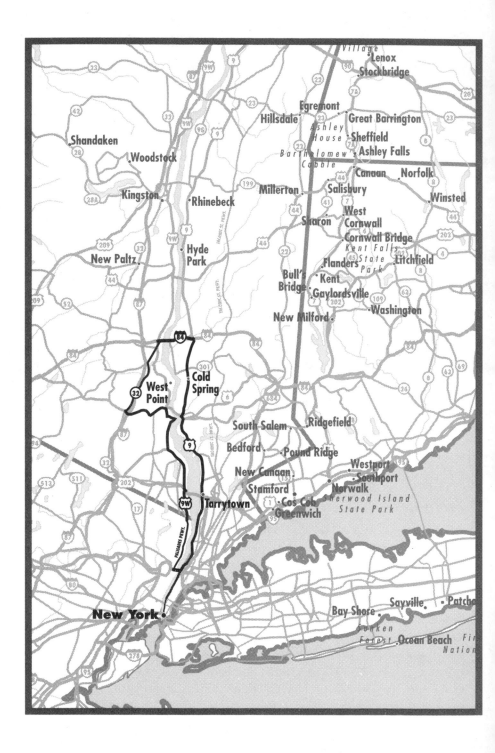

A.M. to 5:00 P.M. between May and October and on weekends only from November through April. You can visit Irving's Hudson River estate **Sunnyside,** on West Sunnyside Lane (914–631–8200), which is open daily between March and December. This estate, along with several of the other properties that follow, is under the care of Historic Hudson Valley, a nonprofit organization, which will gladly provide you with more information (see address and telephone number under "For More Information"). In nearby North Tarrytown you'll find **Philipsburg Manor,** on US 9 (914–631–8200), a beautifully restored seventeenth-century manor house with a mill and mill pond. It's also open daily between March and December. Also in North Tarrytown is **Kykuit,** a Rockefeller estate (914–631–8200), which has been opened for public viewing. It's a forty-room Colonial Revival mansion, on eighty-seven lush acres, dotted with sculpture by modern masters including Alexander Calder, Henry Moore, and Lois Nevelson. It's pronounced "kye-kit." Nearby you'll find **Union Church of Pocantico Hills,** with stained-glass windows by Marc Chagall and Henri Matisse. It was commissioned by members of the Rockefeller family.

Continue up Route 9 to **Van Cortlandt Manor,** in Croton-on-Hudson (914–631–8200), which is a restored baronial manor offering insight into the life of a wealthy family in the early 1800s.

From there carry on to **Garrison,** which is home to **Boscobel,** 4 miles north of Garrison on NY 9D (914–265–3638), an early eighteenth-century country home open for touring. It's an acclaimed example of Federal architecture. There are guided tours indoors and gardened grounds outside overlooking the Hudson River.

Just to the north is the village of **Cold Spring,** where you can settle in for a wonderful lunch, a relaxing afternoon, and the night. The town is filled with historic nineteenth-century buildings.

LUNCH: Plumbush Inn, Route 9D (914–265–3904), is a beautiful Victorian restaurant on five woodland acres. Lunch is a bit of a splurge, but worth it. The cuisine is largely continental. Open Wednesday through Sunday.

Afternoon

Spend the afternoon poking around the many antiques and crafts shops in Cold Spring and check out the **Foundry School Museum,** 63 Chestnut Street (914–265–4010), which displays Hudson River School paintings. The museum is open March through December, Tuesday and Wednesday from

Views of the Hudson River from Bear Mountain are sensational.

10:00 A.M. to 4:00 P.M., Thursday from 1:00 to 4:00 P.M., and on Sundays from 2:00 to 5:00 P.M.

DINNER: Bird & Bottle Inn, Old Albany Road, Garrison (914–424–3000), serves traditional American and continental dishes in a tavern that dates back to 1761.

LODGING: Hudson House, 23 Main Street, Cold Spring (914–265–9355), is an attractive fifteen-room country inn on the banks of the Hudson River.

DAY 2

Morning

BREAKFAST: On Saturday and Sunday mornings, a full breakfast is included in the room price at Hudson House. During the week a continental breakfast is served.

After breakfast drive north via Route 301 from Cold Spring to Route 9 north and then take I-84 west over the river and head into **Newburgh** to see **Washington's Headquarters,** Liberty and Washington streets (914–562–1195). From here Washington commanded his troops from 1781 to 1782. The headquarters are open between April and October, Wednesdays through Saturdays from 10:00 A.M. to 5:00 P.M., and on Sundays from 1:00 to 5:00 P.M.

From Newburgh head south on Route 32 about 7 miles or so until you see a sign for the **Storm King Art Center,** One Pleasant Hill Road, Mountainville (914–534–3190). Plan to spend several hours here: Storm King is the leading outdoor sculpture park and museum in the United States. It sprawls over 400 acres of lawns, terraces, fields, and woods. Visiting hours are from 11:00 A.M. to 5:30 P.M. daily from April 1 through November 15.

LUNCH: On weekends from May through October, you can buy light luncheon fare in the Storm King picnic area.

Afternoon

After lunch continue south to **West Point,** home to the **United States Military Academy.** Founded in 1802, this spectacularly situated academy (it crowns a bluff high above the Hudson) has turned out many prominent leaders including Robert E. Lee, Ulysses S. Grant, and George S. Patton. The best time to visit is during spring or fall when the cadets parade or a sporting event takes place. There's a museum devoted to military history. Visiting hours are from 9:00 A.M. to 4:45 P.M. For special events (sports and parade information), contact the Public Affairs Office, Building 600, USMA, West Point, NY 10996; (914) 938–3614. For general information call (914) 938–2638.

From West Point take Route 9W South and get off at the Haverstraw exit to reach **Bear Mountain Park** (914–786–2701), a 5,067-acre park that extends westward from the Hudson. Here you'll find an excellent **Trailside Museum,** which consists of several small museums including a reptile museum, a nature-study museum, a geology museum, and a history museum. There are also hiking trails, picnic areas, a mountain-top observatory, and a breathtakingly beautiful drive up the mountain—called **Perkins Memorial Drive.**

Once you've feasted on the serenity of the park, you can head back into Manhattan (which is a mere 45 miles away), taking the dramatically scenic Palisades Parkway south to the George Washington Bridge.

ESCAPE TWO
NEW YORK

THERE'S MORE

Hiking. Hudson Highland State Park, just north of Cold Spring, has lots of trails to wander along, as does the Manitoga Nature Preserve, south of Garrison. In nearby Carmel the Appalachian Trail cuts right through Clarence Fahnestock State Park.

Fahnestock State Park is off the Taconic State Parkway on Route 301 in Cold Spring. Extra challenging is Breakneck Ridge, a hike just north of Cold Spring. The first half mile is straight up (though it's not really rock climbing, you do have to use your hands sometimes to hold onto rocks), but it's well worth it. The views—up and down the Hudson and inland a bit—are astonishingly beautiful. If you have time (you'll need a total of two or three hours), do the entire loop trip. You'll sleep well afterward. Also check out Croton Point Park, off Route 9 in Croton-on-Hudson.

Horse racing. Yonkers Raceway, Yonkers Avenue and Central Avenue in Yonkers, on I–87, between exits 2 and 4 (914) 968–4200. Harness racing.

Hudson River Cruises. River Valley Tours, Inc., P.O. Box 743, New Paltz, NY 12561; (914) 255–1955. One way to explore the historic Hudson Valley region is by car. Another way is on a sleep-aboard cruise. For information on scheduled cruises, call or write.

Hudson River History. The Hudson River Museum of Westchester, 511 Warburton Avenue in nearby Yonkers; (914) 963–4550. This museum includes Glenview Mansion, a Hudson River house overlooking the Palisades; a planetarium; and regional art, history, and science exhibits.

SPECIAL EVENTS

Early October. Autumn Crafts & Tasks Festival, Van Cortlandt Manor, Croton. Demonstrations of house and farm labor in the 1700s.

October. Annual Arts and Crafts Festival, Bear Mountain State Park. A juried indoor and outdoor show.

December. Candlelight Tours at Sunnyside, Philipsburg Manor, and Van Cortlandt Manor. English Christmas celebration.

OTHER RECOMMENDED RESTAURANTS AND LODGINGS

Bear Mountain

Old Bear Mountain Inn, Bear Mountain State Park; (914) 786–2731. Though a magnet for tourists, this rustic, sixty-room hunting lodge has its charms. You can stay overnight or grab a simple meal.

Stormville

Harrald's, Route 52; (914) 878–6595. This restaurant is northeast of Cold Spring (about 5½ miles east of the Taconic Parkway), but well worth the detour. It's well known and respected for its game dishes.

FOR MORE INFORMATION

Hudson Valley Tourism, P.O. Box 2840, Salt Point, NY 12578, (800) 232–4782.

Historic Hudson Valley, 150 White Plains Road, Tarrytown, NY 10591; (914) 631–8200, extension 99.

Westchester Convention & Visitors Bureau, Ltd., 222 Mamaroneck Avenue, Suite 210, White Plains, NY 10605; (914) 948–0047 or (800) 833–WCVB.

Orange County Tourism, 20 Matthews Street, Suite III, Goshen, NY 10924; (914) 294–5151, extension 1647, or (800) 762–8687.

Putnam County Chamber of Commerce, P.O. Box 597, Carmel, NY 10512; (914) 225–7134.

New York Department of Economic Development, Division of Tourism, One Commerce Plaza, Albany, NY 12245; (518) 474–4116 or (800) CALL–NYS.

Hudson River Valley III
THE WEST BANK

2 NIGHTS

Mountain scenery • Wineries • Hiking • Horseback riding
Sports resorts • Skiing (downhill and cross-country)
International cuisines • Antiques shops

Back in 1820 author and historian Washington Irving wrote the tale of "Rip Van Winkle," in which Rip joins a party of gnomes in the Catskill Mountains and falls asleep for twenty years. These modest but magical mountains, which can have a calming effect on anyone who visits them, can be reached in less than two hours from Manhattan.

Though the real magnet of the area is **Catskill Park,** which covers 705,500 acres, there are several river towns just to the east and south that are not only gateways to the park but are attractions in themselves.

For this trip we suggest you start just south of the park, exploring the countryside around New Paltz, then head north to Kingston, which, back in 1777, was New York State's first capital. From there we take you into the Catskill Forest, to Shandaken in the mountains and Woodstock, which is the Catskills' most famous town.

DAY 1

Morning

Take the Henry Hudson Parkway up to the George Washington Bridge and cross over to the Palisades Interstate Parkway. Take that to the New York State Thruway north up to exit 18, which is **New Paltz.**

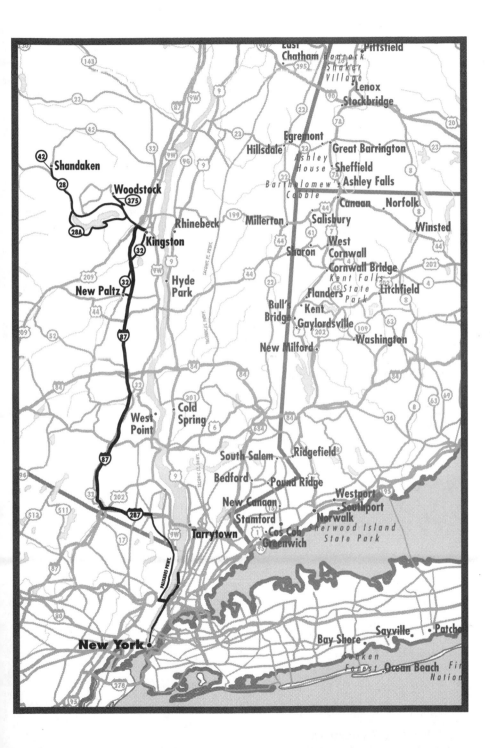

Head right for the Mohonk Mountain House, your home for the night, where you'll have a chance to wander about its wooded trails and feast your eyes on the lake for which the resort is named (*mohonk* means "lake in the sky"). For the best view of all, climb the cliff-top observation tower.

LUNCH: Mohonk Mountain House, Mountain Rest Road, New Paltz (914–255–1000), has a hot and cold buffet for lunch.

Afternoon

Spend the afternoon visiting the wineries and other attractions along the **Shawangunk Wine Trail,** a 30-mile loop (well marked with signs) that includes five Ulster County wineries. Bear in mind that you could make an entire day out of this, so the sooner you head out after lunch, the better. The wineries included are: **Adair Vineyards,** 75 Allhusen Road, New Paltz (914–255–1377); **Rivendell Winery,** 714 Albany Post Road, New Paltz (914–255–0892); **Brimstone Hill Vineyards,** 49 Brimstone Hill Road, Pine Bush (914–744–2231); **Baldwin Vineyards,** 110 Hardenburgh Road, Pine Bush (914–744–2226); and **Walker Valley Vineyards,** Route 52, Walker Valley (914–744–3449). Visiting hours vary from vineyard to vineyard, but generally the vineyards are open during summer months until 5:00 P.M.

DINNER: Mohonk Mountain House, Mountain Rest Road, New Paltz (914–255–1000 or 800–772–6646 from 212, 516, and 718 area codes). Dinners in the dining room are usually traditional American dishes, though there are often other choices featured as daily specials.

LODGING: Mohonk Mountain House, Mountain Rest Road, New Paltz (914–255–1000), is a big old-fashioned country hotel surrounded by the arrestingly beautiful scenery of the Shawangunk Mountains (right next to the Catskill Mountains). There's golf, tennis, hiking, and horseback riding—you name it.

DAY 2

Morning

BREAKFAST: Start the day with a big traditional American breakfast at Mohonk House.

After breakfast head into town to see **Huguenot Street,** which is the oldest street in America where original buildings still stand. New Paltz was

Ulster County is home to several wineries open for tours and tastings.

founded back in 1678 by half a dozen Huguenots who were granted land by the Colonial governor of New York. Huguenot Street is lined with six stone houses and a church, which were built between 1692 and 1799. All are open to the public from Memorial Day through Labor Day, Wednesday through Sunday from 10:00 A.M. to 4:00 P.M. or by appointment.

From New Paltz head north on Route 32 toward **Kingston.** Along the way consider stopping in at **Apple Hill Farm,** 141 Route 32 South, New Paltz (914–255–0917), where you can pick your own apples and pumpkins during the fall season.

Kingston is an old river port that was founded in 1652 as a Dutch trading settlement and became New York State's first capital in 1777. Many of its early buildings still stand today and are open to the public including the **Old Dutch Church,** 272 Wall Street (914–338–6759), and the **Senate House,** 312 Fair Street (914–338–2786). All tour sites are either in or adjacent to the historic district, which is known as the Stockade because of the walls that used to surround it. Other Kingston attractions include the **Hudson River Maritime Museum and Rondout Lighthouse,** One Rondout Landing (914–338–0071), which is devoted to the maritime history of the area (daily May 1 through October 31 from 11:00 A.M. to 5:00 P.M.) and the **Trolley Museum,** 89 East Strand (914–331–3399), which showcases old trolley cars. The Trolley Museum is open between Memorial Day and July 4th on weekends only and in July and August on Monday, and Thursday through Sunday from noon to 5:00 P.M. Also worthwhile is the **Senate House State Historic Site,** 296 Fair Street (914–338–2786), and the **Volunteer Firemen's Hall and Museum of Kingston,** 265 Fair Street (914–331–0866).

LUNCH: Schneller's, 61 John Street (914–331–9800), is a great choice for lunch while strolling through historic Kingston. It's an old German tavern offering homemade schnitzels and wursts. There's also a beer garden.

Afternoon

Once you've had a look around Kingston, head west on Route 28 (this route takes you right into the **Catskill Forest Preserve,** which is a large part of the Catskills under the protection of the government), then turn north on Route 42 to reach **Shandaken,** a township that includes several mountain hamlets and is home to **Slide Mountain,** the highest peak in the Catskills.

DINNER: This part of the Catskills has several fine eateries featuring French cuisine and, in fact, is known as "the French Catskills." One of the best is **Auberge des 4 Saisons**, ½ mile north of Shandaken on NY 42 (914–688–2223), which specializes in duck.

LODGING: You can also stay at the **Auberge des 4 Saisons,** NY 42 (914–688–2223), in a simple lodge room with a jaw-droppingly-beautiful mountain view.

DAY 3

Morning

BREAKFAST: Breakfast is included in the room rate at Auberge des 4 Saisons.

After breakfast head back onto Route 28, detouring on Route 28A for some more beautiful scenery around the 12-mile-long Asholkan reservoir, and then follow Route 375 into **Woodstock,** where the famed rock concert took place in 1969. Here you can spend hours browsing through shops and galleries before heading back to New York City. Don't miss the **Woodstock Artists Association Gallery,** 28 Tinker Street at Village Green (914–679–2940). It has been the center of the community since 1920, featuring works by both local and nationally known artists.

LUNCH: Joshua's, 51 Tinker Street, Woodstock (914–679–5533), is right in town and offers a good selection of sandwiches and vegetarian dishes, plus some Middle Eastern dishes as well.

From Woodstock it's a short drive east to Route 87, which you take south back to the New York metropolitan area.

THERE'S MORE

Biking. Mountain bikes can be rented at Catskill Mountain Bicycle Shop on North Front Street, New Paltz (914–255–3859); at Overlook Mountain Bikes, 107 Tinker Street, Woodstock (914–679–2122); and at Woodstock Bicycle Shop, 9 Rock City Road, Woodstock (914–679–8388).

Bird-watching. Slide Mountain is an especially good place for bird-watching. Among its many inhabitants are wild turkeys, ruffed grouse, pileated woodpeckers, yellow-bellied sapsuckers, and several different warblers and thrushes.

Game farm. The Catskill Game Farm, off Route 32, near Catskill (518) 678–9595. This game farm is in the neighborhood where Rip Van Winkle is said to have slept. Kids can feed tame deer, llamas, and other animals.

Golf. Mohonk Mountain House in New Paltz (914–255–1000) and Green Acres in Kingston (914–331–7807).

Hudson River boat tours. In Kingston several boat companies offer river trips. Among them are Hudson River Cruises (914–255–6515), which has music and dinner cruises, North River Cruises (914–679–8205), and the Great Hudson Sailing Center (800–237–1557 or 914–429–1557), which offers sailing trips.

Parks and Preserves. Cohotate Preserve, Greene County Environmental Education Center, Route 385, north of the Rip Van Winkle Bridge, near Athens; (518) 622–3620.

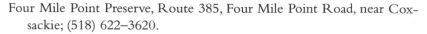

Four Mile Point Preserve, Route 385, Four Mile Point Road, near Coxsackie; (518) 622–3620.

Ramshorn-Livington Sanctuary, off Route 9W, Grandview Avenue, Catskill; (519) 943–6895 or (914) 473–4400. A tidal swamp with more than 480 acres operated by the North Catskills Audubon Society.

Skiing. For downhill and cross-country skiing, there's Belleayre Mountain Ski Center, Highmount (914–254–5600); for cross-country only, Lake Mohonk in New Paltz (914–255–1000).

SPECIAL EVENTS

August. Ulster County Fair, an annual event at the Fairgrounds, 2 miles southwest of New Paltz on Libertyville Road.

September. Hudson Valley Food Festival, uptown Kingston, Wall Street area. Includes music, tastings, and demonstrations.

Hudson Valley Garlic Festival, Cantine Field (exit 20 off the Governor Thomas E. Dewey Thruway), Saugerties. Food, cooking demonstrations, lectures, crafts, and entertainment.

Harvest Moon Festival at the Hudson River Maritime Museum, Rondout Landing, Kingston. Seasonal foods, music, exhibits.

OTHER RECOMMENDED RESTAURANTS AND LODGINGS

High Falls

Depuy Canal House, Route 213, High Falls (914) 687–7700. This very special restaurant is in a landmark historic stone building that used to be a tavern (back in 1797). The menu—some seafood, some meat dishes—changes frequently.

Highland

Rocking Horse Ranch Resort, Highland, NY 12528; (914) 691–2927. A great choice for families, this resort is a dude ranch complete with horseback riding, all-you-can-eat chuck-wagon cuisine, and a whole "alphabet of activities."

New Paltz

Locust Tree Inn, 215 Huguenot Street; (914) 255–7888. An attractive restaurant serving chicken, lamb, and fish dishes. It overlooks a golf course.

FOR MORE INFORMATION

Ulster County Public Information, P.O. Box 1800, Kingston, NY 12401; (914) 331–9300 or (800) DIAL–UCO.

New Paltz Chamber of Commerce, 257½ Main Street, New Paltz, NY 12561; (914) 255–0243.

Woodstock Chamber of Commerce, Box 36, Woodstock, NY 12498; (914) 679–6234.

New York Department of Economic Development, Division of Tourism, One Commerce Plaza, Albany, NY 12245; (518) 474 4116 or (800) CALL–NYS.

Northern Westchester County

HORSE COUNTRY

---

2 NIGHTS

Horse farms • Colonial houses • Hiking
Rural countryside • Antiques shops • Fine dining
Galleries and museums • Concerts

If you thought you had to drive for five or six (well, at least three) hours to get to someplace that's very New England, you'll be pleasantly surprised to discover this little chunk of the world.

Just a little over an hour's drive from Manhattan, there are at least half a dozen little towns or hamlets (including Bedford, Katonah, North and South Salem, and Pound Ridge) that could easily pass for New England. They're small, they're home to antiques shops, galleries, and little bistros selling fragrant soups on chilly days, and they're surrounded by woods and streams and lakes that really do sparkle. Drive down Main Street in South Salem on an autumn day, and yes, you will think you took a wrong turn somewhere and ended up in New Hampshire.

This little corner of southeastern New York, right on the border of Connecticut, is not only scenic but also is culturally very active. There are several museums and galleries, music festivals, and some restaurants that, on their own, warrant a trip to the area. On top of that, however, there are some diversions you can find only in rural areas including pick-your-own orchards, horse shows at sprawling farms, and hundreds of acres of woodland preserved for public use.

Unfortunately, there are really no places to stay, aside from a Holiday Inn in nearby Mt. Kisco. Nevertheless, Ridgefield, Connecticut, which is home to

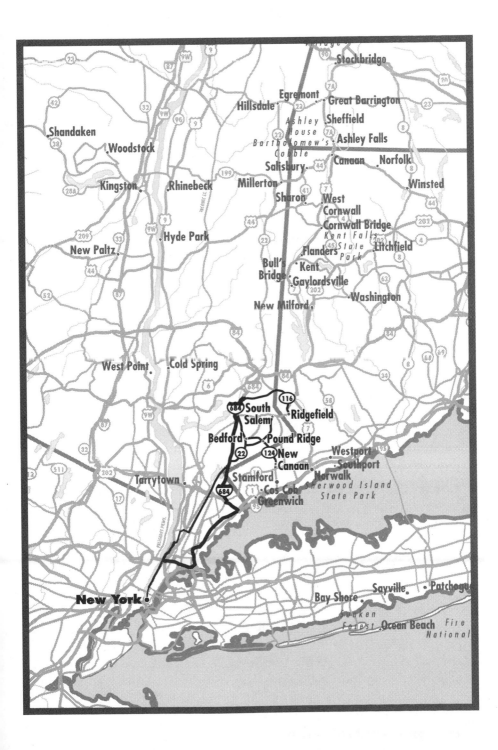

a couple of country inns, is just over the border from both North and South Salem, and New Canaan, Connecticut, is just beyond Pound Ridge, New York. You can very easily combine this trip with our Ridgefield and New Canaan escape (see page 84).

DAY 1

Morning

To reach the area head north on either I–684 or the Saw Mill River Parkway. Both will get you to the Bedford/Katonah exits in just about an hour's time. In fact the Saw Mill River Parkway merges with I–684, where you should exit (exit 6, Katonah/Cross River). Turn right onto Route 35, take it to the first stoplight, and then turn right onto Route 22. About half a mile or so up on the left, you'll see the signs for the **Katonah Museum of Art,** Route 22 East at Jay Street (914–232–9555), your first stop of the day.

Firmly ensconced in local history, this museum, which originally occupied a small room in the Katonah Village Library, showcases between eight and ten exhibitions a year from a variety of periods, cultures, and mediums, many of which have received national recognition. There's also a sculpture garden. Open Tuesday through Sunday from 1:00 to 5:00 P.M. and on Saturdays from 10:00 A.M. to 5:00 P.M.

Right across from the museum, you'll see Jay Street, which takes you right into the town of Katonah, where you can pause for lunch and a look around some artsy shops.

LUNCH: The Baker's Cafe, 17 Katonah Avenue (914–232–8030), is a busy little bistro always packed with locals. The food is on the healthful side (sprouts and such), and the breads and desserts are baked on the premises. There are tables outside for eating *alfresco* when the weather's good.

Afternoon

From town retrace your steps on Jay Street back to Route 22, where you'll turn right. Follow Route 22 for a little more than a mile and you'll see the **John Jay Homestead State Historic Site,** Route 22 (914–232–5651), on the left. This large farmhouse, built in 1787, housed the Jay family up until about forty years ago. Costumed hostesses take visitors around, pointing out the furnishings that belonged to John Jay and the family generations that

Northern Westchester County's Caramoor Center for Music and the Arts

followed. Hours and dates the house are open change through the year, so it's best to call ahead. If you're visiting during the year-end holidays, there are scheduled holiday house tours and marionette shows for both children and adults.

Just beyond the homestead turn left onto Girdle Ridge Road at the concrete dividers. About half a mile down on the right is the **Caramoor Center for Music and the Arts** (914–232–5035), which contains both a house museum and a Venetian theater surrounded by formal gardens. The house, a Mediterranean-style villa painted pink, was originally the country home of Walter Tower Rosen, a lawyer and investment banker. It's filled with artwork and antiques that he and his wife collected from palaces throughout Europe. Entire rooms, in fact, were brought over, including a library from a French château and a pine-paneled room from a home in England. Performances, which include those by concert pianists, chamber groups, and opera

companies, are held during the summer months. For a schedule write Caramoor Center for Music and the Arts, Box R, Katonah, NY 10536 or call (914) 232–5035. The house is open for touring Thursday through Sunday from 1:00 to 4:00 P.M.

One of Bedford's most scenic roads, **Hook Road,** is right behind Caramoor. Well worn by the hooves of horses, the dirt route takes you past big old houses surrounded by woods and gardens and through countryside that feels a million miles away from the concrete chasms of New York City.

Follow Hook Road to the end and you'll be back on Route 22 (called Cantitoe Street here). Turn left and it'll take you right into **Bedford Village,** a treasure box of a town with impeccably cared-for Colonial houses and historic buildings and a flawless green. Bedford Village was settled back in 1680 and became a popular country retreat for wealthy families in the mid-1800s, when the railroad made access to the area very easy. Many of the buildings were built after the Revolution (since most were burned by the British in 1779) and are lovingly preserved by the Bedford Historical Society. These include the 1787 Court House (the oldest public building in Westchester County) and the one-room schoolhouse, which are open for touring Wednesday through Sunday, from 2:00 to 5:00 P.M. Other historic buildings and sites include the old burial ground, the general store (1838), and the Bedford Free Library (1807).

If you're antiquing, allow yourself some time to poke around the shops on the main street. Antiques hunters customarily go from Bedford Village on to Scotts Corners in **Pound Ridge,** which not only has several antiques shops but also quite a few antiques fairs and sidewalk sales. Many people call Pound Ridge the arts and antiques capital of Westchester. There are more than twenty shops and galleries, all within half a mile of one another. To reach Pound Ridge, follow Route 172 east out of Bedford Village, then turn right onto Route 137, then left onto Westchester Avenue. It'll take you right into Scotts Corners, a one-street village center usually lined with Mercedes-Benzes, BMWs, or limousines-in-waiting. Quite a few celebrities (including Christopher Reeves and Ralph Lauren) have homes tucked away in the dense woods that ramble off in every direction around here.

DINNER: The Inn at Pound Ridge, Route 137, Pound Ridge (914) 764–5779, is high on most people's pre- or post-Caramoor list. Formerly Emily Shaw's Inn, it is an old inn in a magnificent country setting with a long history of favorable restaurant reviews. The food is traditional American, and the price might be considered a bit of a splurge. If you're not up for spending the money, head into nearby New Canaan for a softer-on-the-wallet meal (burgers, big salads, light American cuisine) at **Gates Restaurant,** 10 Forest Street; (203) 966–8666.

LODGING: The **Roger Sherman Inn,** 195 Oenoke Ridge, New Canaan (203–966–4541), sits on a lovely stretch of country road just outside the center of New Canaan (not quite a ten-minute drive from Scotts Corners; just follow Route 124). It's a small seven-room inn (some with fireplaces) that dates back to circa 1740.

DAY 2

Morning

BREAKFAST: A continental breakfast comes with the room at the Roger Sherman Inn.

From New Canaan backtrack through Scotts Corners and follow Route 124 to **South Salem.** South Salem is the kind of community where you may find yourself asking directions to the center of town, only to be told, "You're in it." It's made up of a post office, a library, a town hall, a police barracks, a flower shop, a market, two churches, and some beautiful old houses. To reach the center, take a right onto Route 35, and then turn left onto Spring Street. Spring Street runs right into Main Street, which is where "everything" is. Chances are good that you'll pass some horseback riders en route. There are several horse farms in South Salem, and all the roads are used for riding.

In nearby Cross River (which is about 2 or 3 miles west of South Salem, via Route 35), you'll find two of Northern Westchester's most delightful attractions, the Yellow Monkey Village and Ward Pound Ridge Reservation. **Yellow Monkey Village** is a little cluster of eighteenth-century buildings colonized by chic shops selling everything from penny candy to highly valued antiques. Shops include Consider the Cook (which offers everything for the kitchen), The Cheshire Tree (for unusual flowers), Yellow Monkey Antiques (emphasis is on English country pine), and Sweet Expectations for all kinds of sweets. The village shops are open Tuesday through Sunday, from 10:00 A.M. to 6:00 P.M.

LUNCH: If the weather's good, take a picnic to Ward Pound Ridge Reservation (read on for deli directions). Otherwise grab a table at the tiny gourmet eatery at Yellow Monkey Village called **Susan Lawrence,** Yellow Monkey Village, Cross River; (914) 763–8833.

Afternoon

Turn right when you pull out of the Yellow Monkey Village driveway and immediately turn right into the Fifth Division, a little market/deli where you can gather picnic provisions if the weather's nice. Directly opposite the Fifth Division is Route 121. Right after you turn onto Route 121, you'll see a sign at the entrance of **Ward Pound Ridge Reservation,** a 4,700-acre nature preserve. Do yourself a big favor here and stick to the posted speed limit of a mere 15 mph—you will not drive away unticketed if you don't. You can take your pick of places to park and wander the park's trails. They cut through meadows and woodlands, run alongside streams, up hillsides, through deep hemlock ravines, over marsh swamps, by cliffs—you name it. "The Reservation" as the locals refer to it, is rife with birds and other wildlife. There's a small museum called the Trailside Museum with taxidermic mounts, a weather station, and Indian artifacts. Out back there's a wildflower garden. Any time of year is a beautiful time to visit The Reservation. In winter you can cross-country ski or go sleigh riding or tobogganing. Admission is $7.00 a car (open dawn to dusk). A map is provided.

After at least a couple of hours of fresh air, head back toward South Salem, turning left onto Mead Street (about 2 miles east of the Fifth Division) to go into **Waccabuc,** a very exclusive community with a country club as its centerpiece. As you drive up Mead, you'll pass one exquisite home after another. If you can't get enough of the beautiful homes, detour down Schoolhouse Road and you'll see more, though foliage hides a lot during the warm-weather months. Then continue back on Mead Street past the **Mead Street Chapel,** which is beautifully tucked away in a corner of the woods, practically blending into the scenery. To the right you'll spot Lake Waccabuc, which has private access only. Mead Street eventually runs into Hawley Road (which is also known as The Mountain Road). Turn left and then turn right onto 121. You are now in **North Salem,** which seems to have more horses than people. Everywhere you look you see farms, with jump-studded pastures and big old barns. You'll see Auberge Maxime (the restaurant we've chosen for dinner) on the right, at the corner of Route 116. Turn right there and follow Route 116 into Ridgefield, Connecticut, where you can settle into your home for the night. It's just a short drive back to North Salem for dinner and for touring the next day.

DINNER: Auberge Maxime, at the junction of Routes 116 and 121, North Salem; (914) 669–5450. A meal here is worth the trip alone. French chef/owner Bernard Le Bris and his wife, Heidi, have been attracting gourmets from around the world for seventeen years. Not only is the food unfailingly good, but the setting could be the French countryside. When the weather's good, you can dine outdoors. The *spécialité de la maison* is duck, which is prepared in more than a dozen different ways.

LODGING: Elms Restaurant and Tavern, 500 Main Street, Ridgefield; (203) 438–2541. A historic inn, built in the 1760s. Guest rooms are furnished with some antiques and four-poster beds. Consider having a meal here as well, though reservations in advance are a must. The kitchen is run by Brendan Walsh, a former chef of Arizona 206.

DAY 3

Morning

BREAKFAST: Complimentary continental breakfast is served at The Elms.

Return to North Salem, via Route 116, and you can fill several hours just stuffing yourself on the bucolic scenery. Be sure to stop and take a quizzical look at **Balanced Rock** (on Route 116, about a quarter of a mile away from Auberge Maxime), which was left behind from the Ice Age. At the intersection of Routes 116 and 124, go straight on Titicus Road and then turn left onto Mill's Road, which takes you through beautiful countryside that looks more like something you'd expect to find in northern Vermont. At some point you can either turn around or carry on to Purdy's and then follow Titicus Road around the reservoir back to North Salem.

At Salem Center turn left and then turn right onto Deveau Road, which takes you up to the **Hammond Museum and Japanese Stroll Garden,** Deveau Road, North Salem (914–669–5033). The museum, which was founded by Natalie Hays Hammond in 1957, has a schedule of changing exhibits and activities, many focusing on the Far East. Out back there's a Japanese Stroll Garden. The Hammond and its garden are open from 12:00 to 4:00 P.M. Wednesday through Sunday from May through December and 10:00 A.M. to 4:00 P.M. Saturday and Sunday from January through April.

LUNCH: The Hammond Museum, Deveau Road, North Salem (914–669–5033), has a patio terrace where you can have a simple lunch, or you can wait until you get to the **North Salem Vineyard,** Hardscrabble Road, North Salem (914–669–5518), where basket lunches packed with local fruits, home-baked breads, cheeses, and your choice of wine are available. The vineyard is open daily 1:00 to 5:00 P.M. from June through November and Saturday and Sunday from December through May.

Afternoon

Return to Route 124 and turn right. For more stunning scenery take the next right onto Baxter Road, which is one of North Salem's most scenic roads. Along the way you can park and walk (or ski or go horseback riding) on what is called the **Open Land Foundation,** which is open to the public.

Afterward, return to Route 124, turn right, and you'll soon come to the **Old Salem Farm** on the left. This enormous farm (which used to be owned by Paul Newman) is famed in the equestrian world for its shows, and it attracts horse lovers from around the country. For information on horse shows, call (914) 669–5610. Visitors are welcome year-round to walk through the stables and have a look around.

When you pull out of the farm, turn left onto Route 124 and follow it for a couple of miles until you come to Guinea Road on the left. Turn and follow that until you reach **Salinger's Orchard,** Guinea Road, Brewster (914–277–3521). You'll know when you're close when you start seeing apple trees on both sides of the road. Apples, however, are just part of the picture at Salinger's. Here you can get fresh-baked breads and pies, doughnuts, peanut butter, honey, pasta, and scores of other wonderful treats. Be forewarned, however, that during fall weekends the place is packed.

From Salinger's backtrack to Route 124 and follow it back to Hardscrabble Road on the right. A short distance in is the **North Salem Vineyard** on the left (914–669–5518). Free tours and tastings are offered June through October, daily from 1:00 to 5:00 P.M., and November through May, on Saturdays and Sundays only from 1:00 to 5:00 P.M. The Vineyard will prepare a basket lunch, which you can eat indoors or out.

From the Vineyard you can very easily hop back on I–684, heading south toward New York City. You'll find the entrance by turning left out of the Vineyard and following Hardscrabble Road, which crosses right over I–684.

THERE'S MORE

See Southern New England Escape Two, page 70.

Animal farm. Muscoot Farm, Route 100, Somers, NY; (914) 232–7118. This is a turn-of-the-century interpretive farm owned and operated by the Westchester County Department of Parks, Recreation, and Conservation. From Katonah go west on Route 35 to Route 100 and turn right. The farm is 1.5 miles down on the right.

Bicycling. Many of the roads in this area are great cycling routes, though quite hilly. Consider taking your bicycle along. An especially good biking area is Ward Pound Ridge Reservation.

Hiking. In addition to some of the hiking places already described, this part of Westchester has several wildlife preserves with nature trails. In Mount Kisco there are two sanctuaries worth seeking out. The Butler–Meyer Sanctuary is a 604-acre preserve with self-guiding trails and a resident naturalist. This sanctuary is popular for birders; in fact, there is a hawk watch station. To reach Butler: At Bedford Village, bear left on Route 172 for 1 mile to the Shell station and the blinker (still on Route 172) and go 2 miles, under Route 684; carry on another ⁹⁄₁₀ of a mile up the hill, and just before you reach the top of the hill, turn left onto Chestnut Road; go 1.5 miles and you'll see the entrance on the right. Westmoreland Sanctuary (which is opposite Butler), offers 150 acres with 15 miles of trails to explore. There are also a museum, nature programs, naturalists, and guided walks. Another worthwhile preserve is Halle Ravine, on Trinity Pass in Pound Ridge.

Skiing. During the winter months you can cross-country ski in Ward Pound Ridge Reservation and on the Open Land Foundation property in North Salem.

SPECIAL EVENTS

May. Horse Show, Old Salem Farm, Route 124, North Salem; (914) 669–5610. Though there are horse shows throughout the year, this one is the biggest. It usually takes place the last two weeks in May. In addition to all the competitions, there are food stalls and vendors selling everything from curry combs to saddles and great Western wear.

OTHER RECOMMENDED RESTAURANTS AND LODGINGS

Bedford Village

Bistro Twenty-Two, Route 22, Bedford; (914) 234–7333. An expensive but very sophisticated bistro.

Katonah

Blue Dolphin Diner, 175 Katonah Avenue; (914) 232–4791. On a summer weekend evening, the sidewalk in front of this diner becomes an open-air cocktail party, with loyal regulars willing to wait as long as it takes for dinner. Inside it's far from a diner. The food, northern Italian, is consistently and astoundingly good.

New Canaan

The Maples, 179 Oenoke Ridge; (203) 966–2927. This twenty-five-room inn is right next to the Roger Sherman we previously recommended. It has a beautiful wraparound porch.

Ridgefield

Elms Restaurant and Tavern, 500 Main Street; (203) 438–9206. Owned by highly regarded American chef Brendan Walsh (the original chef of New York City's Arizona Cafe), the Elms has earned itself a wonderful reputation. There are several small dining rooms, always abuzz with contented diners. Among the menu offerings: A Connecticut Seafood Stew, Grilled Loin of Cervena Venison, and Thyme Roasted Pheasant.

West Lane Inn, 22 West Lane; (203) 438–7323. A historic inn, dating back to the mid-1800s. All rooms are individually decorated. Its restaurant, the Inn at Ridgefield, features continental cuisine in a very elegant setting.

South Salem

Le Château, Route 35; (914) 533–6631. Some people have never heard of South Salem, but they've heard about Le Château. The castle itself, built in 1907 by J. P. Morgan, is on thirty-two woodland acres. The classic French cuisine is reliably good.

FOR MORE INFORMATION

Westchester County Convention and Visitors Bureau, 222 Mamaroneck Avenue, White Plains, NY 10605; (914) 948–0047.

New York Department of Economic Development, Division of Tourism, One Commerce Plaza, Albany, NY 12245; (518) 474–4116 or (800) CALL–NYS.

Montauk and the Hamptons

LONG ISLAND BEACHES

2 NIGHTS

Ocean beaches and views • Farms • Fresh seafood
Chic boutiques • Art galleries • Estates • Wineries
Museums • Boating • Wildlife • Spa • Tennis

Sun-bleached beaches. Platters piled high with spanking fresh lobster. Sea-breeze-swept verandas. These are just some of the images that come to mind when you mention Montauk or the Hamptons to most New Yorkers. This strip of Atlantic coast on Long Island's eastern end has long been a favorite summer escape for city residents.

Though sharing the same stretch of beach (it goes on for miles and miles), the Hamptons and Montauk are actually very different. The Hamptons, which include Westhampton, Hampton Bays, Southampton, Bridgehampton, and East Hampton, are very upscale, with huge houses surrounded by well-coiffed hedges. They are also very social, attracting celebrities and other boldfaced names from all over. Many New Yorkers either rent, own, or take shares in summer houses and spend a good chunk of their time party hopping or playing tennis with clients. Montauk, on the other hand, is more laid back in both appearance and attitude.

For this escape we combine a visit to both the Hamptons and Montauk. If you'd rather spend more time beaching, consider cutting the journey in half, visiting either just the Hamptons or just Montauk.

By the way, traffic can be painfully uncomfortable, especially going out on Friday afternoons and evenings and returning to the city on Sunday afternoons and evenings. Do yourself a big favor and get a jump-start on your trip.

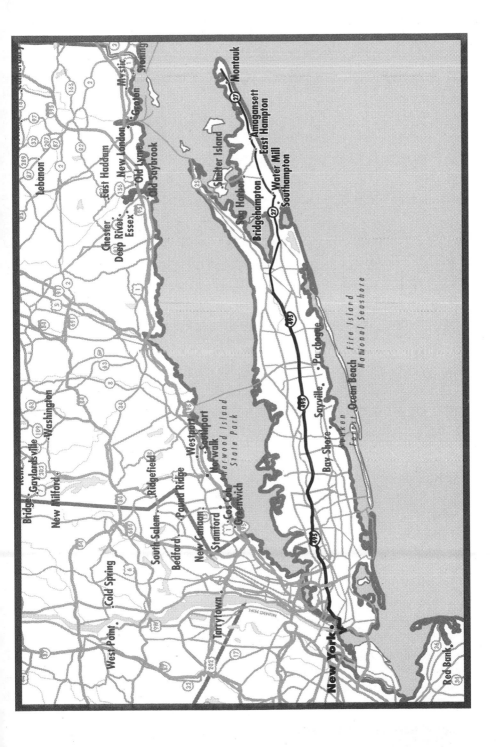

Leave early in the morning or midweek. Also, bear in mind that many inns have a three-night minimum, and some have a one-week minimum during July and August.

DAY 1

Morning

Start by taking the Midtown Tunnel from Manhattan under the East River and follow the Long Island Expressway (I–495) east to exit 70. Follow the signs for Route 27 and then turn left. Route 27, the Sunrise Highway, takes you to the five towns known as "The Hamptons" and on to Montauk at the island's easternmost point.

All five of the Hampton towns have long been a haven for writers, artists, and other celebrities in addition to summer visitors. The main attraction is the beach, which, backed by rolling dunes, stretches out for miles, offering plenty of opportunity for undisturbed sunning.

As you hopscotch from town to town, you'll find that a popular Hampton activity is browsing through the boutiques and galleries; in fact, sometimes it's hard to tell the difference. Here, a perfect ear of corn can be discussed as if it were an objet d'art, filling the better part of a dinner-party conversation. You'll find all sorts of one-of-a-kind must-haves such as heavy pasta bowls and con-versation-piece sweaters that you'll figure out how to clean later. If you're here for the shopping, your best bet is to just pull over wherever you spot a park-ing place in a town. Chances are there will be enough shops to keep you hap-pily amused.

Otherwise make your first stop in **Southampton** at the **Old Halsey House,** 21 South Main Street (516–283–1612). This is the oldest English frame house in New York State. There's also a Colonial herb garden. The house is open every day except Monday, from June through September. Also worth seeing is the **Southampton Historical Museum,** 17 Meeting House Lane, off Main Street (516–283–1612). The main building, which was formerly a whaling captain's home (1843) is filled with period furnishings. There's also a one-room schoolhouse and a carriage house plus a nineteenth-century village street with more than a dozen restored shops.

Southampton's most famous shopping area is **Job's Lane,** where you'll find pricey boutiques competing for your credit card signature. As riveting as shopping can be, don't miss the **Parrish Art Museum,** also on Job's Lane at

The beaches in Montauk are washed by powerful Atlantic waves.

25 Job's Lane (516–283–2118), which has a good collection of nineteenth-
and twentieth-century American paintings along with other changing
exhibits. It's open from mid-June through mid-September, Monday and Tuesday and Thursday through Saturday, plus Sunday afternoons; the rest of the
year, Thursday through Monday.

After a look around the Parrish and a bit of shop-hopping, take time out
to gape at the town's legendary mega-mansions. As with most affluent oceanfront areas, the biggest and the best homes are on the roads that run parallel
to the ocean or intersect them. You can feast your eyes by driving down
Meadow, Gin, Halsey Neck, Copper's Neck, and First Neck Lanes.

LUNCH: Right in the heart of Southampton you'll find **75 Main,** 75 Main
Street (516–283–7575), a busy little bistro headed up by New American chef
Walter Hinds (formerly of New York City's Match) offering a good selection
of pasta and grilled fish dishes as well as pizzas.

Afternoon

Even if you're not a hard-core beach person, consider taking time out to plop down on the beach for an hour or so. There's a wonderful public beach right on Meadow Lane.

Afterward, continue east on Route 27, stopping at shops in the villages of **Water Mill** and **Bridgehampton.** Water Mill is named for its gristmill, which is now a museum called the **Water Mill Museum** (516–726–4625). It's open every day except Tuesday. Closed in winter.

The destination for the day is **East Hampton,** which has an impressive collection of old houses that have been declared historic landmarks. The best way to enjoy them is to stop by the Chamber of Commerce, 4 Main Street (516–324–0362), and pick up a free walking-tour map. Some of the highlights include the oldest houses, some of which can be found on James Lane, which borders the eastern edge of the South End Burying Ground. Most famous of them is the 1680 **"Home Sweet Home" House,** 14 James Lane (516–324–0713), which was the childhood home of John Howard Payne, the composer of the song of the same title. It's open to visitors April through December, 10:00 A.M. to 4:00 P.M. Monday through Saturday and 2:00 to 4:00 P.M. Sunday. There's also a windmill that was built in 1804 out back. **Historic Mulford Farm** is also on James Lane (516–324–6850). It's a living-history museum open daily July and August and on weekends in June and September. The rest of the year, appointments are necessary.

On Main Street you'll find the **Guild Hall Museum,** 158 Main Street (516–324–0806), which is an art museum and the cultural center of East Hampton. It's open daily from June through September and the rest of the year from Wednesday through Sunday. Close by you'll find **Clinton Academy,** 151 Main Street (516–324–6850), the first prep school in New York State. It's now a museum exhibiting a collection of eastern Long Island artifacts. Call ahead; hours vary.

At the end of town on North Main Street stands **Hook Mill,** a wind-powered grist mill, next to a burial ground with tombstones dating back to 1650. There are tours of the mill through the summer.

Before leaving East Hampton take a drive down Lily Pond Lane to see more magnificent homes.

DINNER: Just 3 miles west of East Hampton, you'll find **Sapore Di Mare,** Wainscott Stone Road, Wainscott (516–537–2764), which is a big splurge, but worth it. The food is Tuscan; the clientele, *very* starry.

LODGING: The Maidstone Arms Inn and Restaurant, 207 Main Street (516–324–5006), is a nineteen-room inn across from the green in East Hampton. It's open year-round.

DAY 2

Morning

BREAKFAST: Honest Diner, 74 Montauk Highway; (516) 267–3535. If you're in the mood for a big, all-American breakfast, head for this popular diner in Amagansett, which is just to the east of East Hampton.

Amagansett has more shops to explore plus the **Town Marine Museum,** on Bluff Road, ½ mile south of Route 27 on the ocean (516–267–6544), with shipwreck and undersea exhibits. There are also several town beaches on which to spread your blanket out.

From Amagansett carry on east to **Montauk,** which is truly land's end Though just 120 miles from the chasms and towers of Manhattan, it honestly feels a million miles away. You'll start to feel the difference just after Amagansett, when the shops trickle out.

There's not a long list of things to do in Montauk. The best pastime is to wander along the beach looking for shells or birds, or maybe go for a trail ride on a pair of mares at the Deep Hollow Riding Academy.

The one big sightseeing attraction is the **Montauk Point Lighthouse** in **Montauk State Park,** 6 miles east of town on Route 27 (516–668–2461), which has stood poised atop an ocean bluff for about two hundred years. It was built in 1795 by order of George Washington.

LUNCH: Gosman's Dock, West Lake Drive at the entrance to Montauk Harbor (516–668–5330), is famed for its generous servings of ultrafresh seafood (you can watch them unload catches right on the dock). Try the broiled fluke; it's hard to find elsewhere. There's a take-out counter and some picnic tables outside in addition to the restaurant dining rooms inside. (Gosman's is closed during the winter.)

Afternoon

Consider going on the 2½-hour sail on the *Delta Lady,* a 65-foot schooner, or enjoy the rest of the afternoon wandering the trails of nearby **Hither Hills State Park,** 3 miles west on Route 27 (516–668–2461).

DINNER: Dave's Grill, Flamingo Road on Montauk Harbor; (516) 668–9190. This formerly rundown fishermen's haunt is now a sophisticated bistro. Order the fish of the day or try the Provençal fisherman's stew out on the waterside patio.

LODGING: The Panoramic View, Old Montauk Highway (516–668–3000), lives up to its name. It's spectacularly situated on ten acres with arrestingly beautiful ocean vistas. The rooms are simply but tastefully decorated with maple furniture. They have high, beamed ceilings and knotty-pine paneling; most have balconies.

DAY 3

Morning

BREAKFAST: A buffet breakfast is set up and open to the public at the **Montauk Yacht Club Resort Marina,** Star Island (516–668–3100), when they're open (between April and January). The buffet starts early, at 7:00 A.M.

After breakfast join in on a whale-watching cruise (see "There's More" for details) or consider spending the day being pampered at **Gurney's Inn Resort & Spa,** Old Montauk Highway (516–668–2345 or 800–847–6397), before heading back to Manhattan.

To return to the city, retrace your steps by following Route 27 west and turning north at Eastport to reach the Long Island Expressway (Route 495), which will take you back to the Midtown Tunnel.

THERE'S MORE

Birding. Montauk Point State Park is a good spot to take your binoculars.

Cruises to Block Island. The *Viking Starliner* takes passengers on 1½-hour-long cruises to Block Island and back. The trips leave at 9:00 A.M. July through October.

Fishing. In Montauk charter boats will take anglers out to fight for blues, marlin, swordfish, and even sharks.

Horseback riding. Deep Hollow Ranch in Montauk offers horseback riding through 4,000 acres of trails to the beach. For more information call (516) 668–2744.

Spa. Gurney's Inn Resort & Spa, Old Montauk Highway, Montauk; (516) 668–2345. In addition to a long menu of spa treatments (seaweed body wraps, herbal wraps, facials, massages), Gurney's is home to a drop-dead gorgeous beach the likes of which you'd be hard-pressed to find anywhere else.

Whale-watching. From May through September the Okeanos Ocean Research Foundation in Montauk, Viking Dock (516–728–4522), offers whale-watching cruises aboard the *Finback II.* The waters off this coast are feeding grounds for humpback, minke, and fin whales, plus dolphins, seals, and sea turtles.

SPECIAL EVENTS

July 4. Southampton's Parade. The town's antique auto museum shows off its classic cars in an annual parade.

Labor Day weekend. Powwow. At the Shinnecock Indian Reservation, just off NY 27A (near Southampton). Dances, ceremonies, displays.

OTHER RECOMMENDED RESTAURANTS AND LODGINGS

Amagansett

The Lobster Roll, Montauk Highway (look for flagpole); (516) 267–3740. In summer months this is a must. A no-frills, roadside seafood eatery, its lobster sandwiches and salads are worth every minute you stand in line. There are also wonderful pies for dessert.

Bridgehampton

Bridgehampton Motel, on Route 27, past the center of Bridgehampton; (516) 537–0197. Owned by Alexis Stewart, the daughter of home-entertaining author and editor Martha, this roadside Fifties motel has been updated in a "retro" style. Just because it wears the name "motel" doesn't mean it's cheap, however. Room rates are steep, especially during weekend nights in season. The motel is open on a part-time basis only.

East Hampton

The Maidstone Arms Inn and Restaurant, 207 Main Street; (516) 324–5006. The food here is contemporary American with a Pacific Rim influence. Among its star-studded clientele are Billy Joel, Alec Baldwin and Kim Basinger, Steve Guttenberg, and Kevin Costner—just to drop a few names. The most popular dishes are Seared Prime Rib-Eye, with pommes Anna and port wine Stilton cheese sauce; Grilled Atlantic Monkfish on a confit of tomato and fresh fennel with a parsley butter; and Stir-fried Tiger Prawns, with Thai black bean sauce and steamed garlic rice.

Nick & Toni's, 136 North Main Street; (516) 324–3550. A popular place to see and be seen, Nick & Toni's serves Tuscan cuisine.

Montauk

East Deck Motel, Ditch Plains Road; (516) 668–2334. Here you can stay in an efficiency studio. Each one sleeps four to six and has basic cable and a full kitchen and dining area. They're perfect for families or couples traveling together. There's a pool and adjacent beach, which has a lifeguard on duty from 10:00 A.M. TO 5:00 P.M. The motel is ½ mile east of the plaza on Montauk Highway; go right on Ditch Plains Road. Open mid-June to early September.

Hotel Montauket, 88 Firestone Road; (516) 668–5992. Overlooking Gardiner's Bay, this is a basic hotel (no pool, TV, private phones, or air conditioning, and some guests share bathrooms), but it's friendly, clean, and inexpensive. The bar and restaurant are popular with locals. From the Plaza take Edgemere Street north; make a left on Fleming Road and then a right on Firestone Road.

Montauk Manor, 236 Edgemere Street; (516) 668–4400. An English Tudor–style castle, Montauk Manor originally was erected by industrialist Carl Fisher as the centerpiece for what he had hoped to be an elaborate summer-resort community. Unfortunately, the Depression squelched his plans. Nevertheless, the building remains, renovated inside to be a modern luxury hotel. Ask for a room with a terrace or patio.

Montauk Yacht Club Resort Marina, Star Island; (516) 668–3100. Now public, the Montauk Yacht Club is a truly deluxe hotel complete with tennis, water sports, spa treatments, and lots more. Back in the twenties and thirties, it was frequented by the Vanderbilts, Astors, and Whitneys.

Oceanside Beach Resort, South Eton Street at Montauk Highway; (516) 668–9825. A two-story motel, here you'll find both standard rooms and units with kitchens. As the name implies, it's steps from the beach.

The Harvest on Fort Pond, 11 South Emery Street; (516) 668–5574. Tuscan cuisine prepared with locally grown garden and fresh seafood—this is a real find.

The Oasis at Ditch Plains Beach, Otis Road (off Ditch Plains Road); no telephone. One does not normally associate healthful food with beachside trailers. Nevertheless, this trailer beach stand, which is parked all summer long at Ditch Plains Beach, is locally famed for its health-conscious and deliriously good menu items, which include burritos, pita sandwiches, tofu dogs, and vegetarian chili.

Southampton

Basilico, 10 Windmill Lane; (516) 283–7987. A trattoria specializing in nouvelle Italian cuisine.

FOR MORE INFORMATION

City Lights Bed & Breakfast, Ltd., P.O. Box 20355, Cherokee Station, New York, NY 10028; (212) 737–7049. This company can arrange for you to stay at bed and breakfasts throughout the Hamptons.

East Hampton Chamber of Commerce, 4 Main Street, East Hampton, New York 11937; (516) 324–0362.

Village of Southampton, P.O. Box 303, Southampton, NY 11969; (516) 283–1612.

Montauk Chamber of Commerce, P.O. Box 5029, Montauk, NY 11954; (516) 668–2428.

Long Island Convention and Visitors Bureau, 350 Vanderbilt Motor Parkway, Suite 103, Hauppauge, NY 11788; (516) 951–3440.

New York Department of Economic Development, Division of Tourism, One Commerce Plaza, Albany, NY 12245; (518) 474–4116 or (800) CALL–NYS.

Shelter Island

A TOTAL GETAWAY

1 NIGHT

Beaches • Seafood • Biking • Peace and quiet

If you want to go some place for the weekend and just "be" rather than "do," Shelter Island is a good choice. Tucked between the north and south forks on the east end of Long Island, it's reachable only by ferry. About a third of the island is nature preserve (Mashomack Forest), and the rest is beautifully unspoiled, thanks to residents who are committed to keeping it that way.

Some say the name Shelter Island comes from an Indian word; others say it was named by Quakers who were persecuted by the Puritans in New England and sought refuge there. Whatever. There is a monument to the Quakers and a graveyard with seventeenth-century stones if you're interested. That's about it in the way of man-made attractions on the island. The island's real attraction is its natural beauty: miles of white sand beaches, rolling wooded hills, and lots of beautiful views of the water.

If you want to avoid the summer traffic, plan to head out to the island between May (except Memorial Day weekend) and early June or after Labor Day through October (except for Columbus Day weekend).

Consider combining this trip with a visit to Montauk or the Hamptons (see New York Escape Five).

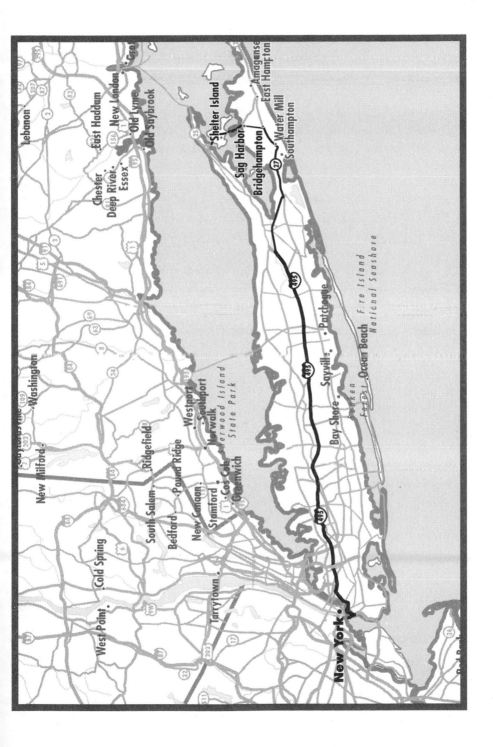

DAY 1

Morning

From Manhattan take the Midtown Tunnel to the Long Island Expressway (I–495). Follow it out to exit 70 and pick up Route 27 east; turn left in Bridgehampton following signs to Sag Harbor. From downtown Sag Harbor cross the bridge and follow signs to the ferry. Ferries shuttle between North Haven and Shelter Island several times throughout the day between 6:00 A.M. and 11:45 P.M. For information call (516) 749–1200 between 9:00 A.M. and 5:00 P.M. on weekdays. The price for one car with a driver is $6.00 each way plus $1.00 for each additional passenger. There are also ferries from Greenport on the North Fork.

Once you arrive on Shelter Island, follow Route 114 to **Shelter Island Heights,** where you'll find the island's handful of stores and restaurants including the Chequit Inn, where you can take time out for lunch.

LUNCH: Chequit Inn, Grand Avenue (516–749–0018), has a terrace from which you can gaze out at sailboats in Dering Harbor. The restaurant specializes in grilled seafood, though lighter fare is available at lunch.

Afternoon

After lunch and maybe a short walk around The Heights, head to the eastern tip of the island, where you'll find a causeway leading to Ram Island, so named because it's shaped like a ram. Check into your hotel and spend the afternoon parked on its private beach or swinging in a hammock under a shady tree in the backyard. If you feel ambitious, there's a tennis court and sailboats to take out. You can also rent bikes (or take along your own) and do some pedaling around this 12-square-mile island.

DINNER: Ram's Head Inn, 108 Ram's Island Drive; (516) 749–0811. This restaurant, where reservations are a must, is alone worth the trip to Shelter Island. The cuisine is contemporary American, and the setting (it overlooks Coecles Harbor) is dreamy.

LODGING: The **Ram's Head Inn,** 108 Ram's Island Drive, (516–749–0811), is marvelously situated in a whole little world of its own. Rooms are nothing extraordinary (though they're perfectly adequate), but are more than compensated for by the setting.

Summertime is when Dering Harbor on Shelter Island is its liveliest.

DAY 2

Morning

BREAKFAST: Continental breakfast is included in the room rate.

Enjoy the morning on the beach, then grab a ferry back to **Sag Harbor,** which is an old whaling town filled with nineteenth-century architecture and history. In fact tiny Sag Harbor used to rival New York as an international port. There are a handful of sights to see including the **Custom House,** Garden Street (516–941–9444), which operated as a customhouse and post office during the late eighteenth and early nineteenth centuries. In July and August it's open daily except Monday; between May and June and September and October, it's open on Saturdays and Sundays only. On the corner of Garden Street and Main, you'll find the **Sag Harbor Whaling and Historical**

Museum (516–725–0770), which tells the story of the island's whaling past. The museum is open daily from mid-May through September.

LUNCH: A Sag Harbor must, **The American Hotel,** 25 Main Street, Sag Harbor (516–725–3535), is renowned for its Old World charm. The food is largely contemporary American.

From Sag Harbor head back to Bridgehampton and retrace your steps back to New York City.

THERE'S MORE

Bicycling. On Shelter Island you can rent bikes at Piccozzi's, right in the center of The Heights on Bridge Street; (516) 749–0045.

Hiking. The Mashomack Preserve, off Route 114 on Shelter Island, has trails and a visitors center. It's open daily. For more information call (516) 749–1001.

SPECIAL EVENTS

Mid-June. 10K Run. This is always an exciting day on Shelter Island, when runners come from all over to race. It starts in the center of the island near the high school.

Late August. Arts and Crafts Show. Every year the playground near the American Legion in the center of the island turns into a showcase for artists and artisans.

OTHER RECOMMENDED RESTAURANTS AND LODGINGS

Belle Crest House, 163 North Ferry Road; (516) 749–2041. This is a bed and breakfast inn with ten rooms in the main house plus a one-bedroom cottage (named the Honeymoon Cottage). Most rooms have canopy beds, some have antiques and private baths. A full breakfast is served outside on the terrace during the summer. The inn is within walking distance of the village (Shelter Island Heights) and the beach.

Chips, Route 114, Shelter Island; (516) 749–8926. Slightly outside of the center of town, Chips is a very casual spot specializing in seafood. Bring your own alcohol. During the summer it has tables set outdoors.

The Azalea House, 1 Thomas Avenue, (516) 749 1252. This is a five-room bed and breakfast in the island's center. Thanks to one of its owners, who comes from Finland, it's full of tasteful Finnish touches including light pine furniture. An extended continental breakfast is included in the room rate.

The Beechtree House, 1 South Ferry Road; (516) 749–4252. Owned by the same people who own The Azalea House, this is a lovely pre-Victorian house with three apartments for guests (two of them have full kitchens). It's named for the monumental beech tree in front, which dominates the yard and is one of the biggest trees on the island.

The Dory, Route 114, Shelter Island Heights; (516) 749–8871. This is a busy waterfront restaurant (with a dory on top) where the seafood is unfailingly good. It's necessary to have reservations during the summer months.

FOR MORE INFORMATION

Sag Harbor Chamber of Commerce, 459 Main Street, Sag Harbor, NY 11963; (516) 725–0011.

Shelter Island Chamber of Commerce, Box 577, Shelter Island Heights, NY 11965; (516) 749–0399.

Long Island Convention and Visitors Bureau, 350 Vanderbilt Motor Parkway, Suite 103, Hauppauge, NY 11788; (516) 951–3440.

New York Department of Economic Development, Division of Tourism, One Commerce Plaza, Albany, NY 12245; (518) 474–4116 or (800) CALL–NYS.

The Adirondack Area

TOWNS AND COUNTRY

3 NIGHTS

Backwood wilderness • Lakes • Quiet • Hiking
Canoeing • Thoroughbred racing • Family amusements
Old fort • Performing arts

Look at any color map of New York State and you'll see an enormous green area taking up a good chunk of its northern region. That's the Adirondack Park, the largest natural preserve in the East, in fact, covering some six million acres.

You could easily spend weeks here, dividing your time between the different fresh-air activities (including hiking through birch and balsam forests and paddling canoes on lakes) and poking around the attractions near Lake George and in nearby Saratoga Springs, or you could devote an entire week or two to an all-out vacation on a hidden mountain lake.

For this trip we combine a brief visit to Saratoga Springs with a short stay on Lake George and Blue Mountain Lake. All three places could be weekend (or longer) destinations in themselves; we've just mentioned the highlights. Keep in mind that in August, when the New York Racing Association has its equine competitions, Saratoga Springs' population swells to two or three times its normal size.

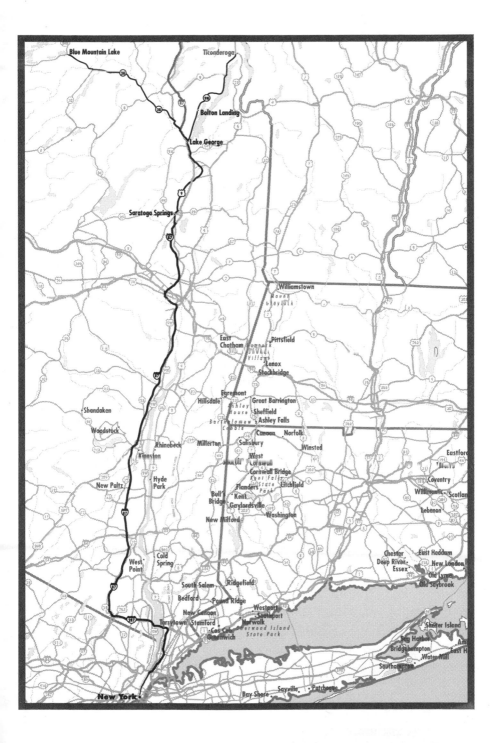

DAY 1

Morning

Take I–87 north to exit 13N. Go left. At the fourth stoplight turn left into **Saratoga Spa State Park** in **Saratoga Springs,** which is home to your hotel for the night.

Saratoga Springs, a town with a beautiful mixture of Victorian and Greek Revival architecture in the foothills of the Adirondack Mountains, has three major magnets: its thoroughbred racing, its performing arts scene, and its mineral baths, for which the town is named. If you'd like to try the latter, you'll find some right in the park—the **Roosevelt Mineral Baths** (518–584–2011). Here you can "take the waters" or, more specifically, soak in naturally carbonated water and follow with a half-hour rest on heated sheets on a cot nearby. The experience should leave you feeling relaxed and revived and ready to get out and wander around the town's museums and shops.

LUNCH: The dining room of the **Gideon Putnam Hotel,** in Saratoga Spa State Park (518–584–3000), is a pleasant spot to have lunch. A large variety of offerings includes burgers, sandwiches, crepes, and the like.

Afternoon

Spend the afternoon checking out the sights and shops in town (follow US 9 north into town from the park). Many of the shops on Broadway are in buildings that have been impeccably restored to their original Victorian appearance. On North Broadway, Circular Street, and Union Avenue, there are many mansions that were originally built in the 1800s. Be sure to wander into **Historic Congress Park,** on Broadway (518–584–6920), which is home to two worthwhile museums: the Museum of the Historical Society and the Walworth Memorial Museum. They trace the history of the city's growth. From June through October they're open daily; during the rest of the year, they're open afternoons only, Wednesday through Sunday.

If you're interested in the history and highlights of horse racing, be sure to check out the **National Museum of Racing and Thoroughbred Hall of Fame,** Union Avenue (518–584–0400), and, of course, the **Saratoga Race Course,** also on Union Avenue, which is the oldest operating thoroughbred racetrack in the country (it was founded in 1863). For information on events call (718) 641–4700.

If you have time, try to visit Saratoga's wonderful dance museum, the **National Museum of Dance,** on South Broadway in Saratoga State Park (518–584–2225). It's the only museum in the country devoted exclusively to professional American dance.

DINNER: Eartha's Kitchen, in town at 60 Court Street (518–583–0602), specializes in sensationally good grilled fare.

LODGING: The **Gideon Putnam Hotel,** in Saratoga Springs State Park, ½ mile south of town on US 9 (518–584–3000 or 800–732–1560), is one of Saratoga Springs' *grande dame* hotels, surrounded by therapeutic pools, tennis courts, and golf courses. Legendary Sunday brunches take place here in glass-walled rooms overlooking the greens.

DAY 2

Morning

BREAKFAST: A great way to start the morning in Saratoga is by having breakfast at the track (for information call **Breakfast at Saratoga,** 518–584–6200). A buffet is served from 7:00 to 9:30 A.M., during which you can watch the early-morning workouts. A more formal champagne breakfast is offered during racing season in a dining tent called **At the Rail Pavilion** (call 718–641–4700 for restaurant information).

After breakfast head north on I–87 to exit 20 and follow Route 9 north, which will take you through the commercialized town of **Lake George** (shops, entertainment arcades, family attractions) and to **Bolton Landing,** where you can settle in for an all-out relaxing stay at the lakefront **Sagamore** resort. (See "Lodging.") Check-in time is not until 3:00 P.M., but the front desk will hold your bags while you have lunch.

LUNCH: Mr. Brown's Pub at the Sagamore (518–644–9400) is an informal spot where you can order chicken wings, burgers, or sandwiches.

Afternoon

Spend the afternoon enjoying the resort facilities at the Sagamore or drive up to see **Fort Ticonderoga,** the military fortress and its museum (follow Route 9N to Ticonderoga; 518–585–2821).

Afterward, follow the scenic drive up to the top of **Mount Defiance.**

During the warm-weather months, Lake George swells with pleasure boats.

DINNER: For a splurge make a reservation at the Sagamore's **Trillium** (518–664–9400), where you can feast on formal dishes such as lobster Napoleon, quail on polenta, or rack of lamb.

LODGING: The Sagamore, Bolton Landing; (518) 664–9400 or (800) 358–3585. Established more than one hundred years ago, this Victorian landmark has been described by just about every travel writer as a *grande dame* hotel. Indeed it is. Designed to preserve the ecological integrity of the area, it was originally built as a social center for the wealthy residents of mansions along the west coast of Lake George, which was known as Millionaire's Row. Over the years it went through its share of troubles, which included two fires. In 1981 age had taken a real toll on the property, and it had to close. Fortunately, the property was rescued by Norman Wolgin, a Philadelphia-based real estate developer and longtime summer resident of Bolton Landing, who formed a partnership to restore the property. The restoration, which cost a

lofty $75 million, left the Sagamore looking more beautiful than ever, qualifying it for the National Register of Historic Places. Its grandeur is apparent the minute you drive across the short bridge that connects Bolton Landing with Sagamore Island.

Though you have the six million acres of the Adirondack Park at your fingertips, the Sagamore prides itself on its own combination of sporting activities. Among the offerings are an 18-hole course designed by Donald Ross, seven tennis courts (two indoors), a racquetball court, a miniature golf course, an indoor swimming pool, plus walking and jogging trails. There's also a beach where you can swim or take your pick of water sports. There are motor boats for rent, fishing guides, sailboat charters, snorkeling trips, parasailing, and waterskiing, just to name a few. Come winter, there's cross-country skiing right on the grounds, ice skating, and complimentary transportation to nearby Gore Mountain for downhill skiing. On top of all that, there's a spa with a whole menu of services including massage (Swedish, athletic, and aromatherapy body massage), facials, foot reflexology, salt-glos, herbal wraps, seaweed body masks, natural mud body masks, hydrotherapy, and salon services. Also part of the spa is a state-of-the-art fitness center with exercise equipment for strength, endurance, flexibility, and cardiovascular fitness.

If you have children in tow, you'll find the Sagamore is the answer to your prayers. Kids ages three through thirteen can join the Teepee Club, which offers more than a dozen different diversions: arts and crafts, pirate picnics, karaoke, scavenger hunts, clown shows, facepainting—the list goes on. The program is run both in the daytime and evenings. For children under three there are babysitting services. The resort offers children's menus in all of the dining areas.

In addition to one hundred guest rooms and suites in the main building, there are Lakeside Lodges with wood-burning fireplaces and private terraces. All guest rooms have air conditioning and in-room cable movies; many of them have write-home-about views.

DAY 3

Morning

BREAKFAST: A huge buffet is offered at the Sagamore.

To sample some of the Adirondack's most densely scenic landscape, head west on Route 28, making your destination **Blue Mountain Lake,** where there's an outstanding museum devoted to the Adirondacks. Set on the shores of Blue Mountain Lake, **The Adirondack Museum,** Blue Mountain Lake (518–352–7311), is a complex of twenty-two buildings on thirty acres. One of the most popular exhibits is a display of the successive generations of Adirondack boats.

Afternoon

LUNCH: Stop in the grocery store in town and get picnic makings to take on a hike up Blue Mountain.

The head of the trail leading to the summit (3,800 feet) is about 1½ miles north of town. The 3-mile-long hike will take you through delicious Adirondack scenery.

DINNER: Big family-style meals, with homemade breads and desserts, are served in the dining room at **Hemlock Hall,** on Route 28N, Blue Mountain Lake (518–352–7706). Open Memorial Day through October 15.

LODGING: At **Hemlock Hall** on Route 28N, Blue Mountain Lake (518–352–7706 or, in winter, 518–359–9065), you can stay in a motel-like unit, a lodge room, or a cabin on the lake. Open Memorial Day through October 15.

DAY 4

Morning

BREAKFAST: Pancakes, hot cereals, eggs with bacon or sausage—big American breakfasts are served in the dining room at Hemlock Hall.

Before heading back to New York City, take time to enjoy the lake and its exquisite scenery. Right at the hotel you can take your pick of canoes, sailboats, paddleboats, and rowboats.

From Blue Mountain Lake retrace your steps back on Route 28 to I–87, heading south.

If you have even more time (another day or two), consider heading further north up to the **Lake Placid** area. You can visit several Olympic attractions including the Olympic Sports Complex, Ski Jumps, and **The 1932 & 1980 Lake Placid Winter Olympic Museum** (518–523–1655, extension 263), which includes video highlights of the 1932 and 1980 games, athletes' uniforms, sports equipment, and other Olympic memorabilia. All around the area you'll find lots of hiking and mountain biking trails.

THERE'S MORE

Horseback riding. Pine Hill Riding Stable, off I–87, exit 21 on 9N (Lake George area), has trail riding. For information call (518) 668–2711.

Mountain biking. High Peaks Cyclery: Mountain Adventure Center, 331 Main Street, Lake Placid; (518) 523–3764. Here you can rent mountain bikes and be sent on your way, choosing anything from an easy 10-mile rolling-hill route to a 75-mile loop with steep ascents. The adventure center can also set you up for in-line skating, skating, camping, and rock climbing.

Performing arts. Saratoga Performing Arts Center, Saratoga Spa State Park; (518) 587–3330. The center hosts a wonderful summer mélange of cultural events including the New York City Opera in June, the New York City Ballet in July, and the Philadelphia Orchestra in August, as well as concerts by a variety of rock, pop, folk, and jazz artists.

Polo matches. Saratoga Polo Association, Saratoga Springs; (518) 584–8108. Matches take place in August.

Scenic flights. Lake Placid Airport, Route 73, Lake Placid; (518) 523–2473. Twenty-minute aerial tours are offered. Passengers can opt for the High Peaks Tour or the Whiteface Mountain Tour; $20 per person (minimum two people).

Skiing. The Adirondacks are home to a dozen alpine ski centers including Lake Placid, which has hosted the winter Olympic Games twice.

Steamboat rides. The Lake George Steamboat Company offers narrated cruises on the lake. For information call (518) 668–5777.

SPECIAL EVENTS

June. Lake Placid Horse Show, Lake Placid. This show, combined with the I Love New York Horse Show held the first week of July, make this a popular destination for equestrians.

June. No-Octane Regatta, Blue Mountain Lake. A grand parade of boats. Events include War Canoe Race, Hurry Scurry Race, Guideboat Race, Jousting Competition, Paddling Races, Sailing Canoe Races, and Great Versatility Race.

Mid-July. Ticonderoga Memorial Military Tattoo, Fort Ticonderoga. Eighteenth-century military music in honor of the Scots who served here.

Mid-September. Adirondacks National Car Show, Lake George Village. Hot rods, custom-made cars, and other special-interest cars are paraded here annually at the Fort William Henry Motor Inn.

OTHER RECOMMENDED RESTAURANTS AND LODGINGS

Blue Mountain Lake

Potter's, on the lake; (518) 352–7331. A string of housekeeping cottages, some smack dab on the water's edge (others just across the street). Though extremely simple and bare boned, these cottages have charm, especially their front-porch views of the smashingly scenic lake. There's also a motel complex and restaurant plus a tennis court.

Chestertown

The Balsam House, Friends Lake, Chestertown; (518) 494–2828. This is a rambling Victorian inn with a wraparound porch. There are twenty rooms decorated with Laura Ashley fabrics and some antiques. It's about a minute's walk from Friends Lake, where guests can swim and canoe. The dining room serves continental cuisine.

Friends Lake Inn, Friends Lake Road; (518) 494–4751. Just across the road from Friends Lake, this is a fifteen-room inn. All rooms are decorated in a country motif; some have four-poster beds. The restaurant is well respected for its sophisticated cuisine and award-winning wine list.

Keene Valley

The Bark Eater Inn, Alstead Mill Road; (518) 576–2221. About a mile or so outside the village of Keene is this down-home inn. There are nineteen simply furnished rooms. Meals are served family-style. Horseback riding is the biggest draw; the inn has a couple of dozen horses and an extensive trail system.

Noonmark Diner, Route 73; (518) 576–4499. Though it looks like a regular old house on the outside and a regular diner on the inside, the Noonmark is locally famed for its homemade goodies—sandwich breads, soups, and pies.

Lake Placid

Lake Placid Lodge, Whiteface Inn Road; (518) 523–2700. Propped up on the shores of forever placid Lake Placid is the rustically elegant Lake Placid Lodge, an Adirondack log-and-stone hotel. Guests can take their pick of a variety of accommodations from lakeside cabins to three-room suites with fireplaces and decks. Absolutely every detail of the Lodge is lovingly tended to from the outrageously comfortable feather beds that are in every room to local artwork everywhere. Meals are served in the Lake Placid Lodge dining room, which has sweeping views of the lake and Whiteface Mountain. For lunch you can have the dining room prepare a picnic, or during the golf season, you can eat at the Whiteface Grill, next to the pro shop.

Saranac Lake

The Point, Saranac Lake; (518) 891–5674 or (800) 255–3530. Located in the northern Adirondacks on an isolated peninsula on Upper Saranac Lake, The Point was built in 1933 as a country getaway for William Avery Rockefeller. Constructed of massive logs and stone, it is a very exclusive retreat with eleven guest rooms, each with a fireplace and museum-quality Adirondack furniture. Extraordinarily good meals are served in the Great Hall, a spectacular high-ceilinged room with hunt trophies adorning the walls.

Saratoga Springs

The Adelphi Hotel, 365 Broadway; (518) 587–4688. A grand old Victorian hotel. Complimentary continental breakfast is served in your room.

The Inn at Saratoga, 231 Broadway; (518) 583–1890. A very simple, historic hotel within easy reach of Saratoga's attractions.

FOR MORE INFORMATION

Adirondack Regional Information: 800–487–6867.

Lake George Chamber of Commerce, Route 9, Lake George, NY 12845; (518) 668–5755.

Saratoga Springs Chamber of Commerce, 494 Broadway, Saratoga Springs, NY 12866; (518) 584–3255.

Warren County Tourism, Municipal Center, Lake George, NY 12845; (518) 761–6366 or (800) 365–1050.

The New York State Department of Economic Development, Division of Tourism, One Commerce Plaza, Albany, NY 12445; (518) 474–4116 or (800) CALL–NYS.

Fire Island

With or Without a Car

LIFE'S A BEACH

---

1 NIGHT

Beaches • Nature walks • Seafood • People-watching

Nicknamed New York's Key West, Fire Island has long been known as a care-free, barefoot kind of place, attracting a combination platter of humanity. Its occupants are made up of the year-rounders, summer home owners, summer renters, and short-term visitors including day-trippers.

A barrier island stretching 32 miles along the southern side of Long Island and only a quarter-mile wide, Fire Island has a rich social and cultural history. Resort development began here back in the 1890s with the establishment of a Chautauqua Assembly, a movement for Christian betterment through learning and the arts. After that tracts of land were bought up by developers and sold to city folk who were seeking vacation lots. Before long the island became a patchwork of neighborhoods for different communities, often over-lapping and coexisting harmoniously, whether involved in boating, fishing, family, and/or gay life.

Fortunately, the island hasn't changed much since its early days. No cars were allowed then—or now. The only means of transportation are feet, wagon, bicycle, and boat (golf carts and trucks for contractors). Though only 40 miles from New York City, it is a remote destination with wonderfully wide sandy beaches and unspoiled maritime forests. Most of the land is now protected by the federal government and has been designated the Fire Island National Seashore. Keep in mind that many hotels and restaurants close for the cold-weather months.

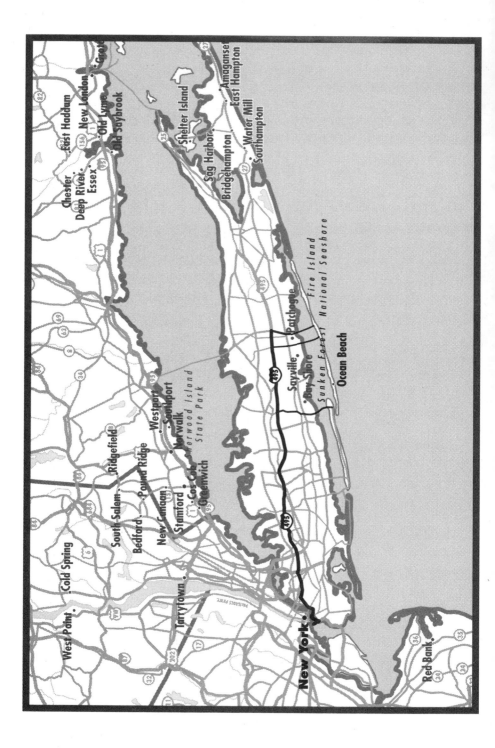

There are several ways to reach the island from Manhattan if you don't have a car. You can take either the Long Island Railroad or a jitney to the ferries at Bay Shore, Sayville, or Patchogue. You can also take a taxi from Manhattan (without spending a fortune) to Bay Shore Ferry. If you're driving your own car, take the Long Island Expressway to exit 53 for Bay Shore, exit 59 for Sayville, or exit 63 for Patchogue. There's a parking field at the ferry dock with daily charges. See "For More Information" at the end of this escape for more details.

DAY 1

Morning

Once on the island, you'll find the largest concentration of hotels and restaurants in **Ocean Beach,** Fire Island's de facto capital. Don't, however, wait very long before making hotel reservations on summer weekends. The rooms fill quickly.

LUNCH: You can have a simple seafood sandwich, a burger, or a salad *alfresco* at **Maguires on the Bay** (Bay Number 1, Bungalow Walk; 516–583–8800).

Afternoon

After lunch relax a bit on your hotel's beach and then head over (by foot or bike) to take a walk at the **Sunken Forest** (516 589–0810), a National Park Service site in Sailors Haven. The Sunken Forest is truly a site to behold. It is made up of 36 acres of dense trees and vines and laced with a boardwalk.

DINNER: **Mathew's Seafood House** (On the bay, Ocean Beach; 516–583–8016) is a good choice for . . . you guessed it! Seafood.

LODGING: Four Seasons Bed and Breakfast, 468 Dehnhoff Walk, Ocean Beach; 516–583–8295. This little B&B is open year-round and has eight rooms (with shared baths).

DAY 2

Morning

BREAKFAST: Breakfast at the Four Seasons Bed and Breakfast.

After breakfast head over by the water taxi to **Watch Hill** (516–597–6455), the island's other National Park Service site, which is about seven miles east of the Sunken Forest. Situated between the bay and the ocean, Watch Hill is made up of wild salt marsh and dense groves of pitch pine and holly and is lovely to walk around.

Then return to Ocean Beach and plant yourselves on the beach until lunch.

LUNCH: Albatross (Bay Walk, Ocean Beach; 516–583–5697) has patio tables that make great perches for people-watching.

After lunch check out the current exhibit at the **Ocean Beach Historical Society** (Bayview and Cottage Walks, Ocean Beach; 516–583–8972).

Later, after more sun and relaxation or perhaps a bike ride (by the way, the Four Seasons provides bikes for your use), head back to the mainland and Manhattan.

THERE'S MORE

Walking. Besides Watch Hill and the Sunken Forests, there are several wonderful walks on Fire Island. There's a 7-mile walk from Watch Hill east to Smith Point, a 7-mile boardwalk trail at Smith Point, and a 4-mile walk east from Smith Point to Moriches Inlet.

Lighthouse. The Fire Island Lighthouse (Fire Island National Seashore; 516–661–4876) is located on the western end of Fire Island. You can visit the visitors center in the keeper's quarters next to the nineteenth-century lighthouse.

OTHER RECOMMENDED RESTAURANTS AND LODGINGS

Clegg's Hotel, 478 Bayberry Walk, Ocean Beach; (516) 583–5399. Directly across from the ferry dock, this very simple (not luxurious) hotel was built in the 1920s by the grandfather of the current proprietor.

The Inn Between, corner of Oneida Street and Bay View Avenue, Ocean Bay Park; (516) 583–8088. An informal restaurant on the bay.

Place in the Sun, 987 Surfview Walk, Ocean Beach; (516) 583–5716. Here you'll find five guest rooms with two shared baths plus an outdoor shower and sauna, open to nonsmokers only.

Fire Island Lighthouse is part of Fire Island's charm.

FOR MORE INFORMATION

Fire Island National Seashore, 120 Laurel Street, Patchogue, NY 11772; (516) 289–4810. South of Montauk Highway, off West Avenue.

Fire Island Tourism Bureau, 49 Main Street, Sayville, NY 11782; (516) 563–8448.

GETTING THERE

By train: The Long Island Railroad provides daily service from Pennsylvania Station to the three towns (one-way fares range from $6.00 to $11.00, depending on whether you go peak or off-peak). The trains leave every thirty to sixty minutes, beginning at 6:36 A.M. weekdays and 7:15 A.M. on weekends. The ferry terminal at Patchogue is within walking distance of the railroad station, and the ferries at Bay Shore and Sayville are a short taxi ride away. The Long Island Railroad also offers packages that include the train and ferry. For information call (718) 217–5477 or (516) 822–5477.

By taxi: Tommy's Taxi takes you from a variety of Manhattan locations to the Bay Shore ferry. Departures from Manhattan are from 8:00 A.M. to 9:00 P.M. daily, from April through the end of October. Fares are approximately $15 one-way Mondays through Saturdays and $18 one-way Sundays and holidays. For more information call (516) 665–4800.

David's Taxi operates regularly between the Bayshore ferries and 68th Street and Third Avenue in Manhattan. One-way fare is $15 Mondays through Saturdays and $18 Sundays. For more information call (516) 665–4384 or (516) 665–1515.

By ferry: For current ferry fares and schedules, call one of the ferry companies.

Bay Shore Ferries: (516) 666–3600 or (516) 665–3600.

Sayville Ferries: (516) 589–0810.

Patchogue Ferries: (516) 475–1665.

SOUTHERN
NEW ENGLAND
ESCAPES

Lower Fairfield County

EXPLORING THE GOLD COAST

2 NIGHTS

Magnificent homes and estates • Antiques and crafts shops
Tag sales • Beaches • Marine life

Big old Victorian houses on golf course–like lawns, estates poised on the shores of Long Island Sound, tidal rivers swollen with yachts and sailboats. This little chunk of Connecticut, colonizing the state's southwestern corner, is home to a small galaxy of prosperous towns.

Unfortunately, many would-be visitors skip over the whole area, assuming it's a pocket of bedroom communities. Indeed, thanks to its proximity to New York (most of the towns can be reached in less than an hour), many of its residents commute into the city daily; nevertheless, lower Fairfield County is a good fit for a weekend escape. Within the span of two days, you can hopscotch from town to town (including Greenwich, Norwalk, and Westport), sampling exceptionally good restaurants and discovering truly top-notch museums and shops. On top of that you'll find plenty of opportunities to wander around in gardens, in woodland preserves, and along the shore.

Many of the communities along the coast were established in the 1700s, when the area was a thriving commercial center. Most of them are linked by the Boston Post Road (which dates back to the eighteenth century), also known as US Route 1 and frequently referred to as the Boston Post Road, Old Post Road, or simply The Post Road. To confuse visitors even more, US Route 1 has a variety of other names in various communities it passes through on the East Coast between the states of Maine and Florida. Its original purpose—to connect the communities and provide food and lodging for weary

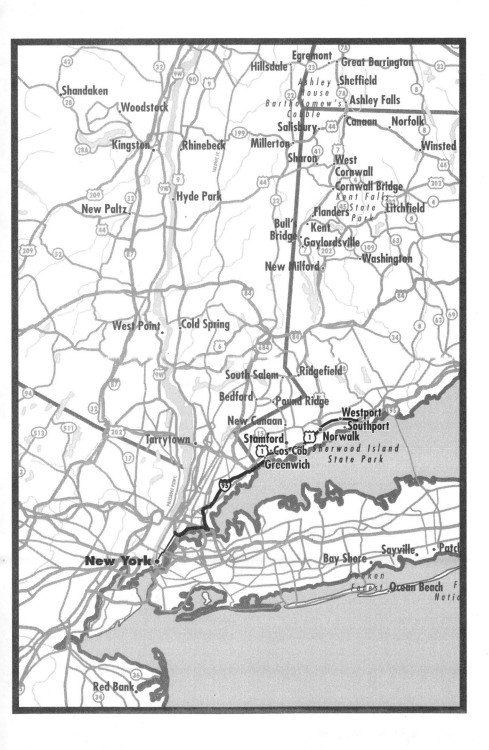

travelers along the way—is still very much alive, though in a nineties version. Along the way you'll pass big-name stores like Staples and Stew Leonard's, as well as fast-food chains, gas stations, movie theaters, and the usual combination platter of suburban retailers.

DAY 1

Afternoon

If you want to do as the locals do, skip out of Manhattan early on a Friday afternoon to beat the rush-hour traffic. Make your destination **Greenwich** (a mere 28 miles from Times Square, I–95, exit 3), which is the first town you come to when entering the state from the southwest.

DINNER: Chef-owned **Restaurant Jean-Louis,** 61 Lewis Street, between Mason Street and Greenwich Avenue (203–622–8450), is a splurgey but well-worth-it choice. For gourmets Chef Jean-Louis needs no introduction: He is widely acclaimed for unfailingly good French cuisine, for which he combines both classical and contemporary techniques. Don't even think of not making reservations. To reach the restaurant, turn left off exit 3 onto Arch Street; cross Greenwich Avenue and then turn left onto Mason Street. Lewis Street is the second street down on the left.

LODGING: The **Homestead,** 420 Field Point Road (203–869–7500), is a fully restored 1799 farmhouse mansion beautifully furnished with country-inn decor and antiques.

DAY 2

Morning

BREAKFAST: One of the beauties of setting out on Friday is that you can take your time to greet the day. Consider lounging around on the wraparound porch of the Homestead before having a light breakfast at **Rue de Croissant,** 95 Railroad Avenue (203–629–1056), a ceramic-tile-floored bistro with fresh-baked breads, muffins, and, of course, croissants.

Devote the morning hours to exploring the town itself, which is centered on Greenwich Avenue, making up an easily strollable historic district complete with wide streets, historic buildings, and stone churches. The shops, of which there are many and all kinds especially on Greenwich and Putnam

The Homestead in Greenwich is a beautifully restored inn dating back to 1799.

avenues, are on the pricey side (with some exceptions such as the consignment shops). Take time out to browse around **Just Books,** 19 East Putnam Avenue (203–869–5023), which purveys titles that appeal to the local clientele (on entertaining, gardening, decorating, and such).

Farther out on East Putnam Avenue is **Putnam Cottage,** 243 East Putnam Avenue (203–869–9697), which was known as Knapp's Tavern during the Revolutionary War and was a meeting place of leaders including General Israel Putnam. The building itself, which dates back to circa 1690, is an attraction (the rare scalloped shingles are especially noteworthy), but indoors there are exhibits as well. Do call in advance, as hours are very limited.

Afterward consider driving around the so-called "country roads" of Greenwich, which are punctuated with massive estates, especially along Lake Avenue, North Street, and Round Hill Road. Many peer out from behind high stone walls, crisp white fences, and iron gates.

One former estate open to the public is the **Bruce Museum,** One Museum Drive (203–869–0376), which had a major renovation. It's a museum of art and science, with exhibits changing about four times a year. The museum is open year-round from 10:00 A.M. to 5:00 P.M. Tuesday through Saturday, and on Sundays from 2:00 to 5:00 P.M.

In nearby Cos Cob you'll find the **Bush–Holley House,** 39 Strickland Road (203–869–6899), a National Historic Landmark (1732) that was originally the home of David Bush, a successful farmer and mill owner. Later, from 1890 to 1925, it was a boardinghouse, owned and operated by the Holley family, where writers and artists gathered. The house is open year-round, Tuesday through Friday from noon to 4:00 P.M. and Sunday from 1:00 to 4:00 P.M.

LUNCH: Travel east on the Post Road or I–95 to **Stamford** (exit 7), where you can take your pick of cuisines from around the globe (Thai, Indian, Italian, Mexican, German, Chinese, Japanese, French, American—you name it) or join the regulars at **Bull's Head Diner,** 43 High Ridge Road (203–961–1400), which boasts a nine-page menu of mainstream favorites, including lots of Greek specialties.

Afternoon

Stamford is home to more than twenty Fortune 500 corporations, which have colonized its forest of very new-looking office towers. It's also home to several worthwhile attractions such as the **Whitney Museum of American Art at Champion,** in Champion Plaza at Atlantic Street and Tresser Boulevard (203–358–7652), a local branch of New York's prestigious Whitney Museum, offering changing exhibits and free gallery talks. It's open year-round, Tuesday through Saturday from 11:00 A.M. to 5:00 P.M. The talks are held on Tuesdays, Thursdays, and Saturdays at 12:30 P.M. Also in Stamford is a unique fish-shaped church designed by Wallace K. Harrison. The **First Presbyterian Church,** 1101 Bedford Street (203–324–9522), was built in 1958; its stained-glass windows are by Gabriel Loire of Chartres, France. **Cavalier Galleries & Sculpture Garden,** One Landmark Square (203–325–3009), is a sculpture garden with more than thirty large-scale sculptures. It's open year-round, Tuesday through Friday from 10:00 A.M. to 4:30 P.M. and Saturday from 10:00 A.M. to 4:00 P.M.

One of Stamford's most popular attractions, as well as a one-of-a-kind shopping experience, is **United House Wrecking,** 535 Hope Street (203–348–5371), which purveys the spoils of demolitions and estate sales (antiques, architectural items, old lighting and plumbing fixtures—you have to see this place). It's open year-round, Monday through Saturday from 9:30 A.M. to 5:30 P.M., and Sunday from noon to 5:00 P.M.

Once you've "done" Stamford, hop back on I–95 and take exit 15 to get to **Norwalk.** Norwalk has a very pronounced maritime feel to it. It's home to an exceptionally informative maritime museum, which is called, not surprisingly, the **Maritime Center at Norwalk,** located at 10 North Water Street (203–852–0700) in **SoNo** (South Norwalk). Half an hour in this place and you'll have a healthy respect for Long Island Sound and Norwalk's busy harbor life. Among its highlights: an aquarium with sharks and seals, an IMAX theater, a boatbuilding demonstration, and several interactive displays. Walk out the door and you're a couple of blocks away from SoNo's thriving epicenter, which is crammed with funky galleries, boutiques, and a selection of restaurants and bars. SoNo is a revitalized nineteenth-century seaside neighborhood listed on the National Register of Historic Places. If time permits, visit the **Brookfield/SoNo Craft Center,** 127 Washington Street (203–853–6155), which displays works by more than 300 artists. It's open year-round, Tuesday through Saturday from 10:00 A.M. to 5:00 P.M. and on Sunday from noon to 5:00 P.M. Another truly worthwhile attraction in Norwalk is the **Lockwood-Mathews Mansion Museum,** 295 West Avenue (203–838–1434), a fifty-five-room Victorian mansion built by financier LeGrand Lockwood. Hours are limited, so do call ahead.

Plan to overnight in **Westport,** a town about which one resident summed up beautifully: "If you live in Westport, you don't have to go away to vacation." Indeed the town, which is a summer weekend escape for many New Yorkers, has a resorty feel to it, especially in the warm-weather months. The most scenic way to reach it from Norwalk (scenic, but not overwhelmingly time-consuming—we're talking maybe a ten-minute drive) is to follow Saugatuck Avenue.

Turn right onto Riverside Avenue and follow for less than half a mile to the Bridge Street Bridge, which is noteworthy only in that it's fabulously redundant. Cross over the Saugatuck River and turn right onto Compo Road South, which puts you in the **Compo Beach** neighborhood. As you approach the water, you'll suddenly begin to feel as if you've been miraculously transported to Nantucket, Martha's Vineyard, or some other idyllic seaside community, especially on a sunny day. You see physically fit people of all ages walking designer dogs, balancing on in-line skates, zipping along (clad in Spandex) on bikes, or cruising in antique cars.

Carry on east of Compo Beach to the **Greens Farms** area, which is home to one megahome after another, especially along Beachside Avenue. By the way if you have bikes to take along, this is a great biking route. Beachside Avenue takes you right into **Southport,** one of Connecticut's most picturesque communities. It's filled with Federal, Greek Revival, and Victorian houses and a couple of very grand churches. The best way to enjoy it is to park your car by the harbor and just wander around.

DINNER: If it's summer, try the **Beach House,** 233 Hillspoint Road (203–226–7005), which sits smack dab on the beach. It's open year-round but is especially festive during the warm-weather months, when it's abuzz with tanned Westporters talking tennis, golf, and sailing.

During the colder-weather months, choose the **Bridge Cafe,** 5 Riverside Avenue (203–226–4800). Located on the Saugatuck River, this festively decorated American-Mediterranean restaurant serves fresh seafood, steak, and chicken dishes, as well as a selection of inventive salads.

After dinner consider taking in a show at the **Westport Country Playhouse,** 25 Powers Court (203–227–4177). This sixty-two-year-old theater has had many a name-name on its stage including Bette Davis, Helen Hayes, and Douglas Fairbanks Jr. The **Westport Arts Center,** Morningside Drive (203–222–7070), also hosts frequent theatrical events as well as exhibits, as does **The White Barn Theatre,** Newtown Turnpike (203–227–3768), and the **Fairfield County Stage Company,** 25 Powers Court (203–227–1290). During the summer months there are free concerts at the **Levitt Pavilion for the Performing Arts** (off Jesup Road, behind the library; 203–226–7600).

LODGING: The **Inn at National Hall,** Two Post Road West (203–221–1351), in Westport is a restored historic landmark building (originally built in 1873) right on the shores of the Saugatuck River. There are fifteen truly luxurious, individually designed guest rooms, seven of which are suites. Absolutely every inch of the inn is artistically designed with lots of trompe l'oeil, handcrafted stenciling, and arched ceilings.

DAY 3

Morning

BREAKFAST: If you stay at the Inn at National Hall, a full breakfast is included; otherwise, take your pick of places for coffee and consider brunching later.

Coffee And, 343 Main Street (203–227–3808), is locally famed for its home-made doughnuts and muffins (try the chocolate-frosted doughnut), but the coffee's better at the local **Starbucks,** One Parker Harding Plaza (203–454–3205).

After breakfast take a walk around the center of town, which has been called a "Mall without Walls" because of the number of shops—many of them parts of major chains. There's a Barneys of New York, Eddie Bauer, J. Crew, Williams-Sonoma, and Banana Republic. There are also several one-of-a-kind shops including Uproar, full of innovative home furnishings and accessories, and The American Hand, a crafts shop. In addition you'll find many antiques shops in this part of town as well as along the Post Road. Westport is also home to the headquarters of the international humanitarian group **Save the Children,** 54 Wilton Road (203–221–4000), where you can find all sorts of one-of-a-kind gifts including pottery, musical instruments, and jewelry crafted by children from around the world.

If you're a bird-watcher, consider parking yourself on a bench along the banks of the Saugatuck River at **Levitt Pavilion,** a park right by the library. During migration seasons you may see more exotic birds here in half an hour than some people see in a lifetime. You're likely also to see scullers sliding over the water like water spiders and hardworking oarspeople rowing to the commands of a coxswain. Westport is home to the Saugatuck Rowing Association, a training facility for both competitive and recreational rowers.

BRUNCH: A great Sunday brunch choice is **Cafe Christina,** One Main Street (203–221–7950). Here you'll find traditional brunch dishes as well as pasta salads, sandwiches, and pizzas. It's located in Westport's renovated former town library. Prices are moderate.

After brunch head over to **Sherwood Island State Park** or back to **Compo Beach** for a day at the beach. Sherwood Island State Park is a 238-acre public playground where you'll pay about $6.00 to park, whereas Compo Beach is a more exclusive beach, where parking costs a whopping $25. For a break from the sun, take a look around the brand-new **Department of Environmental Protection Museum,** which is housed in a former concession stand on the West Beach of Sherwood Island. In it are a wide variety of items from state parks all over the state including a pipe used to transfer water at the Burlington Fish Hatchery, a perch-hatching tray dating back to 1930, and a 1935 lobster pot. Admission is free. Hours are 10:30 A.M. to 4:30 P.M., Wednesday through Sunday year-round; during summer months hours are extended. Call (203) 226–6983 for information. Or stop by the **Nature Center for Environmental Activities,** 10 Woodside Lane (203–227–7253), a sixty-two-acre wildlife sanctuary with a museum in Westport. To return, hop back on I–95 to get back to New York City.

THERE'S MORE

Nature walks. Look at a map of Fairfield County and you'll see green patches everywhere. It's home to quite a few nature preserves including the following:

Audubon Center of Greenwich, 613 Riversville Road, Greenwich (Route 15, exit 28; 203–869–5272), is a must for bird-watchers. It's a forty-eight-acre sanctuary with 15 miles of woodland trails.

Barlett Arboretum, at 151 Brookdale Road off High Ridge Road (1 mile north of Route 15, exit 35), in Stamford; (203) 322–6971. Here you'll find sixty-three acres of natural woodland and gardens to explore.

The Nature Conservancy's Devil's Den Preserve, 33 Pent Road, Weston; (203) 226–4991. Wander through 1,746 acres woven with more than 20 miles of well-marked trails through predominantly deciduous forests.

Stamford Museum & Nature Center, at 39 Scofieldtown Road, Stamford; (203) 322–1646. This museum is home to a nineteenth-century working farm, a country store, and several galleries exhibiting farm tools, some artwork, and assorted Americana. It sprawls over 118 acres, offering many trails and picnic areas.

Sheffield Island Lighthouse can be reached by ferry from Hope Dock, which is at the corner of Washington Street and North Water Street in Norwalk. The lighthouse, which dates back to 1868, has four levels and ten rooms to explore and is surrounded by three acres of prime picnic grounds. For more information call (203) 838–9444.

Stargazing. Rolnick Observatory, 182 Bayberry Lane, Westport; (203) 227–0925. Two nights a week, Wednesdays and Thursdays (or by appointment), the public can take in a free view of the night sky via a powerful telescope. Operated by Westport Astronomical Society.

SPECIAL EVENTS

August. SoNo Arts Celebration, Washington Street in South Norwalk. A big block party with food, crafts, arts, and entertainment.

Mid-September. Septemberfest, Greenwich Common, Greenwich. Carnival rides, entertainment, international food festival, a pet show, and more.

Norwalk Oyster Festival, Veterans Park, Norwalk. This annual event celebrates Long Island Sound's seafaring history with entertainment, arts and crafts, boat trips, oyster shucking, and lots of foods.

Late July–early August. Pequot Library Book Sale, Southport. This is the largest book sale in the state of Connecticut. It features more than ninety thousand volumes in forty-five categories and attracts more than ten thousand people. For more information call (203) 259–0346.

OTHER RECOMMENDED RESTAURANTS AND LODGINGS

Fairfield

Centro, 1435 Post Road; (203) 255–1210. A great choice for dinner, Centro attracts a beautiful-people crowd who come for the pasta, gourmet pizzas, and other reliably good dishes. You can also count on good, chewy bread and olives for appetizers.

Spazzi Trattoria and Wine Bar, Brick Wall Plaza, 1229 Post Road; (203) 256–1629. A lively spot where festive pasta dishes are prepared by artistic cooks. Be sure to save room for the desserts; they're truly magnificent.

Greenwich

Bertrand, 253 Greenwich Avenue; (203) 661–4459. A top French restaurant with a beautiful-people clientele.

La Grange, at the Homestead Inn, 420 Field Point Road; (203) 869–7500. This local favorite serves classic French cuisine.

Norwalk

Barcelona, 63 North Main Street, South Norwalk; (203) 899–0088. Go with friends to this delightful Spanish tapas bar.

Meson Galicia, 10 Wall Street; (203) 866–8800. For more formal Spanish dining, this restaurant is a special treat.

Stamford

Siena Ristorante, 519 Summer Street; (203) 351–0898. A Tuscan restaurant, Siena is locally famed for its *risotto* and pasta dishes. Also wonderful are its desserts, which include pannacotta (a cooked-milk custard made with vanilla bean) served with a purée of fresh fruits.

Weston

Cobb's Mill Inn, 12 Old Mill Road; (203) 227–7221. Housed in an eighteenth-century mill, this restaurant draws a large sentimental crowd who have traditionally been coming for holidays, birthdays, anniversaries, and other occasions. Though the food is not remarkable, the view—of the pond and waterfall—and the atmosphere are every bit Fairfield County.

Westport

Cotswold Inn, 76 Myrtle Avenue; (203) 226–3766. A tiny (four rooms) inn tucked away on a back street with wall-to-wall charm.

Promis, 1563 Post Road East (203) 256–3309). Located on the Westport/Fairfield line, this restaurant is well liked locally for its unfailingly good cuisine that is French-inspired Continental. The menu includes a selection of seafood, chicken, duck, and lamb dishes. Signature dishes are its *risottos* and soufflé desserts.

Sol e Luna Ristorante Toscana, 25 Powers Court; (203) 222–3837. If you're in the mood for great Northern Italian cuisine, head straight to Sol e Luna. Located right next to the Westport Playhouse, it tends to attract a pretheater crowd during the season.

FOR MORE INFORMATION

Connecticut Department of Economic Development, 864 Brook Street, Rocky Hill, CT 06067–3405; (800) CT–BOUND.

Fairfield County Tourism District, 297 West Avenue, Norwalk, CT 06850; (203) 854–7825 or (800) 8–NORWALK.

Greenwich Chamber of Commerce, Two Lafayette Court, Greenwich, CT 06830; (203) 869–3500.

Yankee Heritage District, The Gatehouse, Mathews Park, 297 West Avenue, Norwalk, CT 06850; (203) 854–7825.

Westport Chamber of Commerce, 15 Imperial Avenue, Westport, CT 06880; (203) 227–9234.

Ridgefield and New Canaan

TWO TOWNS TO TOOL AROUND

1. NIGHT

Historic villages • Stately homes
Antiques and crafts shops • Rural countryside

Not too many towns can say they have a gourmet sidewalk hot-dog vendor. Well, Ridgefield can. Right in the heart of town, at Chez Leonard's cart, you can take your pick of a variety of gourmet hot dogs including Le Hot Dog Alsacienne (with sauerkraut, French mustard, and caraway seeds), Le Hot Dog Suisse (with Swiss fondue cheese), Le Hot Dog Mexicaine (with chili and Bermuda onions), and Le Hot Dog Excelsior Veneziano (sautéed peppers, onions, olives, tomatoes). Chez Leonard's hot-dog stand is not the only place in town with "good taste," however. The whole village, with its wide Main Street lined with buildings that range from pre-Revolutionary to Victorian, epitomizes good taste. There are no major interstates, parkways, or railroads that take you right there, which may have something to do with the town's wonderful unblemished quality. Nevertheless, as lovely as Ridgefield is, it has been growing quickly; in fact, many longtime residents talk about how beautiful it "used" to be.

Less than half an hour's drive away is **New Canaan,** which is also an attractive residential community. The two are just over the New York border, less than 60 miles from Manhattan in the southwest corner of the state. Together they make up a simple, but charming weekend getaway with plenty of shops, restaurants, and scenery to keep you happily busy.

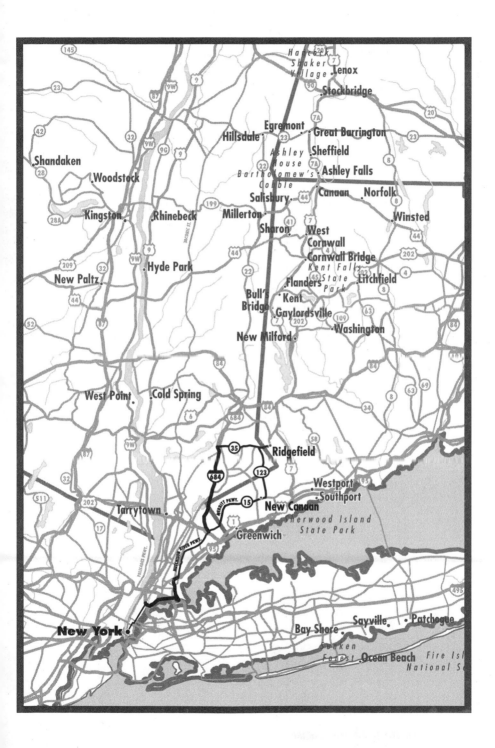

Ridgefield's Keeler Tavern Museum dates back to 1715.

DAY 1

Morning

If you start out early in the morning, you'll have the whole day to poke around Ridgefield's shops and galleries. The drive should take no more than an hour and a half. Though there are several ways to get there, we recommend taking I–684 north and getting off at the Katonah/Cross River exit. Turn right and follow NY 35, which becomes CT 35 and takes you right into Ridgefield. If you have more time, consider combining this trip with our Northern Westchester escape (see page 26). The two fit together beautifully.

Once you get to Ridgefield, start by grabbing a parking spot (there's a lot behind the Ridgefield Bank and Town Hall) and then set out to explore by foot. The hub of town can best be seen by walking down one side of Main Street (starting at the corner of Market Street, opposite St. Stephen's Church) to Ballard Park, then returning on the opposite side. Though it's just a 2- or 3-block walk, allow yourself plenty of time to meander in and out of the shops. Some standout shops include **Hunter's Consignments,** 426 Main Street (the entrance is actually in an alleyway linking Main Street with the aforementioned parking area), and **The Silk Purse,** 470 Main Street. Both are consignment shops crammed with everything from silver cigarette holders to monster armoires.

Though you'll be tempted to lunch at Gail's Station House, 378 Main Street, consider saving it for Sunday brunch. If it's a beautiful day, you may want to take a couple of Leonard's hot dogs into **Ballard Park,** which is a lovely green with lots of inviting benches. If you really want to go gourmet, gather picnic items at **Hay Day,** 21 Governor Street (accessible from the aforementioned parking area). Don't be shocked, however, if your picnic ends up costing a bundle. Hay Day, which prides itself on its ultrafresh fruits and vegetables, home-baked breads and desserts, and astounding selection of wines, cheeses, and prepared dishes, is on the pricey side. Still, its foods and wines are nonpareil. The adjoining **Hay Day Cafe,** 21 Governor Street (203–438–2344), is a good alternative to a picnic lunch. There's a satiating selection of salads, pastas, and soups, as well as entrées of seafood, beef, lamb, and chicken—all made with the freshest ingredients imaginable. Beware of the desserts, however; they are not for the calorie-conscious.

Afternoon

After lunch wander up the street to the **Aldrich Museum of Contemporary Art,** 258 Main Street (203–438–4519), which has changing exhibits along with a sculpture garden that elicits all sorts of puzzled looks and "Is this really art?" kinds of comments.

From the museum it's a fifteen-minute walk (or couple-minute drive) to the **Keeler Tavern,** 132 Main Street, at the junction of Routes 33 and 35 (203–438–5485). Here you can learn all about the town's history, which has its roots in Colonial times, when it was a way station on the carriage road between New York and Boston. The Keeler Tavern (which dates back to 1715) was an inn providing accommodations for the carriage passengers. Now it's a museum complete with guides dressed in period costumes. One of its most noticeable features, however, is a cannonball lodged in a wall. During the Battle of Ridgefield (1777) in the Revolutionary War, it was "sent" by the British.

To see a small but stop-in-your-tracks-and-stare collection of some of Ridgefield's most stunning homes, detour over to High Ridge Road (from the Keeler Tavern head west on Route 35, turn right onto Parley, and then right onto High Ridge). These magnificent mansions, surrounded by flawless lawns, are especially attractive during the year-end holidays, when each one vies for your attention with wreaths adorning every window.

DINNER: A popular choice for wedding receptions and other celebrations, **Stonehenge,** Route 7 (203–438–6511), combines both good looks (its photogenic pond and grounds are every bridal couple's dream backdrop) and quality French cuisine. Dinner entrées run from $18 to $30.

LODGING: Elms Restaurant and Tavern, 500 Main Street, Ridgefield; (203) 438–2541. A historic inn, built in the 1760s. Guest rooms are furnished with some antiques and four-poster beds. The kitchen, which in recent years was taken over by chef Brendan Walsh, is one of the best in Fairfield County.

DAY 2

Morning

BRUNCH: If it's Sunday, make sure you beat the après-church crowds for brunch at **Gail's Station House,** 378 Main Street (203–438–9775), and if you can, grab one of the tables by the front windows so that you can watch the passersby or a table outside if it's a nice day. Also . . . go starved. This funky little restaurant serves huge portions (try the Texas Pink) and yummy homebaked goods.

Afternoon

After brunch you can take your time driving back to New York, stopping in New Canaan (and any antiques shops or tag sales) along the way.

To reach New Canaan, follow Route 35 west. Just after you cross the New York border, turn left onto Route 123. Several miles down, you'll cross the border again, into New Canaan. This route takes you through serenely scenic landscapes, passing horse farms, a golf course, and quite a few megahomes.

New Canaan, the center of which you can reach by turning right onto Locust Avenue, is a spick-and-span tidy residential community where most residents look as though they could model for a Ralph Lauren catalog. This is Connecticut just as you pictured it. The side streets are lined with large multichimneyed houses with wraparound porches, graceful columns, and the kind of gardens you see featured in glossy magazines.

New Canaan is home to the **Silvermine Guild Arts Center,** 1037 Sil-vermine Road (203–966–5617), which is an art school with galleries show-casing the works of member artists and artisans. There is also the **New Canaan Historical Society,** 13 Oenoke Ridge Road (203–966–1776), which oversees the original town hall, library and drugstore among other buildings. Both of the above have limited visiting hours, so call ahead.

If it's a beautiful day, take time out to walk around the **New Canaan Nature Center,** 144 Oenoke Ridge Road (203–966–9577). Here there are more than forty acres of woodland, meadows, and ponds plus gardens and hands-on exhibits.

Before heading back consider stopping at **Gates Restaurant,** 10 Forest Street (203–966–8666), for a cup of cappuccino. Then return to Route 123, which will take you back to the Merritt Parkway for your return trip home.

THERE'S MORE

Antiques. Ridgefield is rife with antiques shops including the Ridgefield Antiques Centre in Route 35's Copps Hill Common, which houses two dozen dealers.

Crafts. Brookfield Craft Center, 286 Whisconier Road, Brookfield; (203) 775–4526. About fifteen minutes away from Ridgefield, this craft center is worth a detour. Here you'll find a school for craftsmanship, an exhibition gallery, and a gift shop. It's located in a historic gristmill complex on Route 25, just east of the four corners intersection with Routes 7 and 202, a few miles north of I–84.

Mall shopping. The Danbury Mall, which used to be The Danbury Fair, is not far from Ridgefield (follow Route 7 north). It has all the big stores—Macy's, Lord & Taylor, Sears—as well as a variety of food vendors.

Sightseeing flights. Scenic small-plane and helicopter rides can be sched-uled at the Danbury Municipal Airport. Trips generally start at about $45 each (based on two people). For information call (203) 743–3300.

SPECIAL EVENTS

Mid-May–mid-June. Art of Northeast USA Exhibition, Silvermine Guild Arts Center, 1037 Silvermine Road, New Canaan; (203) 966–5617. A juried competition with paintings, drawings, and sculpture by participants from the Northeast states.

June–September. Chamber Music Festival, Silvermine Guild Arts Center, 1037 Silvermine Road, New Canaan; (203) 966–5618 (programs). Evening concerts.

September. Annual Fairfield County Region Antique Car Show, East Ridge Middle School, Ridgefield. An annual event, held the first Saturday after Labor Day from 10:00 A.M. to 3:00 P.M. The longest-running antique car show in America. It is the last pre–World War II antique car show in America, which means entries are restricted to unmodified 1942-and-older vehicles. The show usually draws more than 200 cars.

OTHER RECOMMENDED RESTAURANTS AND LODGINGS

New Canaan

The Maples, 179 Oenoke Ridge; (203) 966–2927. A twenty-five-room inn with a grand wraparound porch.

Roger Sherman, 195 Oenoke Ridge; (203) 966–4541. An antiques-furnished inn with just seven rooms; some with fireplaces.

Tequila Mockingbird, 6 Forest Street (between East Avenue and Locust); (203) 966–2222. A Mexican-style cafe with terra-cotta tiled floors, a gaily painted mural, and a good selection of Southwestern and Mexican dishes.

Ridgefield

Stonehenge, Route 7; (203) 438–6511. In addition to being a wonderful restaurant (see description on page 88), Stonehenge is also a lovely country inn.

Thirty Three and A Third, 125 Danbury Road; (203) 438–3904. Tucked away in a shopping center, it's a surprise to find such sophisticated cuisine here. At lunch there are all sorts of salads and sandwiches, and at dinner, a good selection of seafood, steaks, and other dishes. If they're serving *risotto* the day you're there, don't hesitate to order it.

West Lane Inn, 22 West Lane; (203) 438–7323. A historic inn, dating back to the mid-1800s. All rooms are individually decorated. Its restaurant, the Inn at Ridgefield, features continental cuisine in a very elegant setting.

ESCAPE TWO

SOUTHERN NEW ENGLAND

FOR MORE INFORMATION

Connecticut Department of Economic Development, 864 Brook Street, Rocky Hill, CT 06067–3405; (800) CT–BOUND.

Ridgefield Chamber of Commerce, 7 Bailey Avenue, Ridgefield, CT 06877; (203) 438–5992.

Lower Connecticut River Valley

RIVER VALLEY TOWNS

1 NIGHT

River views • River history • Antiques shops
Art galleries • Eighteenth- and nineteenth-century houses
Traditional New England fare
Vintage steam train • Riverboat cruise

With its roots back in the settlement of the New World, this little piece of south-central Connecticut is densely historic. Back in the early 1600s, many colonists settled along the banks of the Connecticut River, from which trading (with ports as far away as the West Indies and the Mediterranean) became a popular activity for centuries to follow.

Today the area is punctuated with small scenic towns that were originally established as shipbuilding and merchant communities. Along the way there are several worthwhile restaurants specializing in New England cuisine, shops where you can buy crafts, antiques, and artwork, and truly warm and welcoming inns.

This two-day excursion takes you to the highlights of the area including Essex, which is one of Connecticut's most visited towns. Be advised that during summer weekends it can be uncomfortably crowded.

DAY 1

Morning

The quickest and most direct route to the area from Manhattan is I–95, which roughly follows the Connecticut shoreline. Get off at Westbrook (exit 65) and

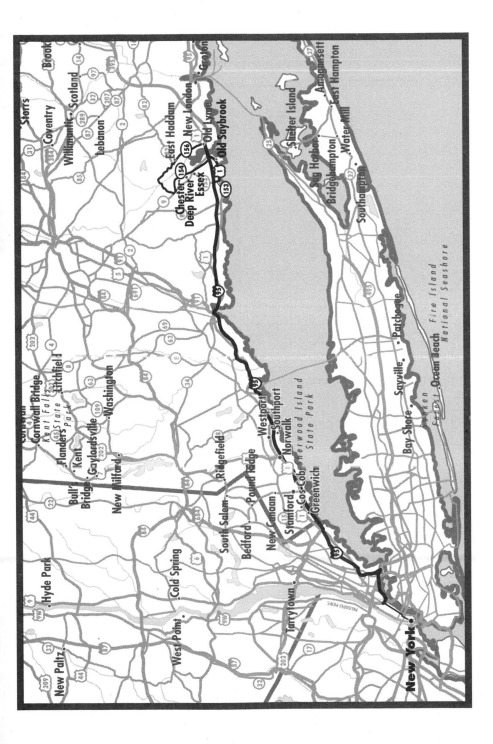

turn right onto Route 153. Follow Route 153 until you come to Route 1, which is locally known as the Shore Route, a steadily scenic road that takes you past picturesque marinas and salt marshes and into **Old Saybrook,** your first stop of the day.

Once a shipbuilding and fishing town, Old Saybrook is now a popular spot for summer vacationers. If you're traveling during a summer weekend, take time out to see the Georgian-style **General William Hart House,** 350 Main Street (860–388–2622), which was once the residence of a prosperous merchant and politician. It's open from mid-June through mid-September, Friday through Sunday, from 12:30 to 4:00 P.M. Those in the market for antiques might want to check out **Essex Saybrook Antiques Village,** 985 Middlesex Turnpike (Route 154) (860–388–0689), where about 125 dealers display their wares.

Afterward continue along Route 154 to head inland to **Essex,** which is home to a stunning collection of beautiful Colonial and Federal houses that were built as far back as the town's eighteenth-century shipbuilding days. The best way to enjoy Essex is to wander about on foot. Main Street is lined with shops selling sweets, jewelry, antiques, artwork, clothing—you name it. To see some of the town's oldest houses, walk up Pratt Street. One of the landmark buildings in town is the **Griswold Inn,** 36 Main Street, where you can settle in for lunch. Dating from 1776, this Essex institution is affectionately referred to as the Gris (pronounced "Griz"). To reach it, walk down Main Street (from Essex Square).

LUNCH: The **Griswold Inn,** 36 Main Street (860–767–1776), is well known and respected for both its accommodations and its food. At lunchtime you can try its own brand of sausages or order a sandwich or salad plate for less than $10.

Afternoon

From the Griswold Inn walk to the riverside end, which is known as the Foot of Main, and you'll come to the **Connecticut River Museum,** Steamboat Dock (860–767–8269). It is housed in a restored 1878 warehouse where steamboats used to stop on their trips between New York and Hartford, unloading passengers and/or freight. A noteworthy attraction in the museum is a full-size reproduction of the *American Turtle,* the world's first submarine. Hours are 10:00 A.M. to 5:00 P.M., Tuesday through Sunday.

From downtown Essex follow Route 154 (Railroad Avenue) west toward Ivoryton, and you'll come to the **Valley Railroad Station,** One Railroad Avenue (860–767–0103). There you can climb aboard a vintage steam train that hoots and whistles its way through the countryside to Chester and back. The trip takes about an hour and a half. You can also combine the train ride with a riverboat sightseeing cruise by getting off at the Deep River station. The combination train/boat ride adds up to about three hours of your time. The main season for the steam train and riverboat is May through October; call for information on their Christmas schedule.

Afterward you can continue upriver by following Route 154 (just keep bearing right when the road forks). It'll take you right to **Deep River,** your home for the night.

LODGING: **Riverwind Country Inn,** 209 Main Street, Deep River (860–526–2014), has just eight rooms (all with private bath), each beautifully decorated with antiques and stenciling. There are also several common rooms with fireplaces.

DINNER: In nearby Ivoryton you'll find **The Copper Beech Inn,** 46 Main Street (860–767–0330), for an elegant French meal.

DAY 2

Morning

BREAKFAST: A Southern buffet breakfast (ham, biscuits, hot casseroles, fresh fruit, coffee cake) is included in the room rate at the Riverwind.

Return to Route 154 and follow it to **Chester,** an attractive village most writers cannot resist calling picture-postcard perfect. Indeed it is. Turn left from Route 154 onto Main Street and you'll find a handful of shops, galleries, and restaurants in the buildings that line the street. One outstanding find is Carol LeWitt's **Ceramica** store, 36 & 38 Main Street (860–526–9978), which is packed with magnificent Italian pottery.

Just east of the town center, on Route 148, you can climb aboard a ferry that's been shuttling between the east and west banks of the Connecticut since 1769. The five-minute crossing operates throughout the day, from April through November, at a nominal charge.

Once on board, all eyes turn on **Gillette Castle,** 67 River Road, Hadlyme (860–526–2336), which looms over the river on the east bank. It was

The Goodspeed Opera House overlooks the Connecticut River.

built as a dreamhouse-come-to-life by the actor/playwright William Gillette. When he died, the state of Connecticut purchased it and turned it and the surrounding land into a state park. There are picnic grounds, rest rooms, food concession stands, and canoe rentals. Call for more information. The Castle is open during the summer months.

In nearby **East Haddam,** you'll find the **Goodspeed Opera House,** Route 82 (860–873–8668), which has a statewide (and actually, even wider) reputation for reviving old American musicals. The opera house itself, a Victorian jewel, is exquisite both inside and out. Tours are given on Mondays and Saturdays in July, August, and September. The theater season runs from April to December.

East Haddam is an attraction in itself, with many impeccably preserved buildings dating back to steamboat days. There's also a little red schoolhouse where Nathan Hale taught in 1773–74, before he was hanged as a spy by the British.

Head south on Route 156 to **Old Lyme,** which is right near the mouth of the river, across from Old Saybrook. Its popularity began in the days of clipper ships and the China trade, but later, like all beautiful places, was discovered and colonized by quite a few artists including Childe Hassam, Willard Metcalf, and Henry Ward Ranger, who called themselves American Impressionists. These artists stayed at "Miss Florence's" boardinghouse, which is now the **Florence Griswold Museum,** 96 Lyme Street (860–434–5542). Florence Griswold, an art lover, was the daughter of a ship captain. The house, which was built in 1817, is filled with period furnishings and showcases changing exhibitions including New England furnishings and decorative arts. It's open from June through October, Tuesday through Saturday from 10:00 A.M. to 5:00 P.M. and Sundays from 1:00 to 5:00 P.M. The rest of the year it's open Wednesday through Sunday from 1:00 to 5:00 P.M.

LUNCH: Right next door to the Florence Griswold Museum is the **Bee and Thistle Inn,** 100 Lyme Street (860–434–1667), a very welcoming inn that dates back to 1756. You can order a simple sandwich or perhaps a more elaborate seafood dish (there are usually daily specials).

Other worthwhile stops in town include the **Congregational Church** on Lyme Street, which is a 1910 copy of the original 1816 structure that was destroyed by fire, and the **The Lyme Academy of Fine Arts,** 84 Lyme Street (860–434–5232), which has changing exhibits during the summer months. Hours are Monday through Friday from 9:00 A.M. to 5:00 P.M., Saturday from 9:00 A.M. to 4:00 P.M., and Sunday from 1:00 to 4:00 P.M.

From Old Lyme you can easily hop back on I–95 south and return to New York City.

THERE'S MORE

Cruises. Camelot Cruises, 1 Marine Park, Haddam (860–345–8591), offers lunch, dinner, Sunday brunch, and special-theme cruises (mystery outings, fall foliage trips) aboard the 400-passenger cruise ship *Camelot.*

Parks. The Selden Neck State Park is a 528-acre park in the Connecticut River that you can reach only by water. It's located 2 miles south of Gillette Castle State Park in East Haddam, from which you can get additional information and permits (call 860–526–2336). Canoes and kayaks can be launched at the ferry slip below the castle.

SPECIAL EVENTS

Mid-July. Annual Ancient Muster, Deep River. Fifty to sixty fife-and-drum corps recall Revolutionary War days in this annual parade that has been taking place for more than 120 years.

Late July. Annual Arts and Crafts Show, Old Saybrook. Held on the Town Green and Main Street, this annual event attracts more than twenty-five thousand people.

Mid-October. "Historic Homes Along the River." A house tour including ten to twelve historic homes. For details call (860) 873–8995.

December. Victorian Christmas at Gillette Castle in Hadlyme. Every year the castle is decorated with evergreens and Victorian ornaments. Musical groups perform on weekend afternoons; (860) 526–2336.

Mid-December. Torchlight Parade, Old Saybrook. This parade is a tradition that dates back to the early colonial days. Fife-and-drum corps march down Main Street to meet townspeople on the Town Green to sing carols.

OTHER RECOMMENDED RESTAURANTS AND LODGINGS

East Haddam

Bishopsgate Inn, Goodspeed Landing; (860) 873–1677. Right across from the Goodspeed Opera House, this early nineteenth-century shipbuilder's house has half a dozen tastefully decorated rooms, all with theatrical names.

Essex

Griswold Inn, 36 Main Street; (860) 767–1776. In addition to dining (see page 77), "The Gris" is a fine choice for staying the night. It's every inch New England, with exposed rough-hewn rafters, low ceilings, and hooked rugs. Its Sunday morning "Hunt Breakfasts" are legendary, with help-yourself, unlimited servings of all sorts of breakfast favorites including kippers and grits.

Old Lyme

Old Lyme Inn, 85 Lyme Street; (860) 434–2600. Dating from the 1850s, this clapboard farmhouse is beautifully furnished with canopy beds, marble-topped dressers, and antique pieces. The dining room is open for lunch and dinner.

Old Saybrook

Saybrook Point Inn, 2 Bridge Street; (800) 243–0212 or (860) 395–2000. A sixty-two-room contemporary hotel with eighteenth-century repro English decor. Ask for a room facing the marina.

FOR MORE INFORMATION

Connecticut Department of Economic Development, 864 Brook Street, Rocky Hill, CT 06067–3405; (800) CT–BOUND.

Connecticut Valley Tourism Commission, 393 Main Street, Middletown, CT 06457; (860) 347–6924 or (800) 486–3346.

Old Saybrook Chamber of Commerce, P.O. Box 625, Old Saybrook, CT 06475; (860) 388–3266.

Southeastern Shoreline
MARITIME MYSTIC AND MORE

1 NIGHT

Historic ships • Submarines • Sea and river ports
Maritime museum • Aquarium • Shopping
Beaches • Seafood dining

Connecticut's maritime roots are most visible in this part of the state, especially in the towns of New London, Groton, Mystic, and Stonington.

You could easily spend a whole day alone at Mystic Seaport; however, there are many other attractions in the area. Consider combining this trip with the Southern New England Escape Three, which takes you to the nearby towns in the Lower Connecticut River Valley.

DAY 1

Morning

Like the rest of the Connecticut shoreline, this area can be easily reached by taking I–95 north. Set out as early as you can, as there is a lot to squeeze into two days.

Make your first stop **New London** (exit 83), a former whaling town. The number-one attraction here is the **United States Coast Guard Academy,** 15 Mohegan Avenue (860–444–8270). Visitors can tour the grounds, the visitors center and museum, the chapel, and the tall ship *Eagle* when it's in port. The latter is used by cadets for training purposes.

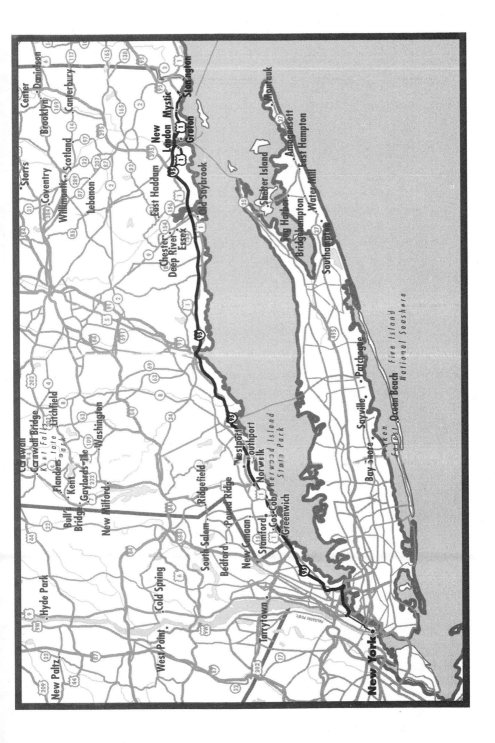

Whale Oil Row, 105–119 Huntington Street, is another interesting attraction in New London. It's a collection of four 1832 temple-front mansions.

Also in town is the **Monte Cristo Cottage,** 325 Pequot Avenue (860–443–0051), which was the boyhood home of playwright Eugene O'Neill as well as the setting for two of his plays, *Ah! Wilderness* and *Long Day's Journey into Night.*

From New London it's a short drive east to **Groton,** which is known as "The Submarine Capital of the World." Indeed, this shore-hugging community is home to the **USS *Nautilus* Memorial, U.S. Naval Base,** Route 12, Groton (800–343–0079). The USS *Nautilus* was the world's first nuclear-powered submarine and is now a National Historic Landmark, permanently berthed. There are meticulously assembled museum displays recounting the history of the U.S. Submarine Force. It's open for touring year-round, but hours vary; call ahead.

From Groton drive east on Route 1 to **Mystic,** where you'll find the famed **Mystic Seaport,** 50 Greenmanville Avenue (860–572–0711), a huge open-air museum. Start by taking time out for lunch.

LUNCH: The Seamen's Inne, 105 Greenmanville Avenue (860–536–9649), located right next to the seaport entrance, serves New England fare.

Afternoon

Once you've fortified yourself with a good lunch, head into the seaport. Here you'll see more historic seagoing vessels, from a dugout canoe to America's sole surviving wooden whaling ship, than most people see in a lifetime. The star attraction for many is the 113-foot *Charles W. Morgan,* a whaling ship that was built in 1841. The height of America's shipbuilding and whaling prosperity is magnificently captured at this seventeen-acre living-history museum. On land there are dozens of nineteenth-century buildings that were brought to the seaport and restored. Highly skilled men and women, in period costume, demonstrate various maritime skills such as sail handling, oystering, and rope-work. Allow at least a couple of hours (even three or four) to roam around. Admission prices vary.

Shoppers shouldn't miss the **Mystic Seaport Museum Store,** which is right at the main gate (South Gate). There are two floors where you can find all sorts of must-haves from simple old-fashioned candies to multi-thousand-

Built in 1841, the Charles W. Morgan *is the last surviving wooden whaling ship.*

dollar lightship baskets. It's open daily from 10:00 A.M. to 5.00 P.M. You'll find more shops inside the seaport, but this one gets first prize.

DINNER: Abbott's Lobster in the Rough, 117 Pearl Street, Noank (860–536–7719), is a must if you love seafood. It's a huge, massively popular seaside restaurant with picnic tables upon which huge platters of spanking-fresh seafood are devoured. Expect to wait in line. Noank is about ten minutes south of Mystic.

LODGING: The Old Mystic Inn, 52 Main Street, Old Mystic (860–572–9422). Not to be confused with the Inn at Mystic, this eight–room inn is in nearby Old Mystic (1½ miles north of I–95 on Route 27), which makes it within easy reach of the seaport and all the other area attractions, but sets it apart from the crowd. The building, which was built in the early 1800s, was originally the Old Mystic Book Shop.

DAY 2

Morning

BREAKFAST: A country breakfast is included in the room rate at the Old Mystic Inn.

After breakfast take a look around the **Mystic Marinelife Aquarium,** Coogan Boulevard, Mystic (860–536–3323), which is home to all sorts of amphibians and other marine habitants including sea lions, seals, and penguins. The aquarium is open from 9:00 A.M. to 5:30 P.M. daily in July and August, and from 9:00 A.M. to 4:30 P.M. September through June.

If you feel like doing a little shopping, head for **Olde Mystick Village** (entrances are on Coogan Boulevard in Mystic; 860–536–4941). The village is a collection of Colonial-style buildings housing about sixty shops that sell an assortment of souvenirs, local food products, and other items.

From Olde Mystick Village drive east on Route 1 for about 5 miles, and you'll come to **Stonington,** a traditional New England seacoast village that deserves a walk around. To get the lay of the land, start by climbing the stone steps to the top of the tower at the **Old Lighthouse Museum,** 7 Water Street (860–535–1440). Inside the 1823 granite lighthouse, there are displays of maritime history and memorabilia of the Orient trade and whaling and fishing days. It's open from May through October, Tuesday to Sunday from 11:00 A.M. to 4:30 P.M. Then wander about admiring the eighteenth- and nineteenth-century architecture throughout the town. Water Street is the town's main street, where you'll find several boutiques, antiques shops, and restaurants.

LUNCH: The **Yellow House,** 149 Water Street (860–535–4986) is a perfect place to stop for a sandwich or salad lunch or later for tea and a snack.

Afternoon

After lunch head back to New York on I–95.

THERE'S MORE

Beach and amusement complex. Ocean Beach Park, near Harkness Memorial State Park south of New London, exit 75–76 from I–95; (860) 447–3031. A beach, a boardwalk, amusement rides, an Olympic-size pool.

Casino. The Foxwoods Casino in Ledyard and the Mohegan Sun Casino in

Montville attract thousands of visitors daily.

Hiking. There are more than twenty parks with trails for all levels of hikers throughout the Mystic Coast and County region.

Spa. In nearby Norwich the Norwich Inn & Spa, 607 West Thames Street; (860) 886–2401 or (800) ASK–4SPA. Facilities include a full-service health spa. You can either stay at the inn or, Monday through Friday, go in for whatever treatments you'd like.

Theater. Eugene O'Neill Theater Center, 305 Great Neck Road, Waterford; (860) 443–5378. An organization devoted to developing new stage works.

SPECIAL EVENTS

Late May. Lobster Weekend, Mystic Seaport, Mystic. Lobster feasts, music, and other entertainment.

Early June. Yale-Harvard Regatta, New London. A rowing regatta with crews from both Yale and Harvard universities.

July 4th weekend. Independence Weekend, Mystic. A re-creation of an 1870s Fourth of July by costumed role-players. Also a parade and other activities.

October. Chowderfest Weekend. Every year Mystic Seaport hosts its annual battle of the chowderpots, where local community groups serve up their own version of the perfect chowder. There's folk music, gallery exhibitions, and all sorts of activities.

OTHER RECOMMENDED RESTAURANTS AND LODGING

Mystic

Captain Daniel Packer Inne, 32 Water Street; (860) 536–3555. A 230-year-old hostelry with a contemporary menu.

The Inn at Mystic, on US 1, at junction of CT 27 (2 miles south of I–95, exit 90); (860) 536–9604. a sixty-seven-room inn ¼ mile from Long Island Sound. Some rooms have fireplaces; some have whirlpools.

The Steamboat Inn, 73 Steamboat Wharf; (860) 536–8300. Located in the heart of Mystic, right on the river. Six of the rooms have fireplaces; four have kitchenettes.

Norwich

Norwich Inn & Spa, 607 West Thames Street; (860) 886–2401 or (800) ASK–4SPA. A luxury inn with complete spa facilities.

FOR MORE INFORMATION

Southeastern Connecticut Tourism District, P.O. Box 89, 27 Masonic Street, New London, CT 06320; (860) 444–2206 or (800) 222–6783.

Mystic Chamber of Commerce, 17 Cottrell Street, Mystic, CT 06355; (860) 572–9578.

Mystic Coast and Country Travel & Leisure Council, 325 State Street, New London, CT 06320; (860) 437–7289.

Connecticut Department of Economic Development, 864 Brook Street, Rocky Hill, CT 06067–3405; (800) CT–BOUND.

SOUTHERN NEW ENGLAND

Northeast Corner
A QUIET GETAWAY

---

1 NIGHT

Historic homes • Mill villages • Hilltop vistas • Vineyards
Gardens and nurseries • Hiking • Cross-country skiing

The nickname for the northeastern corner of Connecticut is "The Quiet Corner." Indeed it is quiet. It's also one of the Northeast's most unspoiled chunks of land, made up of fertile pastures, low-rising hills, rivers, forests, and historic villages.

DAY 1

Morning

To reach the area take I–684 north to I–84 east. Get off at exit 67 and go south on Route 31 to the junction of Route 44. Take 44 east to Route 31 again and follow that into **Coventry,** where you'll find **Caprilands Herb Farm,** 534 Silver Street (860–742–7244). The farm, which has an eighteenth-century farmhouse, is owned by author and herbalist Adelma Simmons. Spend some time walking through the herb gardens, check out the shops, and then sip a cup of herbal tea in the dining room. It's open daily from 9:00 A.M. to 5:00 P.M. Garden tours are conducted by request.

Coventry has a handful of other attractions including the **Nathan Hale Homestead,** South Street (860–742–6917), which was the family home of the state hero. It's open from May 15 through October 15, Tuesday through Saturday from 1:00 P.M. to 5:00 P.M. Nearby is the **Strong-Porter House Museum,** South Street (860–742–7847), a farmhouse that was built around

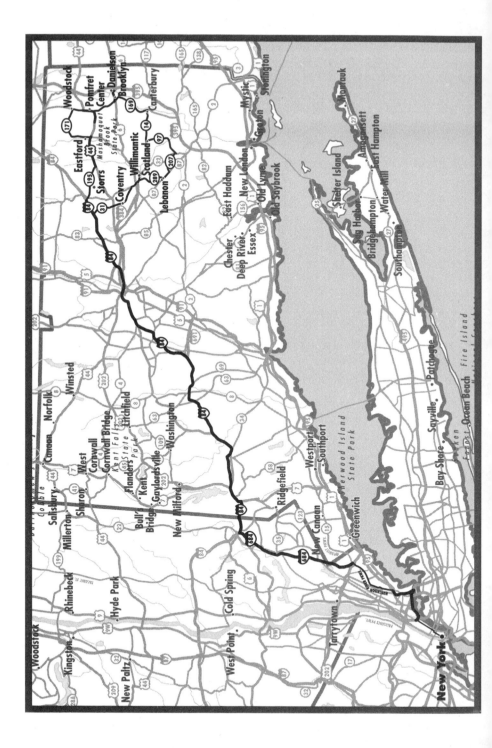

1730 by a great-uncle of Nathan Hale. There are several outbuildings to tour including a carpenter's shop, a carriage shed, and a barn with exhibits. You can buy a combined ticket for admission to both this museum and the Nathan Hale Homestead. In Coventry there's also an old one-room schoolhouse called the **Brick School House,** Merrow Road (860–742–7847), which was built between 1823 and 1825. It's open mid-May to mid-October from 1:00 to 4:00 P.M. daily.

LUNCH: Bidwell Tavern, 1260 Main Street, Coventry (860–742–6978), is located right in the heart of Coventry's antiquing district. It's a historic restaurant serving New England cuisine including a wonderful Yankee pot roast.

There's also a winery—the **Nutmeg Farm Winery,** 800 Bunker Hill Road (860–742–8402)—where you can take a tour followed by a tasting. It's open year-round on weekends, from 11:00 A.M. to 5:00 P.M.

Afternoon

From Coventry drive a short distance south to **Willimantic,** where you can stop to see the **Windham Textile and History Museum,** 157 Union-Main Street (860–456–2178). It's a fascinating museum, with exhibits devoted to textile production at the height of the Industrial Revolution. There's a re-created 1880s mill shop floor, a company store, a tenement home, a library dating back to 1877, and a mill agent's mansion. Hours vary; call ahead.

Make your next stop in the town of **Lebanon** (follow Route 289 south). There are some very worthwhile attractions here including the **Jonathan Trumbull House,** West Town Street, on the Green (860–642–7558), and the Trumbull family's store, which is known as the **Revolutionary War Office,** West Town Street (860–642–7558). Trumbull was the only colonial governor who supported America's war for independence. The war office stocked war supplies and became a meeting place of the Council of Safety. The Trumbull house is open between May 15 and October 15, Tuesday through Saturday, from 1:00 to 5:00 P.M.; the Revolutionary War Office is open from the end of May to the end of September, weekends only, from 1:30 to 4:30 P.M. Also on West Town Street is the **Dr. William Beaumont House,** West Town Street, on the Green (860–642–7558). This eighteenth-century cottage was the birthplace of the "Father of Physiology of Digestion." Inside there are several displays of early surgical instruments. It's open on Saturdays only, from 1:00 to 5:00 P.M., from mid-May through mid-October.

The Jonathan Trumbull House on the Green in Lebanon

From Lebanon head east on Route 207 and turn left onto Route 97, following it to **Scotland.** Take time out here to visit the **Nutmeg Flower Farm,** 144 Pudding Hill Road (860–423–6454), which has display gardens. Call ahead for hours; they vary.

Carry on east to **Canterbury,** where you'll find the **Prudence Crandall House Museum,** at the junction of Routes 14 and 169 (860–546–9916). This was New England's first school for black women. It's open from January 15 through December 15, Wednesday through Sunday from 10:00 A.M. to 4:30 P.M. Canterbury is also home to **Wright's Mill Tree Farm,** 63 Creasey Road (860–774–1455), which has more than 250 acres of ponds, waterfalls, and mill sites to explore. Open daily from 9:00 A.M. to 5:00 P.M. April through December.

Turn left onto Route 169 and you'll find yourself passing through a densely scenic landscape. This road has been designated by Scenic America as one of the ten most scenic highways in the United States.

Continue about 7 miles to **Brooklyn** and stop to have a look around the **Daniel Putnam Tyler Law Office,** on Route 169 (860–774–7728), where Tyler practiced law from 1822 to 1875. Hours are very limited, however. It's open only on Wednesdays and Sundays, from 1:00 to 5:00 P.M., between Memorial Day and Labor Day. Brooklyn is home to the **New England Center for Contemporary Art,** Route 169 (860–774–8899), which showcases changing exhibits in its pre-Revolutionary barn setting. It's open April through November, from 1:00 to 5:00 P.M., Wednesday through Sunday. Brooklyn also has two beautiful churches to see: the **Unitarian Church** on the green and **Old Trinity Church** (take Route 6 east for a mile and turn left onto Church Street). Both date back to 1771. In nearby **Danielson** (follow Route 6 east of town), you'll find **Logee's Greenhouses,** 141 North Street (860–774–8038), which has more than two thousand varieties of indoor plants including 700 (!) types of begonias. The greenhouses are open daily from 9:00 A.M. to 4:00 P.M. (You'll be coming back to Brooklyn for dinner.)

Continue north to the picturesque town of **Pomfret Center,** which is home to the elite Pomfret Preparatory School. You can tour the village's last mill, which is now a museum known as the **Brayton Grist Mill and Marcy Blacksmith Museum,** Route 44 (entrance is at Mashamoquet Brook State Park). Pomfret Center is also home to **Sandra Lee's Herbs & Everlastings,** Route 97 (860–974–0525), a two-and-one-half-acre herb and flower farm open between May and November, Tuesday through Saturday from 10:00 A.M. to 5:00 P.M. and on Sundays from noon to 5:00 P.M. (closed in August).

Woodstock, about 5 miles from Pomfret Center, is next on your itinerary as well as your stopover for the night. Try to get there before 5:00 P.M. so that you can get in to see **Roseland Cottage,** Route 169 (860–928–4074). Roseland is a Gothic Revival summerhouse that was built by merchant and publisher Henry Bowen. Be sure to take a look inside the barn; it contains what's possibly the oldest indoor bowling alley in the country. The cottage, which is filled with original family furnishings, is open from mid-May to Labor Day, Wednesday through Sunday from noon to 5:00 P.M., and from Labor Day to mid-October, Friday through Sunday from noon to 5:00 P.M.

DINNER: The **Golden Lamb Buttery,** Bush Hill Road, Brooklyn (860–774–4423), is located in a converted barn well known among gourmets. The menu generally includes classic American dishes and whatever's ready to be plucked from the garden. There's usually a wonderful soup to start, followed by a choice of entrées (duck, lamb, various seafood) prepared a different way every day.

LODGING: The Inn at Woodstock Hill, 94 Plaine Hill Road, off Route 169 (860–928–0528), is a twenty-two-room inn listed on the National Register of Historic Places. It's a restored country estate on more than a dozen acres.

DAY 2

Morning

BREAKFAST: A continental breakfast is served at the inn.

If you're interested in antiquing, head east on Route 171 to **Putnam,** which has several antiques shops. Then backtrack west on Route 171. Turn south on Route 198 and stop to see the amazing collection of African violets (600 varieties) at **Buell's Greenhouses,** 11 Weeks Road (860–974–0623) in **Eastford.** Keep in mind, however, that it is not open Sundays. The rest of the week, it's open from 8:00 A.M. to 5:00 P.M.

From Eastford continue south, then turn right onto Route 44 and follow it down to **Storrs,** which is the area's cultural center. You could stay busy for hours browsing through the collections at the **University of Connecticut** alone: the Atrium Gallery of Contemporary Art (860–486–3930); the William Benton Museum of Art, which features European and American works (860–486–4520); and the Connecticut State Museum of Natural History (860–486–4460). By the way "UConn" has a dairy bar where the ice cream is nonpareil.

Nonuniversity attractions in Storrs include the **Gurleyville Grist Mill,** Stone Mill Road (860–487–1658), which is the state's only remaining stone gristmill, and the **Mansfield Historical Society Museum,** 954 Storrs Road (860–429–6575), which has exhibits relating to local history.

LUNCH: The **Depot Restaurant,** Route 44, Mansfield (860–429–3663), has a good selection of soups, salads, and sandwiches plus daily specials such as quiches and seafood crepes.

Afternoon

Return to New York City by heading north on Route 195 to I–84 west. Take I–84 right over the New York border and head south on I–684.

THERE'S MORE

Auto racing. Due north of Storrs, in Stafford Springs, is the Stafford Motor Speedway, Route 140; (860) 684–2783.

Hot-air ballooning. In Woodstock you can take to the skies in a balloon with Brighter Skies Balloon Co., 33 Butts Road; (860) 963–0600.

SPECIAL EVENTS

May. Wright's Mill Tree Farm, Canterbury. Free guided Mother's Day Bird Walk.

Mid-May. Springtime Festival, Danielson. A parade, a road race, arts and crafts, food booths, a petting zoo, and more.

August. Fossils and Minerals Family Day, Jorgensen Auditorium at University of Connecticut, Storrs. Hands-on activities for children, exhibits, slide shows, and more.

Early September. Woodstock Fair, on the fairgrounds at Routes 169 and 171, South Woodstock. This is the state's best-attended family fair. There's a horse show, go-cart racing, vaudeville acts, arts and crafts—you name it.

Mid-September. Juried Outdoor Arts and Crafts Show, Davis Park, Danielson. More than 150 artists and artisans from all over the Northeast show their work here.

OTHER RECOMMENDED RESTAURANTS AND LODGINGS

Storrs

Altnaveigh Inn, Route 195; (860) 429–4490. This is a bed and breakfast in a farmhouse that was built in 1734. It has five rooms very simply decorated in a New England country style. Downstairs the restaurant serves seafood, beef, and chicken dishes. A continental breakfast is included in the room rate.

FOR MORE INFORMATION

Connecticut's Quiet Corner, P.O. Box 598, Putnam, CT 06260-0598; (860) 928–1228.

Connecticut Department of Economic Development, 864 Brook Street, Rocky Hill, CT 06067–3405; (800) CT–BOUND.

The Litchfield Hills

TRADITIONAL NEW ENGLAND

2 NIGHTS

*Antiques shops • New England scenery • Art galleries
Country fairs • Woodland walks • Fine dining*

For lots of wealthy New Yorkers and celebrities (Meryl Streep, Dustin Hoffman, and Henry Kissinger, to name just a few), this little northwestern corner of Connecticut is a "have your cake and eat it too" location. It has all the things that make New England New England, such as white steepled churches, stately old houses, covered bridges, stone walls, fields filled with large-eyed cows, and big old barns sagging with the contour of the land. At the same time the area is home to a surprising number of up-to-urban-standards restaurants (many with European- or Culinary Institute of America–trained chefs), dozens of art galleries and museums, and an impressive collection of inns and other buildings listed on the National Register of Historic Places.

There are more than three dozen towns scattered throughout the Litchfield Hills, most of them with fewer than five thousand inhabitants. This short trip takes you to the area's highlights, on a loop tour that roughly begins and ends in New Milford.

DAY 1

Morning

Less than two hours from Manhattan (about 100 miles), the Litchfield area can be reached by following the Henry Hudson Parkway to the Saw Mill River

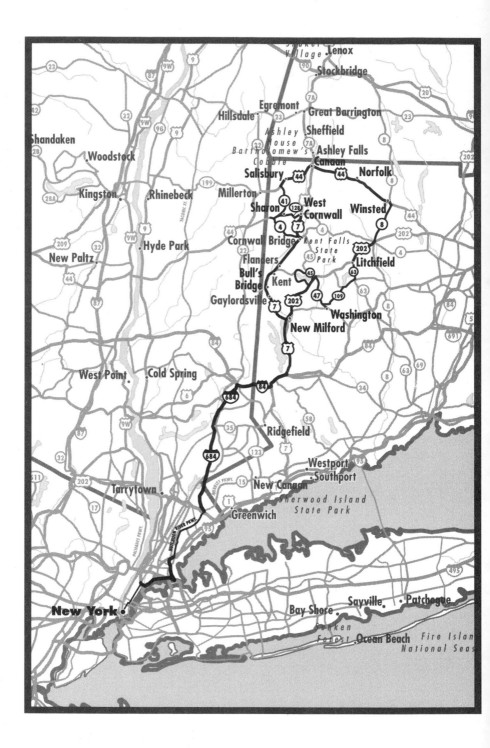

Parkway to I–684 to Route I–84 east, then following Route 7 north (exit 7) to New Milford. (An alternative route is to take Route 684 north to Route 22 and cross over the state line on Route 55, heading into Gaylordsville.)

Either way, as you proceed north, you can't help feeling as though you've left the city far behind. Once you pass New Milford, it's time for passengers to stop reading the map or catnapping and start looking at the scenery. From here on the landscape is steadily scenic—wooded hills, vintage farmhouses, lakes and rivers that really do sparkle, and small villages that inevitably elicit all sorts of cliché adjectives like "charming," "postcard-perfect," and "cute."

If you're a food lover, consider making a stop at **The Silo: The Store and The School,** Upland Road, New Milford (860–355–0300). This former farm is now a cooking school and retail store, with kitchenware from around the United States, Mexico, and Europe. Take a look around the adjoining silo, which usually has marked-down items for sale. Upstairs in the silo there's a gallery showcasing the work of local artists and artisans. On Sundays there are often recitals accompanied by wine and cheese receptions. Call ahead for a schedule of events and, if you're interested in taking a class (on bread baking, low-fat Chinese, even barbecue cuisine), class schedules. All classes, which start in early spring and go on every weekend up to Christmas, are three hours long and self-contained.

Make your next stop **Bull's Bridge,** one of the state's two covered bridges that you can drive through (the other one is in nearby West Cornwall). It's just before Kent and spans the Housatonic River. As well as being very picturesque, the bridge has a historical claim to fame in that Washington crossed it back in 1781. Supposedly one of his horses fell in the river (it was March) and had to be pulled out.

Plan to spend a chunk of time in **Kent** (Route 7 takes you right through the heart of it), especially if you enjoy browsing around galleries and antiques shops. Be forewarned, however; Kent can be a mob scene on fall weekends.

Kent is also home to the **Sloane-Stanley Museum,** Route 7, about 2 miles north of Kent Center (860–927–3849), which has a collection of early American farm and woodworking tools that were amassed by Eric Sloane, the artist and writer. The museum is open from mid-May through October, Wednesday through Sunday. Carry on and you'll come to **Flanders Historic District,** which is a preserved group of houses that were originally part of the center of Kent. One of them, the Seven Hearths, is now a museum filled with artwork by the American portrait painter George Lawrence Nelson.

A bit farther north on Route 7 is **Kent Falls State Park** (860–927–4100), a 295-acre park with a beautiful waterfall that's been featured in many ads and is a location on the TV soap opera *The Guiding Light.* With its webwork of trails and picnic facilities, this is a lovely park in which to while away a couple of hours. You can climb up to the head of the falls (something like 25 feet) on a wide, stepped pathway.

Before leaving the area stop by to pick up a picnic lunch in town.

LUNCH: Picnic in Kent Falls State Park.

Afternoon

Continue north on Route 7 to **West Cornwall,** which many people consider Connecticut's prettiest town, where, on Route 128, you'll find the state's other passable **covered bridge.** It has been in continuous service since 1837. Detour a bit to **Sharon,** west on Route 4 or Route 128, if you'd like to see more beautiful New England scenery and pick your own fruit (strawberries in June and July, raspberries in July and August, and apples in September and October) at **Ellsworth Hill Farm** on Route 4 (860–364–0249). Then stop at the **Northeast Audubon Center,** Route 4 (860–364–0520), a 684-acre sanctuary with self-guiding trails, wildflower and herb gardens, a farm area, an interpretive center, and a gift shop. It's open year-round, Monday through Saturday from 9:00 A.M. to 5:00 P.M.

From Sharon head north on Route 41 to get to **Salisbury,** which is home to a handful of shops and a welcoming little tearoom called **Chaiwalla,** One Main Street (860–435–9758). There are more than a dozen teas imported from around the world, and each one is freshly brewed from Salisbury spring water. Of course, a cup of tea would not be complete on its own, so there is an equally impressive selection of edibles including traditional scones, sausage pies, onion tarts, and a variety of desserts. It's open mid-morning to 6:00 P.M., but closed in winter. Chaiwalla is also a center for tea tastings, lectures on tea, and poetry and short-story readings over tea.

In nearby **Lakeville** you'll find **Lime Rock Park,** where sports-car races take place from April through November. For ticket information call (860) 435–0896.

From Salisbury it's a short drive up to **Canaan,** which is home to the **Housatonic Railroad,** one of the nation's oldest railroads. There are scenic rides throughout the summer and autumn months. For details call (860) 824–0339.

The Covered Bridge in West Cornwall has been in continuous service since 1837.

Carry on east on Route 44 to **Norfolk.** Back in the late 1800s, Norfolk was a scheduled stop on the railroad between New York City and Pittsfield, Massachusetts. At that time it became a popular resort for the affluent, who built many of the large houses you see there today. The village green is surrounded by buildings listed on the National Register of Historic Places. There's a small **Historical Museum** here (860–542–5761), that houses local artifacts and some old Connecticut-made clocks. It's open mid-June through mid-September on weekends only. One of the most enjoyable ways to see the town is to take a horse-drawn carriage (or sleigh, in winter). For schedules stop by or call The Horse and Carriage Livery Service on Loon Meadow Drive, off Route 44 (860–542–6085).

Nearby there are a couple of hiking opportunities including **Haystack Mountain,** 1 mile north on Route 272. From the top there are nonpareil views of the Berkshires and **Campbell Falls,** 6 miles north of Norfolk on

Route 272. Two miles south of Norfolk, on Route 272, is **Dennis Hill,** which is topped by a summit pavilion (it used to be a summer residence) where you can get a far-reaching view of the Litchfield Hills.

DINNER: The Cannery Cafe, 85 Main Street, Canaan (860–824–7333), serves imaginatively prepared American cuisine along with a very good selection of American wines.

LODGING: In Norfolk there are two truly top-notch bed and breakfasts. **Greenwood's Gate,** 105 Greenwoods Road East (860–542–5439), is a beautifully restored 1797 Colonial home furnished with antiques. The **Manor House,** Maple Avenue (860–542–5690), is an English Tudor mansion, with Tiffany stained-glass windows, also filled with antiques.

DAY 2

Morning

BREAKFAST: At your bed and breakfast.

From Norfolk follow Route 44 east to **Winsted,** the self-proclaimed mountain-laurel capital, and then head north on Route 20 to **Riverton** if you're interested in visiting the **Hitchcock Museum,** which is on Route 20 (860–738–4950). Riverton is where the famous Hitchcock chairs are made; in fact, Lambert Hitchcock made his first chair in 1826 on the banks of the Farmington River, which flows through Riverton. The museum showcases painted nineteenth-century furniture. It's open from April 1 to late December, daily from 11:00 A.M. to 4:00 P.M. Nearby you'll find the Hitchcock Factory store and the Lambert House, both with showrooms.

Backtrack to Winsted, where you can get on Route 8 and head south to Route 202 west, which will take you right to the town of **Litchfield.**

Litchfield is about as New England as a town can be, complete with a village green, a spick-and-span white church, and stately eighteenth-century houses lined up along wide maple-tree-lined streets as if contestants in a beauty pageant. The town, which sits on a plateau above the Naugatuck Valley, was spared early industrialization because the railroads laid their main lines down in the valley. Its most famous early resident was Harriet Beecher Stowe, author of *Uncle Tom's Cabin.* She grew up here.

One of Litchfield's most celebrated, and photographed, attractions is the **Congregational Church,** at the junction of Routes 202 and 118. Built in 1828, it's the perfect New England church. Also perfect is Litchfield's **Green,** which was laid out in the 1770s. If time permits, have a look around the **Litchfield Historical Society Museum,** on the Green (860–567–4501), a good source of local history. It's open from April to mid-October, Wednesday through Sunday; closed major holidays. The **Tapping Reeve House and Law School** on South Street (860–567–4501) are worth visiting. Both date back to the 1700s. The law school was America's first and included graduates Aaron Burr and John C. Calhoun. They're open from mid-May through mid-October, Wednesday through Sunday; closed Fourth of July and Labor Day.

Also in Litchfield, just off Route 118 on Chestnut Hill Road, is the **Haight Vineyard and Winery** (860–567–4045), where tours and tastings take place year-round except on major holidays.

For those wanting to get a little fresh air, the **White Memorial Foundation** is a 4,000-acre conservation area 2½ miles west of town on Route 202. There are more than 35 miles of trails threaded through the woodlands.

Just south of town is **White Flower Farm,** Route 63 (860–567–8789), a sprawling retail and mail-order nursery with ten acres of display gardens and thirty acres of growing fields. The display gardens are open from mid-April through October, Monday through Friday from 10:00 A.M. to 5:00 P.M., and on Saturdays, Sundays, and holidays from 9:00 A.M. to 5:30 P.M.

LUNCH: The **West Street Grill,** 43 West Street, Litchfield (860–567–3885). Try the pan-seared sea scallops and grilled apple-smoked Atlantic salmon.

Afternoon

From Litchfield head south on Route 63, then turn right onto Route 109, and follow that to **Washington,** a little village built around a church. There are a handful of sights to check out in the area including the **Museum of the Gunn Memorial Library,** on the green in Washington (860–868–7756), a house built in 1781 containing local-history collections and exhibits, antique furniture, old dolls and doll houses (open Thursday through Saturday in the afternoons), and the **American Indian Archaeological Institute,** Curtis Road (860–868–0518), which houses an impressive collection of Indian artifacts as well as a complete outdoor Indian village. The latter is open 10:00 A.M. to 5:00 P.M. Monday through Saturday and noon to 5:00 P.M. on Sunday. Closed Monday and Tuesday during the winter.

DINNER: The restaurant at **The Mayflower Inn,** Route 47, Washington (860–868–9466), overseen by chef John Farnsworth, is not only beautifully situated at one of the state's best inns, but has wonderful food and wines to match.

LODGING: The Mayflower Inn, Route 47, Washington (860–868–9466), has twenty-five rooms, all overlooking gardens filled with rare flora.

DAY 3

Morning

From Washington take Route 47 north to Route 202, turn left, and then turn right onto Route 45. About 2 miles up on the left, you'll come to North Shore Road. Turn onto it and take the second right onto Hopkins Road, which is home to **Hopkins Vineyard,** Hopkins Road (860–868–7954). There are tours of the winery as well as tastings. Afterward continue on North Shore Road and you'll come to the Inn at Lake Waramaug.

LUNCH: The **Boulders Inn,** East Shore Road, New Preston (860–868–0541), starts serving "dinner" at noon on Sunday. The fare is contemporary New England cuisine.

After lunch (or an early dinner) take a leisurely drive around the lake before heading back to New York City.

THERE'S MORE

Bird-watching. There are plenty of opportunities to pull out the binoculars in the Litchfield area. Here are some of the best spots:

H. C. Barnes Nature Center, 175 Shrub Road, Bristol; (860) 589–6082.

Flanders Nature Center, office at Flanders Road, off Route 6, Woodbury; (860) 263–3711.

Northeast Audubon Center, Route 4, Sharon; (860) 364–0520.

White Memorial Foundation, Route 202, Litchfield; (860) 567–0857.

Car racing. Lime Rock Sports Car Races, Lime Rock Park, Lime Rock. Sports-car and stock-car road races take place April through October. For more information call (860) 435–2571.

Horseback riding. Lee's Riding Stable, Inc., East Litchfield Road (off Route 118), Litchfield; (860) 567–0785.

Skiing. Mohawk Mountain Ski Area, Great Hollow Road, Cornwall; (860) 672–6464. Connecticut's largest ski resort, with 23 slopes and trails.

SPECIAL EVENTS

Mid-June. Laurel Festival. Driving routes for viewing mountain laurels in bloom; laurel queen; parade. For more information call (860) 379–2713.

Mid-June through mid-August. Norfolk Chamber Music Festival, Norfolk. This annual festival takes place on the grounds of a charming nineteenth-century estate. For program and ticket information, call (203) 432–1966.

Mid-July. Annual Litchfield Open House Tour, Litchfield. Tour includes Litchfield homes of historic and architectural interest. Call (860) 567–9423 for more information.

Late September. Fall Festival, Kent. An annual festival on the grounds of the Connecticut Antique Machinery Museum.

OTHER RECOMMENDED RESTAURANTS AND LODGINGS

Litchfield

Tollgate Hill Inn and Restaurant, Route 202 (Tollgate Road); (860) 567–4545. This is both a delightful inn and an award winning restaurant specializing in contemporary American cuisine.

New Preston

Boulders Inn, East Shore Road; (860) 868–0541. The inn has a selection of accommodations in the main house (built in 1895), the carriage house, and guest houses.

Salisbury

The White Hart Inn, Village Green (Routes 41 and 44); (860) 435–0030. Both a welcoming inn and fine choice for meals, the White Hart Inn is a meticulously renovated inn that began operating in the early nineteenth century. Informal meals are served in the Tap Room (be sure to try the house pâté), whereas more elegant meals (dinner only) are served in the Sea Grill Restaurant.

The Under Mountain Inn, 482 Under Mountain Road; (860) 435–0242. This is a gracious little B&B in an eighteenth-century farmhouse. Dinners are prepared by the British-born chef/owner on Friday and Saturday nights.

FOR MORE INFORMATION

Litchfield Hills Travel Council, P.O. Box 968, Litchfield, CT 06759; (860) 567–4506. Also Litchfield Hills Information Booth, located on the Green in Litchfield. Open daily from June through mid-September; weekends only in October.

Connecticut Department of Economic Development, 864 Brook Street, Rocky Hill, CT 06067–3405; (800) CT–BOUND.

Newport

MASTS AND MANSIONS

---

2 NIGHTS

Opulent summer cottages • Historic waterfront
Oldest synagogue in the United States
Renowned restaurants • Sailing • Tennis • Beaches

Gleaming yachts, palatial mansions, beautiful people, tennis tournaments — these are the things that come to most people's minds at the mere mention of Newport. This sensationally situated city (poised on the southern tip of Aquidneck Island and bounded by water on three sides) does offer a slice of the good life.

Newport had two periods of history during which it enjoyed prominence. During colonial days it was a very important trade center. Later on, in the nineteenth-century "Gilded Age," it became a popular resort for old-money families (including the Vanderbilts, Astors, and Belmonts) who built opulent summer "cottages."

Thanks to The Preservation Society of Newport County and the Newport Restoration Foundation, the history of Newport has been beautifully restored and/or preserved. During a short visit you can combine a walking tour of its colonial section in the northwest with a driving tour of its enormous mansions in the southern end.

Newport is a place you can go back to year after year, discovering new places or revisiting old ones. Squeezing everything into one weekend is a tall order, especially if you want to spend some time relaxing on a veranda or a breezy beach.

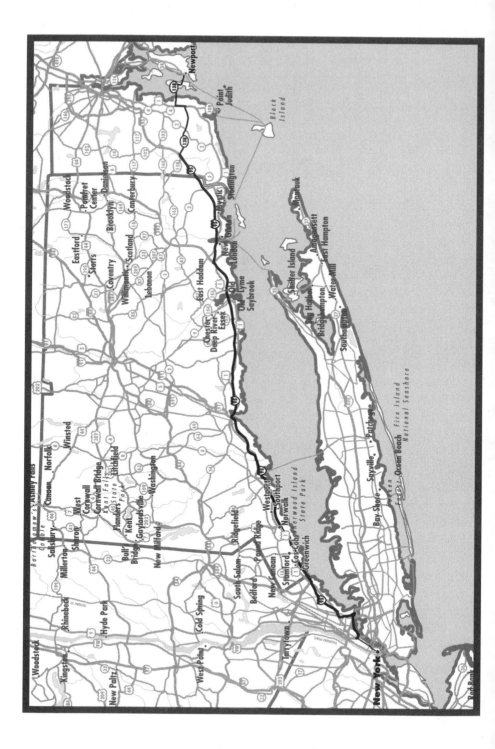

DAY 1

Morning

The fastest way to reach Newport from New York is to take I–95 north to exit 3A, Route 138 east, in Rhode Island. Follow 138 east over the Jamestown and Newport bridges and directly into Newport.

First things first: Ditch your car. If you're staying at The Inntowne, you can park for a nominal fee (free in the off-season). You'll spend today touring **Colonial Newport,** which can best be explored on foot. It's the northwestern section of the city, clustered around the harbor.

A good starting point is Washington Street, which runs from Long Wharf to Battery Park and is lined with old gas lamps and colonial houses. From Washington Square walk north and make your first stop **Hunter House,** 54 Washington Street (401–847–1000). This colonial home dates back to 1748 and has been faithfully restored inside and out. It's open daily May through September from 10:00 A.M. to 5:00 P.M. and weekends only during April and October from 10:00 A.M. to 5:00 P.M.

From Hunter House walk north up Washington to Popular Street, where you'll turn right and follow to Farewell Street. Here there are several ancient cemeteries including an eighteenth-century **Common Burial Ground** on Warner Street (a continuation of Popular Street on the other side of Farewell Street). From there walk south on Farewell Street to Thaymes Street until you reach Washington Square.

Here you'll find the **Brick Market,** which was built in 1760 and has been used in a variety of ways. For some time it was used as a theater, later on it was a town hall, and now it's an exhibit hall devoted to Newport history. It's open Monday through Saturday from 10:00 A.M. to 9:00 P.M. and on Sundays from noon to 9:00 P.M. in summer; hours vary slightly in winter months. Nearby you'll see the **Old Colony House** on Washington Square (401–846–2980), which was the headquarters of the colonial and state governments. The Declaration of Independence was read from the balcony of this building. In summer months there are tours Monday through Saturday from 9:00 A.M. to 4:00 P.M.

Newport's oldest house, the **Wanton–Lyman Hazard House,** is a couple of blocks away at 17 Broadway (401–846–0813). There's a museum, eighteenth-century cooking demonstrations, and a Colonial garden. It's open Friday and Saturday only from mid-June through Labor Day 10:00 A.M. to 4:00 P.M., with additional Sunday hours 1:00 to 4:00 P.M. July and August.

The **White Horse Tavern** can be your next stop. Walk west on Broad-way and north on Farewell to Marlborough Street; it's on the corner. This Newport landmark has been in operation since 1687.

LUNCH: The **White Horse Tavern,** corner of Farewell and Marlborough Streets (401–849–3600), combines both historical charm (fireplaces, dark-beamed ceilings, slanting wood floors) and decent food (salads, seafood, some pasta dishes). If it's a beautiful day and you'd rather picnic, stop by the **Market on the Boulevard,** 43 Memorial Boulevard (401–848–2600), where you can pick up picnic fixings.

Afternoon

On the same corner you'll find the **Friends Meeting House,** 29 Farewell Street (401–846–0813), which dates back to 1699. It's the oldest Quaker meetinghouse in America. It's open for group tours by appointment only.

From there walk back through Washington Square and turn left onto Touro Street, where you'll find the **Touro Synagogue,** 85 Touro Street (401–847–4794), the oldest standing temple in the United States. From late June through Labor Day, the synagogue is open from 10:00 A.M. to 5:00 P.M. Monday through Friday and from 10:00 A.M. to 6:00 P.M. on Sunday. For rest of the year, call for hours. The **Newport Historical Society** (401–846–0813) is a couple of doors down at 82 Touro Street. Many of the guided walking tours begin here. For information call (401) 846–0813. Inside there's a museum devoted to local history. Hours are Tuesday through Friday from 9:30 A.M. to 4:30 P.M.

Walk south down Division Street to the corner of Spring and Church streets and you'll spot **Trinity Church** on Queen Anne Square (401–846–0660), a beautiful example of Colonial architecture. When it was built in 1726, it was hailed as "the most beautiful timber structure in America." It's open daily from 10:00 A.M. to 4:00 P.M.

Carry on east along Church Street to the **Redwood Library,** 950 Belle-vue Avenue (401–847–0292) at the beginning of Bellevue Avenue. Not only is this the county's oldest library in continuous use, but it has a wonderful collection of Early American paintings inside. Hours are Monday through Saturday from 9:30 A.M. to 5:00 P.M.

The **Newport Art Museum and Art Association,** 76 Bellevue Avenue (401–848–8200), is on the next block. It showcases changing exhibits by contemporary New England artists. It's open from October through May, Tuesday through Saturday from 10:00 A.M. to 4:00 P.M. and on Sundays from 1:00 to 5:00 P.M., and from Memorial Day through Labor Day daily from 10:00 A.M. to 5:00 P.M.

Turn left onto Memorial Boulevard and follow it to the end where the 3-mile **Cliff Walk** begins. The walk, which is a little challenging (don't attempt it if you're traveling with young children or a handicapped person), takes you along Newport's cliffs, offering fabulous views of many of its mansions.

DINNER: La Petite Auberge, 19 Charles Street (401–849–6669), is a well-established restaurant in town, serving celestial French cuisine.

LODGING: Inntowne Inn, 6 Mary Street (401–846–9200 or 800–457–7803) is located within easy walking distance of many Newport sights. Each of the seventeen rooms in this bed and breakfast, is attractively and individually decorated.

DAY 2

Morning

BREAKFAST: A continental breakfast is included in the price at the Inntowne Inn.

You'll spend most of today exploring the mansions for which Newport is so famous. Because distances between them can be long, your best bet is to drive. Several of them have guided tours that last about an hour. Most of the mansions are open daily between 10:00 A.M. and 5:00 P.M. in summer; winter hours vary.

Start by visiting **Kingscote,** Bowery Street off Bellevue Avenue, which is relatively modest compared with some of the others. It was built in 1840 for a plantation owner. **The Elms,** which is a little farther south on Bellevue, is a classical building surrounded by formal gardens, fountains, and a sweeping lawn. It was built for a coal baron at the turn of the century. Continue south on Bellevue and you'll come to **Château-sur-Mer,** which was the residence of William Shepard Wetmore, who made his fortune in the China trade. The most famous of the Newport mansions, **The Breakers,** is on Ochre Point Avenue (turn left on Victoria and continue to Ochre Point Avenue). This stunning property has seventy rooms. It was built in 1893 for Cornelius Vanderbilt II and his family. Return to Bellevue and continue south to **Rosecliff,** which has been used as a set for several movies, including *The Great Gatsby*. Farther south on Bellevue is **The Astor's Beechwood.** Here you can watch costumed actors and actresses re-create the lives of the Astor family, their guests, and staff. **Marble House** is the next stop continuing down Bellevue. This house, which must be seen to be believed, was designed by Beaux Arts–trained Richard Morris Hunt, whom William K.Vanderbilt asked to create "the very best living accommodations that money could buy." The last mansion to visit on Bellevue Avenue is **Belcourt Castle,** which is filled with European and Oriental treasures.

LUNCH: During the summer months **The Inn at Castle Hill** on Ocean Drive (401–849–3800) serves a great brunch (reservations are a must). Other times of the year, your best bet is to head back into town and take your pick of great lunch spots.

Afternoon

The Ocean Drive follows the coast around to **Hammersmith Farm,** near Fort Adams (401–846–7346), which was the childhood summer home of Jacqueline Bouvier Kennedy Onassis. The house is full of Bouvier/Kennedy memorabilia. The gardens that surround it were designed by Frederick Law Olmsted.

Nearby is the **Museum of Yachting,** Fort Adams, Ocean Drive (401–847–1018), which showcases highlights of the America's Cup and other sailing events. It's open mid-May through October, daily from 10:00 A.M. to 5:00 P.M.

DINNER: There are several good restaurants on the wharves along Newport Harbor including **The Black Pearl,** Bannister's Wharf (401–846–5264), which serves mostly American fare and seafood.

LODGING: Your best bet is to stay put in your first night's hotel since time is limited.

DAY 3

Morning

BREAKFAST: Muriel's, 58 Spring Street (401–849–7780), is a great choice for breakfast. It's located on the corner of Spring and Touro Streets, right near the Touro Synagogue. Menu items include huevos rancheros, eggs Benedict, and French toast. Muriel's is also a great choice for Sunday brunch.

Newport's harbor is always filled with yachts and sailboats.

After breakfast make your way over to **The International Tennis Hall of Fame** and the **Tennis Museum** at the Newport Casino, 194 Bellevue Avenue (401–849–3990). The first National Tennis Championships were held here in 1881.

Then return to the wharves for a look around the shops before heading back to New York City (take Route 138 west back to I–95 and follow that south to the metropolitan area).

THERE'S MORE

Beaches. Newport Beach, on Memorial Boulevard, and King Park and Beach, on Wellington Avenue, are open to the public. There's also a small beach at Fort Adams State Park.

Bikes. Bikes can be rented at Ten-Speed Spokes, 18 Elm Street; (401) 847–5609.

Harbor Cruises. The *Spirit of Newport* (401–849–3575) gives one-hour cruises of Newport Harbor and Narragansett Bay. They depart from the Newport Harbour Inn on America's Cup Avenue every hour and a half.

State Park. Fort Adams State Park on Ocean Drive surrounds Fort Adams. There's beach swimming, fishing, boating, and picnicking.

Vintage Dinner Train. The *Star Clipper,* 19 America's Cup Avenue, Newport, RI 02840; (401) 849–7550 or (800) 462–7452. This is a vintage train designed to take passengers back to an era of grace and romance. As you cruise along enjoying the scenery out a picture window, you'll feast on a gourmet meal replete with crystal, china, and linen.

SPECIAL EVENTS

March. Newport Irish Heritage Month. Throughout the town there are a variety of events including concerts, plays, arts and crafts, a parade, and more.

Mid-August. JVC Jazz Festival, Newport. Outdoor concerts by some of the world's best jazz musicians.

December (month long). Christmas in Newport. Citywide celebration. Concerts, candlelight tours, Festival of Trees, Holly Ball, and visits by St. Nicholas.

OTHER RECOMMENDED RESTAURANTS AND LODGINGS

Newport

Elm Tree Cottage, 336 Gibbs Avenue; (401) 849–1610 or (800) 882–3ELM. A beautiful, historic mansion, now a B&B, within easy walking distance of the beach.

Flo's Clam Shack, 4 Wave Avenue, Middletown; (401) 847–8141. *The* place to go if you're in the mood for fried clams and oysters, lobster rolls, or raw shellfish.

The Francis Malbone House, 392 Thames Street; (800) 846–0392. An inn with eighteen antiques-filled rooms situated around a central garden. The building itself was designed in 1760.

Inn at Castle Hill, Ocean Drive; (401) 849–3800. A classic New England inn with views of Newport Harbor.

Ivy Lodge, 12 Clay Street; (401) 849–6865. This is a small bed and breakfast close to many of the cottages along Bellevue.

Mama Luisa, 673 Thames Street; (401) 848–5257. This restaurant prides itself on its superb Italian food. Try the pumpkin-filled ravioli.

Mill Street Inn, 75 Mill Street; (401) 849–9500 or (800) 392–1316. Located close to the harbor and restaurants, this hotel offers contemporary suites.

Newport Harbor Hotel & Marina, 49 America's Cup Avenue; (401) 849–2600. Located in the heart of town, this hotel has wonderful harbor views as well as a full-service marina.

FOR MORE INFORMATION

The Preservation Society of Newport County, 118 Mill Street, Newport, RI 02840; (401) 847–1000.

The Newport County Convention and Visitor's Bureau has an information center at 23 America's Cup Avenue; (800) 326–6030 or (401) 849–8048.

Rhode Island Department of Economic Development, Division of Tourism, 7 Jackson Walkway, Providence, RI 02903; (800) 556–2484 or (401) 277–2601.

Block Island
With or Without a Car
OFFSHORE TOURING

---

2 NIGHTS

Beaches • Bicycling • Bird-watching • Seafood • Fishing
Horseback Riding • Sailing • Tennis • Windsurfing

Anchored 12 miles off the coast of mainland Rhode Island, this bite-sized island (a mere 11 square miles) is strewn with wildflowers, dotted with shingled cottages and placid pools, crisscrossed by hundreds of miles of stone walls, surrounded by white, duney beaches, and, on one coast, edged by cliffs that rise 200 feet above the sea.

During summer months the island is its liveliest, with at least half a dozen ferries a day shuttling day-trippers over from the mainland. Most of them don't get much farther than Water Street and the nearby beaches, however, which leaves the rest of the island blissfully peaceful. Unlike some northeastern islands, Block Island has not fallen prey to the customary tourist trappings such as fast-food chains and tacky souvenir shops. In fact, there are not even any traffic lights on the island.

If you want to experience the island as the locals do, consider visiting during a weekend in October, when there's a slight nip in the air and not another tourist in sight.

Whatever time of year you go, for a short visit, your best bet is to leave your car on the mainland, ferry over, and rent bikes to get around. You can take a ferry from the Galilee State Pier in Point Judith, year-round, or from New London (Connecticut), Providence, and Newport during the summer months. There are also ferries from Montauk, Long Island, New York.

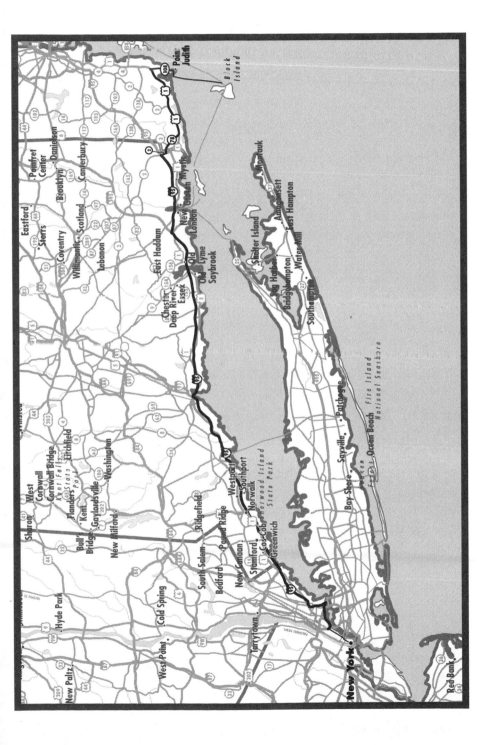

By the way, many places close on Block Island during winter months. Call the Block Island Tourism Council to check (800–383–BIRI or 401–466–5200).

DAY 1

Morning and Afternoon

If you're traveling without a car, you'll probably spend a good chunk of the day traveling to the island. During summer months only, you can take a bus from New York to Providence and then take the four-hour ferry ride. Or take Amtrak to Westerly, Rhode Island and then grab a cab over to the airport and fly to the island (it's a twelve-minute flight). You can also take a bus to New London (Connecticut) and pick up a ferry there, though service is limited. For phone numbers, see "For More Information."

If you're driving your own car, take exit 92 off I–95N. Bear right onto North Stonington Road (Route 2E). Take a right onto Route 78. At the end of Route 78, turn left onto Route 1S. Follow that to the Galilee/Point Judith exit. Turn right onto Route 108 off the exit and then bear right onto Route 108S. Continue on Route 108S to the Block Island Ferry exit. If you want to take your car over to the island, be sure to have reservations well in advance.

DINNER: The Oar, at the Boat Basin in New Harbor; (401) 466–8820. This casual restaurant is owned by the same family that owns and runs the island's successful Hotel Manisses and The 1661 Inn. Specialties include johnnycakes, fresh fish, burgers, New England clam chowder, and a raw bar.

LODGING: An elegant choice is the **Hotel Manisses,** Spring Street (401–466–2421 or 800–MANISSES), a Victorian hotel (built in 1882, but renovated in the 1970s) within walking distance of the ferry landing in Old Harbor. Plan to stay there both nights so that you don't have to waste time moving.

DAY 2

Morning

BREAKFAST: When you stay at the **Hotel Manisses,** Spring Street (401–466–2421), breakfast—which is actually served in **The 1661 Inn,** its sister inn—is included in the room price. It's a buffet breakfast with a

Block Island's Southeast Lighthouse was originally built in 1874.

selection of fish, waffles, French toast, roasted potatoes, corned beef hash, scrambled eggs, fruit juices, and fresh muffins. The setting, on a hill overlooking the water, is a wonderful place to start the day.

Lounging around on a white sandy beach is usually the top priority for most Block Island–bound weekenders. Nevertheless there are a handful of attractions to see as well as sensationally scenic roads to bike along. Right near Ernie's you'll find shops (on Water Street, Dodge Street, and Weldon's Way) that rent bikes. Though mopeds can also be rented, you'll find that the locals are not terribly fond of them because of the noise and the danger (there are several dozen accidents reported annually). Bicycles generally can be rented for between $6.00 (for a three-speed) and $12.00 (for a ten-speed) a day.

Make your first cycling destination **Mohegan Bluffs** and the nearby **Southeast Lighthouse.** You can do the trip in about an hour and get back to town for lunch and a browse around the shops. Start by heading out of town south on High Street. Though the road starts off hilly, it flattens out after a short distance, so don't panic. En route you'll pass the Block Island School, where all students on the island, from kindergarten to twelfth grade, go. The total enrollment hovers around a little more than one hundred students! Shortly after passing the school, the pavement ends and the road changes its name to Pilot Hill Road. Carry on and you'll eventually come to Mohegan Trail. Turn left and follow it until you come to a dirt road on the right. There's a rack where you can lock up your bike and then follow the path out to see the beautiful clay cliffs that drop dramatically into the water. Supposedly, in 1590, local island Indians (the Manisseans) fought off Mohegan Indians by forcing them to plunge over the cliffs to their deaths. The Southeast Light-house, which was recently moved 245 feet inland to save it from erosion, was originally built in 1874. It has one of the most powerful electric beacons on the East Coast, capable of being seen from as far away as 30 miles out to sea.

The return trip to town is largely downhill and takes you past many Victorian houses as well as along a piece of the island's shore.

Take time out to look around inside the **Spring Street Gallery** (across from the Hotel Manisses), where many local artists display their work. There are more galleries in town and several gift shops where you can buy local pottery, watercolors, and other Block Island originals.

LUNCH: Expect to wait for a table at the **Harborside Inn,** Water Street (401–466–5504). It's one of the island's most popular lunch spots, with a terrace cafe where you can get anything from a burger to a local seafood dish (such as broiled scallops or baked stuffed clams). It's right across the street from the ferry dock.

Afternoon

After lunch grab your towels, sun block, and visors and plant yourself on the beach. **Crescent Beach,** which you'll spot as you come in on the ferry, is a popular choice. It stretches from Old Harbor for 3 miles north to the cliffs of Clay Head. For your own isolated piece of beach, simply wander north until the footprints thin out.

Later on if you feel like doing a little more pedaling, head to the southwest part of the island. All said and done, it'll take you about two hours. From Old Harbor take Chapel Street to Old Town Road to Center Road. Turn left and then right onto **Beacon Hill Road,** a rough dirt road leading to the island's highest point, a dizzying height of 210 feet above sea level. Don't laugh; there's a great view of the island from up there.

Turn left when you get back to Center Road and follow it up to West Side Road, where you'll turn left (by the Island Cemetery). This route takes you through some of the island's most densely scenic landscapes. Along the way pull over to see the view at the **West Side Baptist Church.** Carry on to Cooneymus Road where you'll take a left. This takes you to **Rodman's Hollow,** a glacial ravine. If you continue east on Cooneymus, you'll come to Old Mill Road and then **Smilin' Through,** a farmhouse once owned by director Arthur Penn. At the intersection that follows, you'll find the island's **Indian Cemetery,** which dates back some 300 years to the original settlers. Turn south onto Lakeside Drive. When the road turns sharply, consider continuing straight on Snake Hole Road, a dirt road; it leads to a beach area and wilderness preserve. Afterward follow the Mohegan Trail to Southeast Road and Spring Street back into town.

A beautiful way to top off the day is to sip drinks on the veranda of the **Spring House Hotel** (401–466–5844), looking out over the ocean at sunset.

DINNER: For the best food and setting on the island, choose the **Hotel Manisses,** Spring Street (401–466–2836), which is also a beautiful place to stay. The menu changes, but almost always includes a good choice of local fish as well as roast duck and chicken dishes.

After dinner don't miss a Saturday night visit to the **Yellow Kittens,** Corn Neck Road (401–466–5855), which has live bands (rock and roll, country, rhythm and blues—you name it) during summer months.

DAY 3

Morning

BREAKFAST: Either eat at the hotel's dining room again or head for **Ernie's Old Harbor Restaurant** on Water Street (401–466–2473). Portions are huge and include all the traditional breakfast favorites such as eggs, bacon and sausages, home fries, and bottomless cups of coffee. You may have to wait in line, however.

Once you feel revived and ready to roll, hop back on your bike for a trip to the northern part of the island. It's about a three-hour trip, starting and finishing in town near the Old Harbor.

Start by following Water Street and then turn onto Dodge. At the four-way intersection, turn right onto Corn Neck Road. Though it runs alongside

Crescent Beach for about a mile, the view is often obstructed by dunes covered with sea grass. It's easy enough, however, to climb over and feast your eyes on the view. On the left is the **Great Salt Pond,** which is very good for shell-fishing and shell collecting.

For a beach break, turn right onto Mansion Road, a dirt road leading to **Mansion Beach,** so named because it used to offer a view of the Edward Searles Mansion, which, unfortunately, burned down in the early 1960s.

Turn right once you get back to Corn Neck Road. You'll pass West Beach Road on the left and then come to **Clay Head Trail** on the right. Follow it and you'll reach what is popularly known as **The Maze,** a web-work of trails winding through a wildlife preserve.

Once again get back on Corn Neck. After you pass **Sachem Pond** (a favorite swimming area), you'll reach the end of Corn Neck Road and **Settlers' Rock,** which was where Block Island's sixteen original white settlers landed on the island. This area is known as **Cow Cove.** Off in the distance you'll see **The North Light House** on Sandy Point, which has been standing since 1867. Take time to walk out to it, but avoid swimming as the currents are very strong; in fact, this area is also known as the **Palatine Graves,** where a ship sank in the 1700s.

LUNCH: For deliriously good and spanking-fresh seafood and fish dishes, choose **Finn's Seafood Restaurant,** Water Street (401–466–2473), in Old Harbor. They have their own fish market plus indoor and outdoor dining.

Afternoon

If you didn't get enough time on the beach yesterday, spend the afternoon lolling about before catching the ferry back to the mainland. Retrace your route back to New York City.

THERE'S MORE

Fishing. Several marinas on the island have boats for hire. Stop by any of the boat-rental and sport-fishing businesses in New Harbor.

Horseback riding. Rustic Rides Farm, West Side Road; (401) 466–5060. There are guided rides, carriage rides, and pony rides for children.

Tennis. There are tennis courts at the Block Island Club on Corn Neck Road, Champlain's Marina in New Harbor, and The Neptune House on Connecticut Avenue.

Windsurfing. There are a couple of places that rent sailboards, including one at Fred Benson Town Beach, Corn Neck Road; (401–466–3230), and Island Moped on Chapel Street (401–466–2700).

SPECIAL EVENTS

Mid-June. Taste of Block Island Seafood Festival and Chowder Cook-Off. This is a great chance to sample all sorts of local seafood dishes.

June. Race Week on Block Island. An around-the-island race, this annual event is one of the largest sailing events on the East Coast.

July 4th weekend. To celebrate the Fourth, Block Island has fireworks, a parade, and a big barbecue.

Mid-August. Annual Block Island House & Garden Tour. Houses around Great Salt Pond open their doors and garden gates to the public.

Mid-September. Annual "Run Around the Block." This is a 15K road race around the island.

Early October. Block Island Birding Weekend. An ideal bird-watching island, especially during spring and fall. The Audubon Society of Rhode Island organizes a weekend of guided walks.

OTHER RECOMMENDED RESTAURANTS AND LODGINGS

Atlantic Inn, High Street; (401) 466–5883. A mansard-roofed Victorian dating back to 1890, this is a delightful hotel with views of the old Harbor.

1661 Inn and Guest House, Spring Street; (401) 466–2421. Owned by the same family as the Manisses, the 1661 is a large white island house with twenty-eight thoughtfully and tastefully decorated guest rooms.

FOR MORE INFORMATION

Block Island Tourist Council, 23 Water Street, Block Island, RI 02807; (800) 383–BIRI or (401) 466–5200.

Rhode Island Department of Economic Development, Division of Tourism, 7 Jackson Walkway, Providence, RI 02903; (800) 556–2484 or (401) 277–2601.

TO GET THERE

By train: Amtrak (800) 872–7245.

By bus: Greyhound (800) 231–2222.

Bonanza (888) 331–7500.

Rhode Island Public Transit Authority (401) 781–9400.

By air: New England Airlines (800) 243–2460.

By ferry: Interstate Navigation operates ferries from Point Judith, New London, Providence, and Newport. Call (401) 783–4613 for schedules and prices. For ferry information from Montauk, call (516) 668–5709 or (516) 668–2214.

MASSACHUSETTS
ESCAPES

The Berkshires

MUSIC, MANSIONS, AND MORE

2 NIGHTS

Performing arts • Fine dining • Country inns
Antiques and crafts shops • Galleries • Historical homes
Rural scenery • Hiking

The Berkshire Hills are known for both their rural beauty (sprawling farms, tidy little villages, dozen of lakes and ponds, thousands of acres of forest) and their cultural assets (they're home to the Tanglewood Music Festival and Jacob's Pillow Dance Festival). Located in the western quarter of the state, they stretch all the way from Connecticut to Vermont (just south of the Green Mountains). The area, which is now massively popular for weekenders, especially during the summer months, first became famous when Nathaniel Hawthorne wrote *Tanglewood Tales*. Route 7 takes you right through the heart of them, passing through a series of wonderful little towns including Stockbridge, Lenox, Pittsfield, and Williamstown.

During July and August, when the Tanglewood Music Festival and the area's other performing arts are in full bloom, the Berkshires can be very crowded. Many inns require a three-night minimum stay, and there are long waits at restaurants and cultural attractions. Your best bet is to visit midweek.

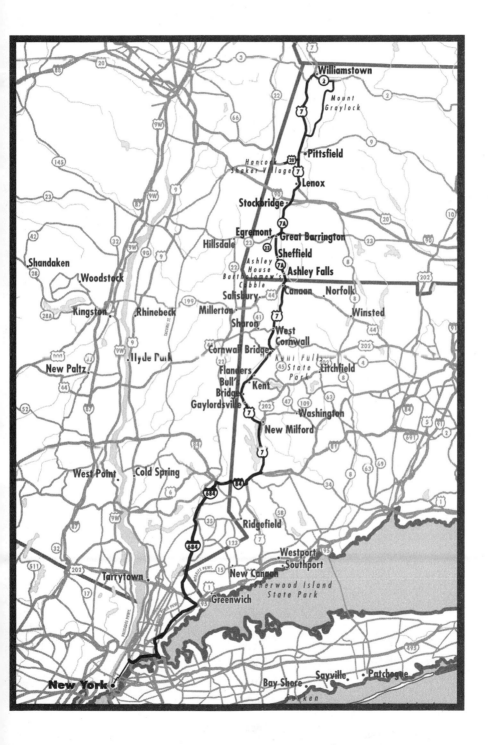

DAY 1

Morning

Head north on Route 684, then east on Route 84 to Route 7 north. Route 7 takes you right to the southern Berkshires.

Shortly after you cross over the Connecticut border into Massachusetts, turn onto Route 7A to reach **Ashley Falls.** Follow the signs from the center of Ashley Falls to your first stop, **Bartholomew's Cobble** (413–229–8600), a 277–acre preserve of 500-million-year-old marble outcroppings above the Housatonic River. You can stretch your legs a bit by following the Ledges Interpretive Trail, which introduces you to some of the preserve's amazing variety of plants and flowers. Just across a field (you'll see signs) is the **Colonel John Ashley House** (also 413–229–8600), which dates back to 1735, making it one of the oldest houses in the county. It's open summers only, from the last week in June through Labor Day, Wednesday through Sunday, 1:00 to 5:00 P.M.

Continue north on Route 7A to get back on Route 7 and **Sheffield,** your next stop. This town is crammed with antiques shops (a directory of who sells what is available in each one). Sheffield is also home to the state's oldest covered bridge (look for the red sign on the right).

Once you've done the shops of Sheffield, keep heading north on Route 7 until you reach Route 23 west. Turn left and follow it into **South Egremont,** where you can pause for lunch and have a look around more antiques shops and galleries.

LUNCH: Gaslight Cafe, Main Street; (413) 528–0870. Here you can grab a big club sandwich, a burger, or try the cafe's special asparagus melt. The cafe is open every day except Tuesday.

Afternoon

Backtrack to Route 7 and carry on to **Great Barrington,** where you'll find more shops, and then press on for about another 4 miles until you see **Monument Mountain** looming before you. If you're feeling up for it, take time out to hike to the summit. Be prepared, however; it could take about two or three hours.

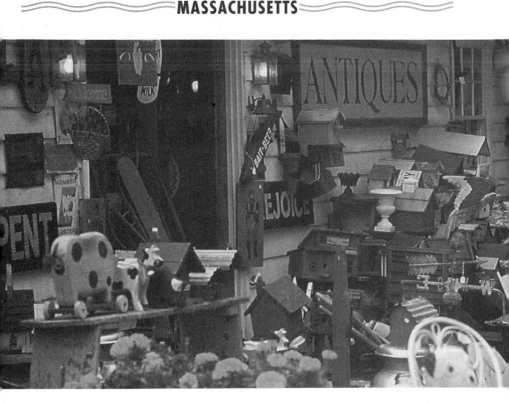

Antiques shops abound in the Berkshires.

The next stop is **Stockbridge,** which many people know from Norman Rockwell's famous illustrations that first appeared on the covers of the *Saturday Evening Post* and *McCall's.* You can see some of the original covers as well as the world's largest collection of the illustrator's works in the **Norman Rockwell Museum,** Route 183 (413–298–4100). Hours are from 10:00 A.M. to 5:00 P.M. daily. Just up the road from the museum is **Chesterwood,** Route 183 (413–298–3579), the summer home of Daniel Chester French, who sculpted the *Seated Lincoln* in the Lincoln Memorial. The museum is open daily from 10:00 A.M. to 5:00 P.M. There are house and studio tours as well as gardens and a museum of the artist's works. Two other top Stockbridge attractions are **The Mission House,** Main Street (413–298–3239), which houses a fine collection of Early American furnishings, and **Naumkeag,**

Prospect Hill Road (414–298–3239), a summer "cottage" that was used during the nineteenth-century "gilded era" when families such as the Vanderbilts and Westinghouses vacationed in these hills. The Mission House is open Tuesday through Sunday from 11:00 A.M. to 4:00 P.M.; Naumkeag is open Tuesday through Sunday from 10:00 A.M. to 4:15 P.M. Both are open from Memorial Day to Columbus Day.

The **Red Lion Inn** on Main Street has been a major Stockbridge landmark for more than 200 years. Consider stopping in for a drink in the courtyard or on one of the rockers on the front porch. Then wander around the shops that crowd around Main Street.

DINNER: Choose **The Old Mill,** Route 23, South Egremont (413–528–1421), which was once a blacksmith's shop as well as a mill. It's one of the most highly regarded restaurants in the Berkshires, with a good selection of fish, chicken, and steak dishes. An alternative is the **Castle Street Cafe,** 10 Castle Street, Great Barrington (413–528–5244), a popular bistro (reservations are a must) known for its deliriously good pasta and grilled fish dishes.

LODGING: Year-round it's important to make reservations at Berkshire inns. During the busy months expect to find many places full. Though pricey, **The Red Lion Inn,** Main Street (413–298–5545), which was originally built in 1773 as a stagecoach stop, is a New England classic.

Evening

In addition to Tanglewood (just north of Stockbridge in Lenox) and Jacob's Pillow (east of Stockbridge in Becket), the southern Berkshires have an abundance of other shows and cultural events. For program information and tickets, call ahead: Berkshire Choral Institute (413–229–8526); Aston Magna Festival (413–528–3595); Berkshire Opera Company (413–243–1343); Stockbridge Summer Music Series (413–443–1138); and DeSisto Estate Dinner Theatre and Cabaret (413–298–4032).

DAY 2

Morning

BREAKFAST: At the inn.

Afterward head north out of Stockbridge on Route 7. About 5 miles up, at the junction of Routes 7 and 7A, you'll find **The Mount,** Plunkett Street at the south junction of Routes 7 and 7A (413–637–1899), which was the summer residence of novelist Edith Wharton. The house, a Classical Revival, is sensationally situated on forty-nine acres. Tours of the house and gardens are offered every day except Monday from late May through Labor Day, and on Saturdays and Sundays between Labor Day and the end of October.

Follow Route 7A to **Lenox,** which is home to **Tanglewood,** on West Street (413–637–1940), where legendary music can be heard under the stars throughout the summer months. Tanglewood is the summer home for the Boston Symphony Orchestra. If you're not planning to attend a performance, do take time to stroll around the grounds (there are 210 acres including formal gardens), which are open daily.

LUNCH: Church Street Cafe, 69 Church Street (413–637–2745), is a very successful bistro with all sorts of eclectic and ethnic dishes. Try to get a table outside if the weather's nice (closed Sunday and Monday).

Afternoon

From Lenox drive north on Route 7, making a stop at the **Berkshire Museum** in **Pittsfield,** right on Route 7 (locally known as South Street) at 39 South Street (413–443–7171). It has a good collection of nineteenth- and twentieth-century paintings as well as some local exhibits. It's open daily in July and August and closed on Mondays the rest of the year. Also in Pittsfield is **Arrowhead,** 780 Holmes Road (413–442–1793), the house where Herman Melville wrote *Moby-Dick.* It's open from Memorial Day through October 31, Monday through Saturday from 10:00 to 4:30 P.M., and Sunday from 11:00 to 3:30 P.M. After Labor Day it's open from Friday through Monday.

About 5 miles west of Pittsfield (at the junction of Routes 20 and 41) is **Hancock Shaker Village** (413–443–0188), a living-history museum devoted to the Shakers. For about 200 years (1781–1960), the site was a Shaker community. Hours are daily between May 1 and October 31, from 9:30 A.M. to 5:00 P.M.

The final stop for the day and your home for the night is **Williamstown,** which is not far from the Vermont border. Among the town's most notable attractions are the **Sterling and Francine Clark Art Institute,** 225 South

Street (413–458–9545), an outstanding collection of French Impressionists (including Renoirs) and Old Masters (open Tuesday through Sunday from 10:00 A.M. to 5:00 P.M.); and **Williams College,** 1 block east of central green (413–597–3131), which has a fine collection of paintings as well as one of the nation's best collections of rare books.

DINNER: The Orchards, 222 Adams Road (413–458–9611) at the inn of the same name, is cloud nine. Anything you order, whether it's poached salmon, grilled sirloin, or braised pheasant and polenta with shiitake-rosemary demiglace, will be flawlessly prepared.

LODGING: The Orchards, 222 Adams Road (413–458–9611), is a top-of-the-line choice with the special touches of an inn (antique furnishings, cordials served in the living room) combined with the amenities of a fine-quality hotel (concierge, in-room movies, exercise room plus golf and tennis privileges).

Evening

During summer months the **Williamstown Theatre Festival** brings professionals and apprentices together for traditional and experimental theater. For program and ticket information, call (413) 597–3400.

DAY 3

Morning

BREAKFAST: The best bet for breakfast is to head over to **Spring Street,** which is 1 block west of Water Street in the midst of Williams College campus. The street is lined with small delis and eateries.

Spend a little time after breakfast browsing around Williamstown shops and then head back south, this time taking Route 2 east. Between Williamstown and North Adams on Route 2, you'll find an access road on the right (Notch Road) to **Mount Greylock.** The ride to the top of the state's highest peak (3,491 feet) takes about half an hour and offers a five-state view. At the summit there's an old lodge called **Bascom Lodge** that's run by the Appalachian Mountain Club. Follow the road back down and you'll wind up in Lanesborough on Route 7, just north of Pittsfield.

Continue south on Route 7, stopping at farm stands along the way to stock up on fresh produce and dairy. Chances are that you'll also see signs for tag sales, at which you may or may not unearth some worthwhile finds. Trace your steps back to Manhattan, taking Route 7 to Route 84 west to 684 south.

THERE'S MORE

Historic railroad. Berkshire Scenic Railway Museum, Willow Creek Road, Lenox; (413) 637–2210. Railroad museum and vintage train rides.

Nature trails. Northwest of Lenox is the Pleasant Valley Sanctuary, which offers several miles of trails to explore. It's open Tuesday through Sunday from dawn to dusk.

Skiing. There's downhill skiing at Butternut Basin, which is about 2 miles east of Great Barrington; Jiminy Peak in Hancock; Brodie Mountain in New Ashford; and other locations throughout the Berkshires.

Waterfalls. Bash Bish Falls, 12 miles southwest of South Egremont (just over the New York line), is a spectacularly scenic valley pierced by 50-foot Bash Bish Falls. A hiker's must at any time of year.

SPECIAL EVENTS

Late January. Tennis Winter Event. A 10K cross country ski race in Kennedy Park in Lenox.

Late June–late August. Williamstown Theatre Festival. Modern classics, contemporary plays, cabarets, and other performances. Call (413) 597–3400 for program and ticket information.

Late June–late August. Berkshire Theatre Festival, at the Berkshire Playhouse, East Main Street in Stockbridge. New and experimental theater. Call (413) 298–5576 for details.

Mid-July. Berkshire Charity Auto Show, Pittsfield. More than 500 antique and special-interest autos are displayed on the grounds of Hillcrest Hospital on West Street.

Berkshire Antiquarian Book Fair. Dozens of dealers display rare books at Stockbridge Plain School on Main Street.

July and August. Tanglewood Music Festival, Lenox. Summer home of the Boston Symphony Orchestra. Outdoor concerts. Write for a program: Symphony Hall, 301 Massachusetts Avenue, Boston, MA 02115; (617) 266–1492. During July and August only, you can call Tanglewood directly at (413) 637–1940.

July and August. Jacob's Pillow Dance Festival, Becket. A summer dance festival featuring ballet, modern dance, jazz, and mime. Contact Jacob's Pillow Dance Festival, P.O. Box 287, Lee, MA 01238; (413) 243–0745.

Mid-July–early August. Aston Magna Festival, Great Barrington. This summer festival takes place at St. James Church on Main Street.

The Berkshire Choral Festival offers five weeks of classical music at the Berkshire School concert shed.

Early August. Berkshire Craft Fair, Monument Mountain Regional High School, Great Barrington. A juried fair with more than one hundred artisans.

Mid-August. Sheffield Antiques Show, Sheffield. More than two dozen dealers from around the Northeast display their prize pieces at this annual event at the Mount Everett Regional High School on Berkshire School Road.

Mid-September. Barrington Fair, Great Barrington. An annual fair with exhibits, agricultural displays, livestock, and entertainment.

Late September. Apple Squeeze Festival, Lenox. Celebration of apples festival.

Early October. Autumn Weekend, Hancock Shaker Village, Pittsfield. Demonstrations of Shaker fall harvest activities.

Late December. House tours of Lenox. Usually the last Saturday of December.

OTHER RECOMMENDED RESTAURANTS AND LODGINGS

Lenox

The Apple Tree Inn, 25334 West Street; (413) 637–1477. A wonderful inn, close to Tanglewood.

Blantyre, 16 Blantyre Road; (413) 637–3556. A 1905 replica of a Scottish castle, this is a magnificently scenic setting for both staying and dining.

Canyon Ranch, 165 Kimble Street; (413) 637–4100 or (800) 742–9000. One of the best spas in the country. Consider spending a couple of nights here, dipping into its various spa treatments.

The Gables Inn, 81 Walker Street, (413) 637–2532. Conveniently located, Gateways is close to Tanglewood, the Berkshire Theater Festival, and Jacob's Pillow Dance Festival.

Wheatleigh, West Hawthorne Road; (413) 637–0610 or (800) 321–0610. This villa, built in sixteenth-century Florentine style, once belonged to a contessa. Today it's one of the Berkshire's most luxurious places to stay.

Williamstown

Field Farm Guest House, 554 Sloan Road; (413) 458–3135. A country guest house set on 254 acres.

FOR MORE INFORMATION

Berkshire Visitors Bureau, Berkshire Common, Box PR, Pittsfield, MA 01201; (800) 237–5747 or (413) 443–9186.

Massachusetts Office of Travel and Tourism, 100 Cambridge Street, 13th Floor, Boston, MA 02202; (617) 727–3201 or (800) 447–MASS.

MASSACHUSETTS

The North Shore

BEAUTY AND THE BEACH

2 NIGHTS

Gracious homes and public buildings • Beaches
Boats • Seafood • Antiques • Witches

For Bostonians the North Shore, which is roughly the area between Salem (immediately north of Boston) and Newburyport near the New Hampshire border, has long been a favorite quick escape. For New Yorkers it's a slightly longer haul (figure about four hours to Boston and another half hour or so to Salem), but well worth it.

Back in the eighteenth and nineteenth centuries, magnificent ships were built in the North Shore towns, and they would set sail for ports in Africa and Asia, bringing great wealth to the area. Today many of the buildings, including majestic sea-captains' homes still stand surveying strikingly beautiful stretches of coastline.

As you explore, you'll see sailboats gliding majestically in the wind, Victorian houses poised on the shores, and old salts puttering around seaside towns. You could easily spend a week exploring the attractions in this area. This short trip takes you to some of the highlights.

DAY 1

Morning

Unless you hit traffic, you should be able to whiz up to the Boston area on I–95 (which becomes Route 128) in about four hours. Just north of Boston

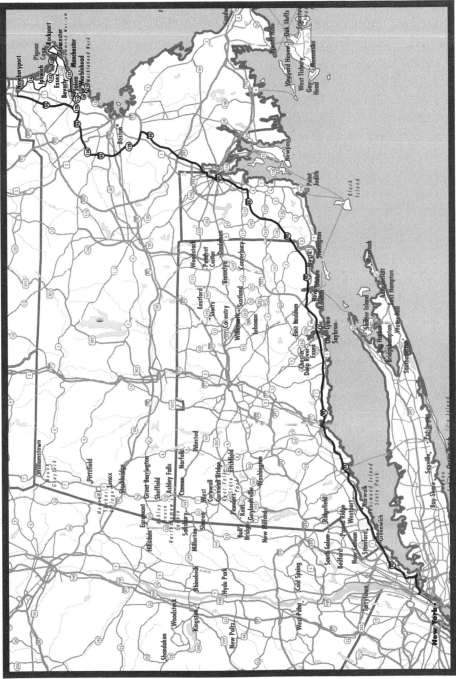

you'll see signs for Route 114 and **Salem,** a great place to begin your explorations as well as have lunch.

LUNCH: You can take your pick of restaurants in Salem. If you want to just grab something simple before setting about your sightseeing, consider heading for **Red's Sandwich,** 15 Central Street (978–745–3527), a diner always crowded with locals. You'll find all the mainstream favorites including burgers, BLTs, and club sandwiches. For a more formal meal, wander over to **The Grapevine Restaurant,** 26 Congress Street (978–745–9335), and, weather permitting, get a table outside in the courtyard out back. Both the lunch and dinner menus include a wonderful selection of northern Italian dishes. If you're eager to get out to see the town and don't want to settle in for a long-drawn-out meal, you can always sit at the bar and order a bowl of linguine tossed with pesto and topped with sautéed vegetables.

Afternoon

Most people automatically think "witches" when they hear "Salem." Indeed this little seafront town was where the famous witch trials took place back in 1692. Ultimately, however, it has never been proven that there were witches in Salem, yet the belief lives on, though many of the locals would just as soon forget the whole ordeal. Those interested in witches will find plenty of opportunities to indulge their fascination. Perhaps the best place of all is **The Salem Witch Museum,** 19½ Washington Square (978–744–1692); there's an audiovisual re-creation of the witchcraft trials every half hour whenever it's open. The museum is located in a Gothic, churchlike building at the intersection of Brown and Hawthorne Boulevard. It's open year-round from 10:00 A.M. to 5:00 P.M. The **Witch House,** 310½ Essex Street (978–744–0180), was the home of Magistrate Jonathan Corwin, one of the judges in the witch trials. Those accused of witchcraft were held in the house before the trials. It's open from mid-March to June, daily from 10:00 A.M. to 4:30 P.M.; between July and Labor Day, daily from 10:00 A.M. to 6:00 P.M.; and between Labor Day and December 1, daily from 10:00 A.M. to 4:30 P.M. **Crow Haven Corner,** 125 Essex Street (978–745–8763), is another must-see witch attraction in Salem. This tiny shop is owned by Laurie Cabot, Salem's most illustrious witch. Here you can buy all sorts of herbs, powders, and seeds to ward off evil or attract love, luck, and money. Also for sale are gargoyles and unicorns, witch books, crystals, moonstones, black cat candles, crystal balls, and magic wands. You can also make an appointment to have a tarot card reading with Laurie Cabot.

Aside from witches, however, Salem has a multitude of other attractions, which makes deciding exactly what to do a bit of a challenge (see "There's More"). In addition to the aforementioned witch sights, be sure to see the **House of the Seven Gables,** 54 Turner Street (978–744–0991), which served as the setting of Nathaniel Hawthorne's novel of the same name (open July through October 31, daily from 9:00 A.M. to 6:00 P.M. and from November through June, daily from 10:00 A.M. to 4:30 P.M. except Sunday, when it opens at noon), and the **Salem Maritime National Historic Site,** 174 Derby Street (978–745–1470), which is a collection of historical buildings, including the Customs House and West Indies Goods Store, and Derby Wharf, overseen by the National Park Service. Start by picking up a copy of their walking map or join in on one of their guided tours (hours vary).

Also extremely worthwhile is **The Peabody Essex Museum,** East India Mall (978–744–3390), which has impressive collections of the art, historical documents, and artifacts from the area's prosperous shipping days. It's open year-round from 10:00 A.M. to 5:00 P.M. weekdays and Saturdays, and on Sundays from noon to 5:00 P.M.

Be sure to take a walk around the waterfront area, **Pickering Wharf,** which has been restored and colonized by several restaurants, gift shops, antiques shops, crystal shops, a New Age bookstore, and the like. And don't miss **Harbor Sweets,** 85 Leavitt Street (978–745–7648), where you can buy sailboat-shaped almond butter crunch chocolates right where they are made (you get to sample the selections beforehand).

From Salem it's an easy drive over to **Marblehead,** your home for the night.

DINNER: **King's Rook,** 12 State Street; (781) 631–9838. This is a great place to have a light dinner—sandwiches, salads, soups. It's also a coffeehouse and wine bar with a long list of desserts.

LODGING: Located between Pearl and Pickett Streets, the **Harbor Light Inn,** 58 Washington Street, Marblehead (781–631–2186), is beautifully situated in the center of Marblehead's historic district. There are twelve guest rooms, each one with either a four-poster or canopy bed, some with views of the harbor.

DAY 2

Morning

BREAKFAST: Roll out of bed and head right for **Driftwood Restaurant,** 63 Front Street, Marblehead (781–631–1145). This full-of-character and full of characters restaurant attracts a crowd of local fishermen and boatbuilders. It's the kind of restaurant where you can order a heaping pile of pancakes and justify it by saying, "Oh well, we're on vacation."

After breakfast wander around Marblehead's cobbled Old Town, which dates back to before the Revolution. It's a wonderful little village, well known among yacht and sailboat owners who come from around the world to race during summer months. Tour **Abbot Hall,** Washington Street (781–631–0000), **Jeremiah Lee Mansion,** near the intersection of Hooper and Washington streets (781–631–1069), and **King Hooper Mansion,** 8 Hooper Street (781–631–2608)—three of Marblehead's landmark buildings.

Then drive the loop around **Marblehead Neck.** This quiet residential community is made up of several grand ocean- and harbor-front homes surrounded by handsome lawns and gardens. Along the way there's an **Audubon Bird Sanctuary** on Ocean Avenue, **Castle Rock** (from which the ocean views are staggeringly beautiful), and, at the tip, **Chandler Hovey Park,** which is home to the Marblehead Light and several benches on which you can sit and look out at the boat-filled harbor with the village as a backdrop.

Carry on up the coast, following Route 1A to Beverly, and then Route 127 to **Manchester,** which is poised on the shores of Cape Ann. Even if you're not a "beach type," don't deny yourself the experience of walking on **Singing Beach** along Beach Street. Not only does the sand "sing," but the coastal scene is arrestingly beautiful. Consider stopping in town first and picking up a couple of sandwiches for a picnic lunch.

Afternoon

North of Magnolia on Route 127, you'll see signs for the **Hammond Castle Museum,** 80 Hesperus Avenue, Magnolia (978–283–2080), a castle that was built by inventor, electrical engineer, and collector Dr. John Hays Hammond Jr. The house is filled with his creations, which are all explained during a forty-five-minute tour. It's open daily from 9:00 A.M. to 5:00 P.M.

Rockport's most photographed attraction, "Motif No. 1."

Continue north to **Gloucester,** a major fishing port. Once in town you'll
see signs directing motorists along the city's **Scenic Tour,** which takes you by
the Harbor Cove, the Inner Harbor, the Fish Pier, and to the city's celebrated
statue of a Gloucester fisherman.

Take time out on your own to see **Beauport,** the Sleeper-McCann
House, 75 Eastern Point Boulevard (978–283–0800), on Eastern Point (across
the bay from downtown Gloucester). The house was built by Henry Davis
Sleeper, an interior decorator and antiquarian of the 1920s. There are hour-
long tours weekdays, from May 15 to October 15 from 10:00 A.M. to 4:00
P.M., and on weekends, from mid–September through mid–October from 1:00
to 4:00 P.M. Another absolutely worthwhile stop in Gloucester is the **Rocky
Neck Art Colony,** a huddle of artists' studios on the water and crammed
together on narrow streets.

From Gloucester continue heading north up the coast to **Rockport,** which started off as a quiet fishing village, was discovered by artists, and has since sprouted into a resort. Rockport got its name because of the local granite—you'll find the durable stone in buildings and markers all over town.

During the summer the **Bearskin Neck,** a narrow peninsula jutting into the water off Dock Square, is practically sagging with tourists. Here you'll find one souvenir shop after another interspersed with art galleries and restaurants. The town's most photographed attraction is called "Motif No. 1," a red fisherman's shack that was named by the first painters who moved to Rockport. Actually the original shack was blown out to sea, so many people jokingly call this "Motif No. 2." If you're interested in seeing paintings, sculpture, and graphics by local artists, stop by the **Rockport Art Association,** 12 Main Street (978–546–6604). The RAA also has free lectures, artist demonstrations, and concerts (see "Special Events").

You might want to note that Rockport is a dry town. This means that no liquor, wine, or beer is served in its restaurants or sold in its inns or shops. You can BYO, but make sure you pick it up in Gloucester or elsewhere on your way up.

DINNER: You'll find seafood abundant in Rockport. If you want to keep the price down, head for **Ellen's Harborside,** just off Dock Square on T-Wharf (978–546–2512). It's always packed with fanatical regulars who pile in for the fresh seafood and homemade desserts (open mid-April through December). The best place to go if you want great seafood with a view is **My Place By-The-Sea,** 68 Bearskin Neck (978–546–9667). It's at the very end of the Bearskin Neck, offering oceanfront dining.

LODGING: Addison Choate Inn, 49 Broadway, Rockport; (508) 546–7543. A sweet little inn in a building that dates back to 1851. It's within easy walking distance of the town's attractions.

DAY 3

Morning

BREAKFAST: Ellen's Harborside, just off Dock Square on T-Wharf (978–546–2512), is the place to go for a big American breakfast or just a corn muffin and coffee.

After breakfast take a drive around the Cape. Head north out of town on Route 127A, making your first stop at **Pigeon Cove.** If you have time, it's a good spot to take a dip. From there carry on to **Halibut Point State Park,** which has an interpretive center, an old granite quarry (now flooded with water), and an observation tower. Beyond the interpretive center there's an Observation Point atop a cliff above the Atlantic. You can go down to the water, but think twice about going in. The waves and rocks can be very dangerous.

From Halibut Point follow Route 127 around the western side of Cape Ann to Route 128. Then turn right onto Route 133 for a scenic drive up to **Essex,** which is a stopover must if you're in the market for antiques. From Essex it's a short drive to **Ipswich,** where you can feast on clams in one of many roadside eateries. Ipswich is a summer resort town with what many consider one of the best beaches on the Atlantic coast. **Crane Beach,** at the end of Argilla Road on Ipswich Bay, is a 5-mile-long sweep of beach open to the public (you pay for parking).

If you're not pressed for time, carry on to **Newburyport** (picking up Route 1A shortly after Ipswich). Newburyport is a museumlike nineteenth-century town filled with shipowners' and captains' houses overlooking a yacht-filled harbor. There are a couple of museums in town—the Coffin House, Cushing House, and Custom House—worth browsing around if you have the time.

From Newburyport you can easily pick up I–95 and head back to the New York area.

THERE'S MORE

Antiques. Pickering Wharf Antiques, Pickering Wharf, Salem; (978) 741–1797. An antiques center displaying the works of more than thirty-five dealers.

Living history. Pioneer Village: Salem in 1630, Forest River Park, Salem; (978) 745–0525. A living-history museum with costumed interpreters.

Whale-watch cruises. Cape Ann Whale Watch operates cruises from Rose's Wharf at 415 Main Street in Gloucester; (978) 283–5110.

SPECIAL EVENTS

Last weekend in June. Festival of St. Peter, Gloucester. A four-day-long celebration with sports events, fireworks, and a Blessing of the Fleet.

June. Rockport Chamber Music Festival, Rockport; (978) 546–7391. Recitals are given Thursday through Sunday throughout the month.

Late July. Old Ipswich Days. Arts and crafts shows, exhibits, clambakes, entertainment.

Last week of July. Race Week, Marblehead. Sailing races.

Mid-August. Heritage Days Celebration, Salem. Band concerts, a parade, exhibits, arts and crafts, and food stalls.

Third weekend in August. Waterfront Festival, Gloucester. Arts and crafts show, military reenactment, food, and entertainment.

Labor Day weekend. Schooner Festival, Gloucester. Races, sailboat parade, and maritime festivities.

OTHER RECOMMENDED RESTAURANTS AND LODGINGS

Gloucester

The Rudder Restaurant, 75 Rock Neck Avenue, East Gloucester; (978) 283–7967. Dinner here is not just a meal, it's a wild party, complete with the zaniest entertainment you may ever see. Closed over the winter months.

Marblehead

The Nautilus, 68 Front Street; (781) 631–1703. A waterfront guest house. Summer weekends fill quickly, so call as far in advance as possible.

Seaward Inn, 62 Marmion Way; (781) 546–3471 or (800) 648–7733. Within easy walking distance of the village, this Cape Ann inn also offers five-course, home-cooking-style meals.

Salem

Hawthorne Hotel, 18 Washington Street West; (978) 744–4080. A major Salem landmark, the Hawthorne is within easy walking distance of all of Salem's attractions and restaurants.

FOR MORE INFORMATION

Massachusetts Office of Travel and Tourism, 100 Cambridge Street, 13th Floor, Boston, MA 02202; (617) 727–3201 or (800) 447–MASS.

Salem Chamber of Commerce, 32 Derby Square, Salem, MA 01970; (978) 744–0004.

Marblehead Chamber of Commerce, 62 Pleasant Street, Marblehead, MA 01945; (781) 631–2868.

Rockport Chamber of Commerce, P.O. Box 67M, Rockport, MA 01966; (978) 546–6575. Information Center on Main Street.

Cape Cod

SEASCAPES AND SEAFOOD

*Beaches • Antiques shops • Seafood • Bicycling • Boating
Boutiques • Galleries • Whale-watching • Nature walks*

Soft breezes off the sea. Acres and acres of salt marshes and cranberry bogs. Clam shacks. For many Cape Cod is synonymous with the word *vacation*. Indeed it is a vacation land, one big open-air sandbox in which both kids and adults can play.

Though rarely referred to as such, Cape Cod is technically an island, separated from mainland Massachusetts by the Cape Cod Canal. Two bridges span the narrow waters—the Bourne to the south (Route 28) and the Sagamore to the north (Route 6). The Cape, which all writers and just about everybody else who has been there or lives there will tell you, looks like a flexed arm on the map. It's just 70 miles from the mainland to Provincetown but is filled with little galaxies to explore.

Keep in mind that you won't be able to see everything in a couple of days on the Cape. This quick escape is just a glimpse of what it has to offer. You'll spend the first half of the trip working your way up the Cape and then meander back down. As many places on the Cape are open only during the summer, be sure to call ahead if you're traveling during any other season.

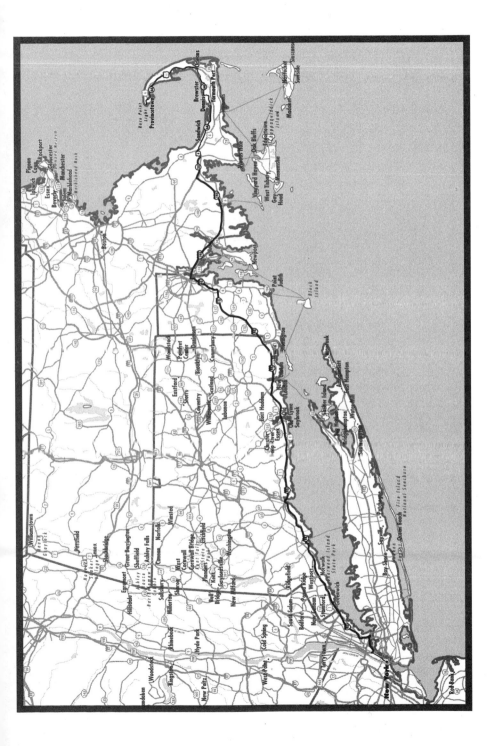

DAY 1

Morning

From New York take I–95 north to I–195. Then take Massachusetts Route 25 to Route 6 east. Route 6 runs right up the Cape, most of the time alongside Historic Route 6A.

One of the first towns you'll come to is **Sandwich,** which calls itself the "oldest town on the Cape." A lot of people skim right by it, heading for Provincetown. Unless you're tired from the drive up and want to get straight to your hotel for the night, consider stopping for a look around its antiques stores, gracious old houses, and beaches. Sandwich is also home to one of the Cape's top attractions: The **Heritage Plantation,** Grove and Pine Streets (508–888–3300), has seventy-six acres of gardens with museums showcasing antique cars, colonial tools, and a working 1912 carousel.

From Sandwich it's a short drive (on historic Route 6A) to **Yarmouth Port,** where you can settle in for the night. Yarmouth Port is home to several old sea captains' houses that line a stretch of Main Street (which is part of Route 6A) known as the "Captains' Mile."

DINNER: Abbicci, 43 Main Street, Yarmouth Port (508–362–3501), is just down the road from the Wedgewood Inn. Though it's not a typical Cape restaurant, a meal here is truly worth it. The cuisine is northern Italian.

LODGING: The **Wedgewood Inn,** 83 Main Street, Yarmouth Port (508–362–5157) is a beautiful old house that was built in 1812. All six rooms are individually decorated with country furnishings. Some have working fireplaces; some have private porches. It's truly a gem.

DAY 2

Morning

BREAKFAST: At the inn (included in the room price).

Start the day by taking a walk on the **Nature Trails of the Historical Society of Old Yarmouth.** The trails take you through some of Yarmouth's most beautiful land and marshes.

Then head out of town north on Route 6A to **Dennis.** If the day is clear, or even partially clear, make your way up to the **Scargo Hill Tower** (from

Cape Cod offers a huge slice of the good by-the-sea life.

Route 6A, turn right onto Old Bass River Road and follow the signs). From the top you can see the Cape stretching out below all the way up to Provincetown.

Brewster is the next stop. Here you'll find three noteworthy attractions. The **Cape Cod Aquarium,** 281 Main Street (508–385–9252), is a wonderful sanctuary for rescued seals, sea lions, and sea turtles as well as an informative marine center. It's open daily from 9:30 A.M. to 5:00 P.M. in summer (hours are slightly shorter the rest of the year). The **New England Fire and History Museum,** 1439 Route 6A (508–896–5711), has one of the world's largest collections of fire-fighting equipment and memorabilia. Hours are from 10:00 A.M. to 3:00 P.M. daily during the summer months and from 10:00 A.M. to 3:00 P.M. on weekends from mid-September to Columbus Day. The **Cape Cod Museum of Natural History,** Route 6A (508–896–3867), is a good place to learn all about the Cape's flora, fauna, and ecology. It's open from 9:00 A.M. to 4:30 P.M. Monday through Saturday and from 12:30 to 4:30 P.M. on Sundays.

A little farther up Route 6A is **Orleans,** which is the midpoint between the Cape Cod Canal and Provincetown. By now it's probably time for lunch and a snooze on the beach.

LUNCH: Stop by a grocery store or deli in Orleans to pick up picnic supplies for the beach.

Afternoon

You can take your pick of beaches in the area. On the ocean side you'll find **Nauset Beach,** a gorgeous beach, with major waves, that stretches on for 10 miles. Over on the bay side **Skaket Beach** is also beautiful but a lot calmer— a good choice for families with young children.

DINNER: Kadee's Lobster and Clam Bar is at 212 Main Street, East Orleans (508–255–6184). The owners also own the next-door East Orleans Fish Market, which means that you can count on wonderfully fresh seafood. You can sit outside and feast on a pile of steamers, corn on the cob, and the best lobster ever—and not spend a fortune. Please note that the restaurant is closed during the winter months.

LODGING: Nauset House Inn, 141 Beach Road, East Orleans (508–225–2195), is just half a mile away from the beach. It's a beautiful country inn surrounded by gardened grounds.

DAY 3

Morning

BREAKFAST: Guests have raved so much about the breakfasts at the Nauset House Inn that innkeeper Diane Johnson has printed the recipes up in a booklet. Breakfast is indeed a treat here and is included in the room rate.

Before leaving Orleans pull into the **Bird Watcher's General Store,** Route 6A; (508–255–6974). Here you'll find everything on birds and birds on everything from postcards to mailboxes, as well as bins of corn, thistle seeds, and sunflower seeds and a good selection of birdhouses.

Continue up the Cape to **Provincetown** at the very tip. Be forewarned, however. During summer months traffic can be crazy. Your best bet is to grab the first parking spot you see as you drive in on Commercial Street. Then you can walk the rest of the way into town, passing one lovely shingled house after another. Most of the in-town inns have parking for guests, but you may be too early to check in.

P-Town, as Provincetown is locally known, is a very lively community with lots of artist types and writers. Though the town is not big, it's crammed with shops, galleries, restaurants, bakeries, night spots—you name it. One of its biggest appeals is people-watching. Sit on one of the benches in front of town hall and chances are you'll see more characters in half an hour than some people see in a lifetime. P-Town is a lot of fun, and during summer months it has a tipsy air of carnival. The rest of the year it is considerably more serene and is the best time to go if you just want to relax and enjoy the profusion of restaurants, night spots, and nearby beaches.

LUNCH: **Café Blasé,** 328 Commercial Street (508–487–9465), is a good outdoor cafe to plant yourself and people watch. The menu has lots of salads, burgers, and quiches.

Afternoon

You can rent bikes right in town at Arnold's Bicycle Shop, 329 Commercial Street (508–487–0844), and pedal around to some of the nearby attractions. Right off Bradford Street (which runs parallel to Commercial Street), you'll find the town's biggest tourist attraction: the **Pilgrim Monument** and **Provincetown Museum,** High Pole Hill (508–487–1310). The museum has some Pilgrim exhibits and a potpourri of other collections (including pieces from whaling-ship days, old costumes, World War I mementos). You can climb to the top of the monument for a far-reaching view of the Cape. Hours for both are from 9:00 A.M. to 9:00 P.M. in summer, and from 9:00 A.M. to 5:00 P.M. in winter.

From the monument it's a short, mostly flat or downhill pedal over to **Herring Cove,** where you can get on the **Province Lands Bike Paths,** a web-work of paved trails that take you over the dunes, through pine groves, and alongside the sea. They include the **Loop Trail** (5¼ miles), **Herring Cove Beach** spur (1 mile), **Race Point Beach** spur (½ mile), **Bennett Pond** spur (¼ mile), and **Race Point Road** spur (¼ mile).

It's worth pedaling back to Herring Cove for the sunset. On a typical day it's an applaudable extravaganza.

DINNER: There are so many restaurants in P-Town that it all boils down to what you feel like eating. Nevertheless, if you want to try a real Cape Cod restaurant, head down to nearby Wellfleet for a traditional New England dinner at the **Wellfleet Oyster House,** East Main Street (508–349–2134). It's a little more formal than your average Cape restaurant.

LODGING: P-Town has lots of small guest houses from which to take your pick, as well as a handful of hotels. Right in the center of town, The **Brass Key Guesthouse,** 12 Carver Street (508–487–9005 or 800–842–9858) has become *the* place to stay in Provincetown. It recently underwent a multimillion-dollar expansion and now offers thirty-three units that are every-inch luxurious. The service is really top-drawer as well. On top of that, there's an outdoor heated pool and a 17-foot whirlpool.

DAY 4

Morning

BREAKFAST: Follow your nose to the **Portuguese Bakery** on MacMillan Wharf, 299 Commercial Street. Here you can start the day with a pastry and coffee.

If you want to get in a couple of hours at the beach, drive over to **Race Point,** which is part of the **Cape Cod National Seashore.** Sprawling over nearly 44,000 acres, the National Seashore was established by President Kennedy in 1961 to protect the area from commercialization.

Then work your way back down the Cape (you can breeze down on Route 6) to return home. En route, consider detouring over to **Chatham,** which is a beautiful little village with gray-shingled sea captains' houses, shops, restaurants, inns, and beaches.

LUNCH: The **Impudent Oyster,** 15 Chatham Bars Avenue (508–945–3545), which is just off Main Street, serves gloriously fresh seafood (be sure to have some Chatham steamers).

THERE'S MORE

Nature walks. The Massachusetts Audubon Society, Route 6, South Wellfleet (508–349–2615), offers naturalist-led wildlife tours, trips to the Monomoy Island Bird Sanctuary, canoe trips, and bay cruises.

Scenic railroad. The Cape Cod Scenic Railroad, Main and Center Streets, Hyannis (508–771–3788), runs between Hyannis and Sagamore, stopping at Sandwich along the way. There are three departures daily, Tuesday through Sunday, from mid-June to late October and weekends in May.

Whale-watch excursions. Whale-watching cruises are offered in Provincetown and Barnstable during July and August. From Provincetown there are several excursions a day. From Barnstable Harbor they leave three times a day.

SPECIAL EVENTS

Early June. Harbor Festival, Bismore Park on Ocean Street in Hyannis. An annual Blessing of the Fleet, clam-shucking and pie-eating contests, and all sorts of activities take place.

July 4. Fourth of July Parade, on Main Street and Old Colony Way in Orleans. This is a 2½-mile theme parade held every year.

Mid-July, late July. Barnstable County Fair. This annual fair takes place on the fairgrounds (Route 151) in East Falmouth but is sponsored by the Barnstable County Agricultural Society. There are horticultural exhibits, livestock shows, a petting zoo, a horse-and-pony show, and more.

Early August. Cape Cod Antiques Exposition, at the Charles F. Moore Sports Center, O'Connor Way (exit 12 off Route 6). This attracts antiques dealers from all over New England.

Late August. Festival of the Arts, Chase Park on Cross Street, Chatham. A juried outdoor event attracting artists from all over.

Late August. Festival Days, Dennis. An annual festival with an antique-car parade, church suppers, crafts fairs, road races, and more.

Early September. Annual Bourne Scallop Festival, Buzzards Bay Park, Buzzards Bay. The largest scallop festival on the East Coast.

Mid-September. Cranberry Festival, Harwich. Races, clambakes, barbecues, a parade—an enormous small-town festival.

OTHER RECOMMENDED RESTAURANTS AND LODGINGS

Barnstable

Beechwood, 2839 Main Street (Route 6A); (508) 362–6618. A very elegant Queen Anne Victorian bed and breakfast shaded by beech trees.

Brewster

Chillingsworth, 2449 Main Street (Route 6A); (508) 896–3640. A top-drawer French restaurant. It's one of the Cape's best.

Ocean Edge Resort & Golf Club, 2907 Main Street; (508) 896–9000 or (800) 343–6074. Unlike most of the inns you'll find on the Cape, this is a major resort with lots of facilities.

Chatham

Chatham Bars Inn, Shore Road; (508) 945–0096 or (800) 527–1884. The doyenne of local hotels, the Chatham Bars Inn is a luxury resort gazing out to sea.

Queen Anne Inn, 70 Queen Anne Road; (508) 945–0394 or (800) 545–4667. A lovely Victorian inn within walking distance of the beach.

Cotuit

The Regatta of Cotuit, Route 28; (508) 428–5715. Housed in a building that dates back to 1790, the Regatta has a very sophisticated menu with dishes inspired by the chef's extensive travels.

East Orleans

Ship's Knees Inn, 186 Beach Road; (508) 255–1312. A restored 1790 sea-captain's home.

Falmouth

The Coonamessett Inn, Jones and Gifford Streets; (508) 548–2300. A very relaxed and comfortable historic inn.

Hyannis

Mildred's Chowder House, 290 Iyanough Road; (508) 775–1045. For simple seafood at its best, head for Mildred's. She offers all the favorites: thick clam chowders, creamy oyster stews, steamers with drawn butter, and lobster rolls that blow all other lobster rolls right out of the water.

Orleans

The Captain Linnell House, 137 Skaket Beach Road; (508) 255–3400. Exceptional seafood and a good wine list.

Provincetown

The Lobster Pot, 321 Commercial Street; (508) 487–0842. Here you can feast on fresh lobster and clam chowder on a waterfront deck.

The Mews Restaurant, 429 Commercial Street; (508) 487–1500. This is an excellent seafood restaurant with a lovely view of the harbor.

Napi's Restaurant, 7 Freeman Street; (508) 487–1145. This is an art gallery/eatery. The cuisine is varied, with lots of foreign influences including the local Portuguese traditions.

Sandwich

Dan'l Webster Inn, 149 Main Street; (508) 888–3622 or (800) 444–3566. A Cape Cod landmark.

FOR MORE INFORMATION

Cape Cod Chamber of Commerce, US 6 and MA 132, Hyannis, MA 02601–0016; (508) 362–3225.

Massachusetts Office of Travel and Tourism, 100 Cambridge Street, 13th Floor, Boston, MA 02202; (617) 727–3201 or (800) 447–MASS.

Martha's Vineyard

A CAREFREE GETAWAY

3 NIGHTS

Beaches • Seafood • Boating • Biking • Historic inns

The Vineyard, as it is locally known and referred to by its fans, lies just off the coast of Cape Cod. It got its name in the early 1600s, when an explorer by the name of Bartholomew Gosnold stepped ashore. Supposedly he, who is said to have had a daughter named Martha, found wild grapes growing, so there you have it! During summer months, the whole island feels like one big open-air party, with vacationers from all over crowding its little streets and duney beaches. Be sure to make hotel reservations in advance.

The island has three main towns: Vineyard Haven is its commercial center and where many of the mainland ferries dock. Oak Bluffs is an old Victorian community filled with gingerbread houses. Edgartown is a museumlike village, with historic houses and inns.

During summer months you have to have a reservation to take your car over to the island. A reservation must be made months in advance, especially if it's over a weekend. It's also costly (at least $80 round-trip in season). The other option is to leave your car on the mainland (figure about $15 a day to park) and rent a car once you get on the island. Either way allow yourself plenty of time to get to the ferry; traffic during summer months can be horrendous. During summer there are more than a dozen ferry trips a day from Woods Hole to Vineyard Haven or Oak Bluffs. The trip takes forty-five minutes.

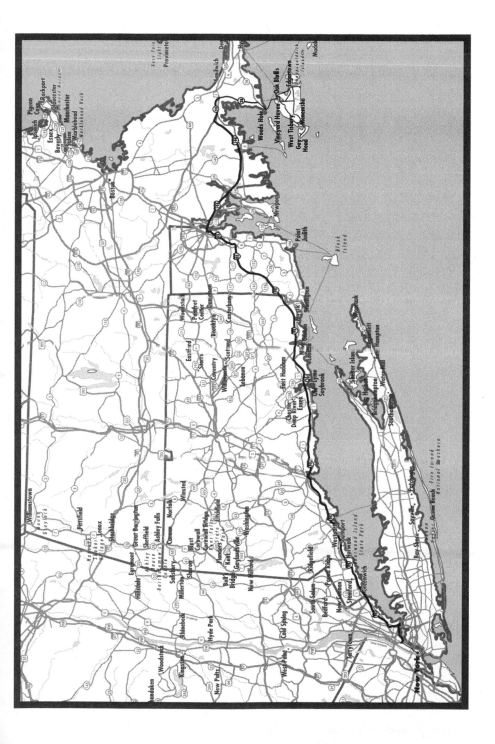

ᔆᑕᴬᴾᴱ ᶠᴼᵁᴿ
MASSACHUSETTS

A trip to Martha's Vineyard can easily be combined with a trip to Nantucket (Massachusetts Escape Five) or to Cape Cod (Massachusetts Escape Three).

DAY 1

Morning

Coming from New York take I–95 north to I–195 to Massachusetts Route 25/28 south, and cross the Bourne Bridge following the signs for Woods Hole. Along the way there are quite a few rotaries, which can get clogged with confused travelers. Take your time.

If you make good time, get your car in line and take a look around **Woods Hole,** which is a mecca for marine biologists. Crowded together near the water's edge are several labs and sea-study centers including the Marine Biological Laboratory, the Woods Hole Oceanographic Institution, the Northeast Fisheries Science Center, and the U.S. Geological Survey's Branch of Atlantic Geology.

LUNCH: If you didn't stop for lunch at a roadside eatery on the way up, head straight for **Shuckers,** 91A Water Street, Woods Hole (508–540–3850). It's a wonderful little seafood eatery with a raw bar. Try the lobster roll; it's celestial.

Afternoon

Depending on which ferry you get, chances are that once you arrive on the island, you won't have much time left in the day for exploring. Your best bet is to check into your hotel and then head out for dinner and a walk around town. For the first night we suggest staying in Oak Bluffs. If you catch a ferry there, you'll be within easy reach of all the inns as well as the town's attractions. If you take a ferry to Vineyard Haven, it's just a short ride over (signs clearly direct you).

LODGING: Choosing just one place to stay anywhere in Martha's Vineyard is truly challenging. You'll find everything from motel-like accommodations to very elegant inns. One favorite is the **Admiral Benbow Inn,** 520 New York Avenue, Oak Bluffs (508–693–6825). Just up the road from the center of town, it's a very comfortable inn that's not overly frilly. It's located in an old house that dates back to the 1870s.

DINNER: Zapotec, 10 Kennebec Avenue (508–693–6800) in the center of town, serves wonderful Mexican cuisine. Another good choice is **Jimmy Seas Pan Pasta Restaurant,** 32 Kennebec Avenue (508–696–8550), where you can take your pick of a wonderful selection of one-pot pasta dishes.

DAY 2

Morning

BREAKFAST: A full breakfast is part of the room rate at the Admiral Benbow.

After breakfast walk past the row of Victorian seafront houses into town and check out **The Flying Horses Carousel,** 33 Oak Bluffs Avenue (508–693–9481). Listed on the National Register of Historic Places, it dates back to 1876, when the horses were hand-carved in New York. Summer hours are from 10:00 A.M. to 10:00 P.M.

From the carousel you can wander over to the **Methodist Camp Meeting Grounds,** just off Circuit Avenue (no phone), which, tragically, many visitors completely miss. Nothing can really prepare you for the sensation of wandering through this community of tiny gingerbread houses painted in every color imaginable. The community originally started as a religious retreat in 1835. Participants stayed in tents clustered together. Many returned year after year and became so passionate about the place that they replaced the tents with more permanent wood cottages. Today it's home to more than 300 cottages, all radiating out from a tabernacle, where there are sing-alongs, religious services, and concerts. There's also a small museum filled with sample furnishings and other bric-a-brac. Do not, under any circumstances, leave the island without seeing this incredible sight. The grounds are open twenty-four hours a day.

Once you've feasted your eyes on the architectural wonders of Oak Bluffs, get back in your car and follow Seaview Avenue around to **Edgartown.** En route you'll pass the **State Beach,** where you can pull over and take a swim or conk out for a couple of hours.

Your best bet for exploring Edgartown is to, once again, go on foot; in fact there are hour-long guided walking tours. For information stop by the visitors center on Church Street across from the Old Whaling Church or call (508) 627–8619. The tour takes you to the village churches, some eighteenth-century houses, and the **Dukes County Historical Society,** Cooke and

One of the many fancifully designed cottages in Oak Bluffs.

School Streets (508–627–4441), which has some informative and interesting displays on the island's history.

Once you've seen Edgartown, consider renting a bike (there are a couple of rental shops in town) and taking it over on the ferry to **Chappaquiddick Island** ("Chappy" to those in the know). It's a mere five-minute ferry ride and costs less than $5.00 round-trip for both you and your bike. Once you set foot on Chappy, head straight across the island on Dyke Road to **East Beach.** This beach is beautifully isolated, has substantial surf, and is prime bird-watching territory.

LUNCH: Picnic on Chappaquiddick.

Afternoon

You'll probably get back to Edgartown with just enough time to check into your inn and freshen up for the evening.

LODGING: The **Captain Dexter House,** 35 Pease's Point Way (508–627–7289), has eleven rooms, all beautifully decorated with antiques, and huge comfortable beds (to get into some of them, you have to literally climb steps).

DINNER: Edgartown has a handful of exceptionally good restaurants including **Savoir Fare,** 14 Church Street (508–627–9864), which has been featured in *Gourmet* magazine. The cuisine is Italian and Californian.

DAY 3

Morning

BREAKFAST: A continental breakfast is included in the price of a room at the Captain Dexter House.

After breakfast set out in your car for **Gay Head,** which is the western tip of the island. Follow West Tisbury Road to Edgartown Road until you reach **West Tisbury.** There you can pause to have a look around **Chicama Vineyards,** Stoney Hill Road (508–693–0309), a thirty-three-acre vineyard. It's open June through October, Monday through Saturday from 11:00 A.M. to 5:00 P.M. and on Sundays, from 1:00 to 5:00 P.M. (closed July 4th and Labor Day). November through May, call for hours.

From there follow South Road to Chilmark and then turn left onto State Road, which will take you right out to Gay Head. There's not much that's man-made on this end of the island except for some beautiful homes tucked away in the duney landscape. Gay Head is known for its dramatic clay cliffs that plunge into the sea. A whole cluster of tourist shops have colonized the crown of these cliffs, offering the customary tourist crop of souvenirs—postcards, beaded belts, T-shirts.

Once you've walked out to the edge of the cliffs and acknowledged the ocean view, you'll be ready to climb back into your car and continue on. From Gay Head it's a short drive to **Menemsha Harbor,** a small working harbor crammed with picturesque shingled houses.

LUNCH: The **Galley,** right on the water in Menemsha Harbor (508–228–9641), is a little shacklike building where you'll find excellent lobster rolls. From its back porch you can sit and watch the harbor activity.

Afternoon

After lunch make your way to **Vineyard Haven,** where you can settle in for the night before heading back to the mainland in the morning. Follow North Road to North Tisbury and then turn left following Vineyard Haven Road to Main Street.

LODGING: The **Captain Dexter House of Vineyard Haven,** 100 Main Street (508–693–6564), is related to the one in Edgartown. It, too, is very attractive, with four-poster beds and some working fireplaces.

DINNER: Chances are that you will have heard of the **Black Dog Tavern,** Beach Street Extension (508–693–1991), by the time you actually eat there yourself. It's the island's most famous restaurant, understandably so. Not only is the food excellent (lots of fresh seafood, home-baked breads and desserts, innovative dishes), but the view (it's inches from the water's edge) is *very* Vineyard. There's also a Black Dog Bakery just steps away.

DAY 4

Morning

BREAKFAST: Included in the room rate at the inn.

Spend the morning hours poking around the shops of Vineyard Haven and then consider picking up lunch at the **Black Dog Bakery** (right near the restaurant). There are sandwiches, wonderful breads, and homemade desserts.

From there you can easily get right on the ferry and head over to the mainland. Once in Woods Hole, retrace your steps back to New York City.

THERE'S MORE

Fishing. There are several charter outfits around the island including Big Eye Charters in Edgartown (508–627–3649) and North Shore Charters in Menemsha (508–645–2993).

Golf. The Mink Meadows Golf Course, off Franklin Street in Vineyard Haven, is a public nine-hole course. Call (508) 693–3057 for more information.

Horseback riding. Both Misty Meadows Horse Farm, Old County Road, West Tisbury (508–693–1870), and Martha's Vineyard Riding Center, across from the airport, West Tisbury (508–693–3770), have horses available for trail rides. Call ahead.

Sailing. There are a couple of boats available for chartering in Vineyard Haven including the clipper schooner *Shenandoah* (call 508–693–1699 for details) and the *Violet,* a restored sailboat that was originally built in 1911 (call 508–693–5597).

Water sports. There are all sorts of rental shops in the Vineyard towns where you can take your pick of seagoing toys such as Sea-Doos (which are like snowmobiles, but they go on the water) and Windsurfers.

Wildlife preserves. There are several nature preserves (for bird-watching and strolling) on the island including Felix Neck Wildlife Sanctuary between Edgartown and Vineyard Haven, Cedar Tree Neck on the north shore, Long Point on the Atlantic shore, Manuel F. Correllus State Forest in the center of the island, and Cape Poque Wildlife Refuge and Wasque Reservations on the island of Chappaquiddick.

SPECIAL EVENTS

June. Illumination Night, Methodist Camp Meeting Grounds, Oak Bluffs, Martha's Vineyard. Every year this Oak Bluffs community strings paper lanterns from Asia throughout the "campgrounds."

Mid-August. Martha's Vineyard Agricultural Society Livestock Show and Fair, at the fairgrounds on State Road. An old-fashioned country fair with crafts, food booths, and exhibits.

OTHER RECOMMENDED RESTAURANTS AND LODGINGS

Edgartown

The Charlotte Inn, 27 South Summer Street; (508) 627–4751. This is a stunning inn, filled with artwork and antiques. Its restaurant, L'Etoile, serves outstanding French cuisine in a glassed-in terrace or in the garden.

Daggett House, 59 North Street; (508) 627–4600 or (800) 946–3400. An antique-furnished inn.

Harbor View Resort, 131 North Water Street; (508) 627–7000 or (800) 225–6005. Overlooking the lighthouse, this is a lovely spot with a veranda from which you can look out at the water.

Menemsha

Beach Plum Inn and Restaurant, North Road; (508) 645–9454 or (800) 528–6616. Set off in a world of its own, this twelve-room inn overlooks Menemsha Harbor, Vineyard Sound, and the Elizabeth Islands. Unlike most of the Vineyard inns, it's surrounded by a substantial amount of property and has its own beach and tennis court. The restaurant, which has a New England menu that changes daily, is a splurgey dinner choice.

FOR MORE INFORMATION

Martha's Vineyard Chamber of Commerce, Box 1698, Beach Road, Vineyard Haven, MA 02568; (508) 693–0085.

Ferry information: The Steamship Authority, P.O. Box 284, Woods Hole, MA 02543; (508) 540–2022.

Massachusetts Office of Travel and Tourism, 100 Cambridge Street, 13th Floor, Boston, MA 02202; (617) 727–3201 or (800) 447–MASS.

MASSACHUSETTS

Nantucket
With or Without a Car
COBBLESTONES AND BEACHES

3 NIGHTS

Beaches • Historic inns • Biking • Gourmet restaurants
Bird-watching • Boutique shopping

In many ways Nantucket is the designer-label island of the Northeast, the Ralph Lauren of islands. Absolutely every inch of Nantucket is attractive. The town of Nantucket itself, where the ferry docks, is a web-work of cobbled streets lined with huge old elm trees, gas lamps, and historic buildings. Inside there are art galleries, boutiques, and restaurants run by top chefs.

The rest of the island is made up of rolling moors (punctuated with bayberry, wild roses, and cranberries) and arrestingly beautiful white-sand beaches. More than a third of it is under protection from development. It's a rather small island, 12 by 3 miles, which makes exploring in a couple of days by bike or foot very manageable.

Like many offshore islands Nantucket has two dramatically different personalities. During summer months the downtown area, as well as many of the island's beaches, is crammed with vacationers. The rest of the year, it's blissfully serene. Do yourself a huge favor and try to go either before June 15 or shortly after Labor Day. That way, you'll be able to enjoy the warm weather without the crowds.

Consider combining an escape to Nantucket with a trip to nearby Martha's Vineyard (see Massachusetts Escape Four) or to Cape Cod. You can

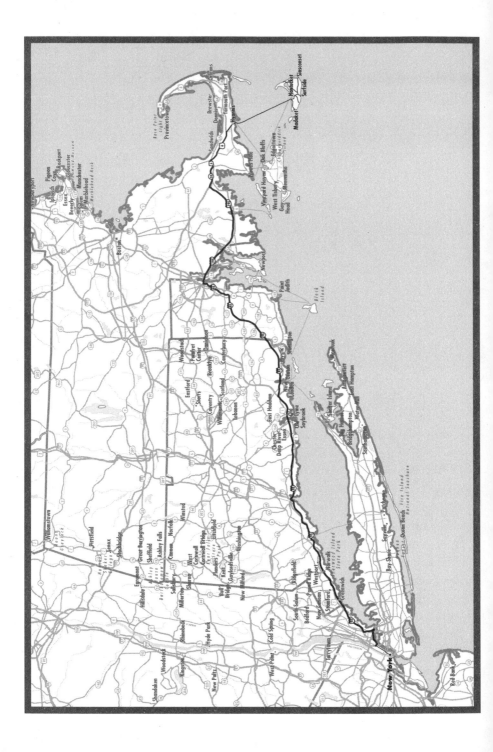

very easily go over on foot for the day. If you have your own bike, consider taking it along; otherwise, you can rent one.

DAY 1

To reach the island you can take a Greyhound Bus (800–231–7245) from the Port Authority in New York to Hyannis. It takes about seven to eight hours. From there you take a ferry over. During summer months ferries run six times daily to the island; other months, they run less frequently. You can also fly Nantucket Airlines over from Hyannis (508–790–0300). If you're driving, from New York take I–95 to I–195. Then take Massachusetts Route 25 to Route 6 east just before the Bourne Bridge. This will take you north and east to the Sagamore Bridge over the canal and right up the Cape. At the rotaries just keep following the signs for Hyannis. Don't even think of taking your car over. It's expensive, there's traffic, and besides, you don't really need one. There's a parking lot right at the ferry docks in Hyannis.

You'll probably catch an afternoon ferry and step ashore sometime just before dinner. Good timing. You can check into your room, which is within walking distance of the ferry, before heading out for dinner.

DINNER: American cuisine—both new and traditional—is what you'll find on the menu at **21 Federal** (21 Federal Street; 508–228–2121). Located in the center of town, it's a popular spot for locals. The fish entrees are especially good.

LODGING: Choosing just one inn in Nantucket is like trying to pick just one chocolate from a sampler. There are many wonderful inns right in town as well as a resort over on the east coast. Prices run the gamut from inexpensive to very expensive. Generally the most expensive ones are very close to the town center. One moderately priced favorite is the **House of the Seven Gables,** 32 Cliff Road (508–228–4706), which is about a ten-minute walk from Main Street. It has ten rooms, some with views of the water.

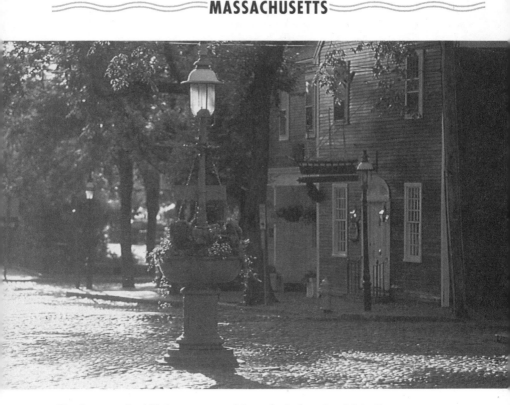

Gas lamps and cobbled streets grace Nantucket's charming Main Street.

DAY 2

Morning

BREAKFAST: A continental breakfast is included in the price of a room at the House of the Seven Gables and at many of the other inns.

After breakfast set out to explore the town by foot. The biggest attraction is the village itself, which is an official National Historic District. Wander around the cobblestone streets and you'll see beautifully maintained mansions dating back to the eighteenth and nineteenth centuries and lots of gardens and window boxes spilling over with fragrant flowers.

There are a handful of museums worth checking out including the **Museum of Nantucket History,** on Straight Wharf (508–228–3889), where you can learn all about the island's background, and the **Whaling Museum,** Broad Street (508–228–1736), which tells the story of Nantucket's whaling past. Both are open daily from mid-June to Labor Day. Hours vary in spring and fall.

There are also several houses that were built during the island's prosperous whaling days including the **Three Bricks** at 93–97 Main Street. These three identical red-brick mansions (which are not open for touring) were built between 1836 and 1838 by a whaling merchant for his three sons.

Across from the Three Bricks, you'll find the **Hadwen House,** 96 Main Street (508–228–1894), a Greek Revival mansion built in 1845–46 that is now a house museum. It's open daily from 10:00 A.M. to 5:00 P.M., mid-June to Labor Day. Hours vary during spring and fall.

Other in-town attractions include the **Old Gaol,** 15R Vestal Street (508–228–1894), a jailhouse dating back to 1805; the **1800 House,** 10 Mill Street (508–228–1894), a nineteenth-century house museum; the **Old Mill,** on South Mill Street (508–228–1894), a Dutch windmill; and the island's **Oldest House,** Sunset Hill (508–228–1894), which dates back to 1686. Most attractions are open from 10:00 A.M. to 5:00 P.M. daily during the high season; hours vary in spring and fall.

For the best view of the island, head for the **First Congregational Church,** 62 Centre Street. It's a ninety-two-step climb to the top of the tower.

LUNCH: The **Espresso Cafe,** 40 Main Street (508–228–6930), right in the center of town, is a good choice for a simple soup-and-salad lunch. Try to get one of the tables in the garden out back.

Afternoon

After lunch either poke around the shops and galleries on Main Street or consider riding a bike to the beach. If you need to rent a bike, you'll find several rental places right in town by the wharf. **Surfside,** on the southern coast, is within easy riding distance (about 3 miles) of town. It's a popular beach with a lunch bar, lifeguards, and a changing facility. If you're up for a longer ride, consider heading out to **Madaket** (12 miles round-trip), at the western tip of the island. The beach here is nonpareil: big white dunes, Atlantic waves, and fewer footprints than at Surfside. It's also prime sunset-viewing territory.

If you decide to browse around the shops, check out the Nantucket Lightship Baskets. The weaving of these baskets, which started back in the nineteenth century, is a real art. They come in all sizes, from small purses to huge picnic baskets. They can be round or oval, open or covered. Many are adorned with scrimshaw and intricately carved and shaped handles. Prices can run anywhere from a couple of hundred dollars for a very simple small basket to several thousands for one decorated with fine scrimshaw.

DINNER: Reservations are a must at **Company of the Cauldron,** 7 India Street (508–228–4016). Fixed-price dinner is offered with only two seatings, at 7:00 and 9:00 P.M. The menu is table d'hôte, so make sure that you ask what's cooking when you call.

LODGING: Your best bet is to stay put in the inn you chose the night before.

DAY 3

Morning

BREAKFAST: At the inn.

Your destination today is **Siasconset** (pronounced "Sconset") on the southeastern side of the island. It's a 7-mile bike trip on bike paths from Nantucket town. As you drive along, you'll pass moors carpeted with blueberry bushes. The blueberries are usually ripest in late July or early August. The village itself is tiny and *very* Nantucket. There's a post office, a rotary, a cafe, a restaurant, and several private homes.

LUNCH: Stop in the **'Sconset Cafe,** Post Office Square (508–257–4008), to get a picnic lunch for the beach. They make all sorts of unbelievably delicious sandwiches with sprouts and dressings you'll want the recipe for.

The beach is just minutes down the road from the village.

Afternoon

The beach here is so wonderful, you'll probably want to stay for a good chunk of time. Afterward head back the same way you came or consider taking the long route up to the Quidnet area and then follow the signs back along the northern shore.

DINNER: The Boarding House, 12 Federal Street (508–228–9622), has a wonderful patio that's great for people-watching and has excellent cuisine. The fare is generally international with Asian and Mediterranean accents.

LODGING: Same inn.

DAY 4

Morning

BREAKFAST: Though breakfast is included in the price of a room, consider eating at the **Morning Glory Cafe,** 14 Old South Wharf (508–228–2212). Here you can have French toast, pancakes, an omelet, or any other breakfast favorite.

Before heading back to the mainland, you can take some time to pick up souvenirs or gifts in town if you didn't get a chance earlier.

Once back on the Cape, retrace your steps to New York City.

THERE'S MORE

Fishing. Several charter companies sail out of Straight Wharf every day in season. Bluefish and bass are the main catches.

Golf. Miacomet Golf Club (508–228–8987) and Siasconset Golf Club (500 257 6596) are two public golf courses with nine holes each.

Walking tours. Historic walking tours of the town of Nantucket are conducted during summer months. For information call Roger Young's Historic Walking Tours (508–228–1062).

Water sports. The Sunken Ship (corner of Broad and South Water Streets (508–228–9226) rents scuba and other sports equipment. Also offers scuba lessons.

Whale-watching. Nantucket Whalewatch, Hy-Line dock, Straight Wharf (508–283–0313), runs excursions in season.

SPECIAL EVENTS

Late April. Daffodil Festival. This spring festival has a parade of antique cars and a prize for the best tailgate picnic.

Early December. Christmas Stroll. Tour Main Street merchants and enjoy special entertainment and carolers.

OTHER RECOMMENDED RESTAURANTS AND LODGINGS

Siasconset

Chanticleer, 9 New Street; (508) 257–6231. French cuisine in a rose garden. What could be more romantic?

Wauwinet

The Wauwinet, Wauwinet Road; (508) 228–0145 or (800) 426–8718. Off in a little world of its own, this resort is spectacularly situated (surrounded by ocean and harbor beaches). Every inch of it is elegant, and its restaurant, Topper's, is perhaps the best on the island. It's a full-service resort but small (only twenty-five rooms plus five cottages). There are tennis courts and all sorts of sports facilities plus jitney service for getting around the island.

FOR MORE INFORMATION

Nantucket Chamber of Commerce, Pacific Club Building, Main Street, Nantucket, MA 02554; (508) 228–1700. Hours are from 9:00 A.M. to 5:00 P.M. weekdays.

Nantucket Information Bureau, 25 Federal Street, Nantucket, MA 02554; (508) 228–0925. Hours are from 9:00 A.M. to 6:00 P.M. daily in summer and from 9:00 A.M. to 4:00 P.M. Monday through Saturday, off-season.

Ferry information: The Steamship Authority, P.O. Box 284, Woods Hole, MA 02543; (508) 540–2022.

Massachusetts Office of Travel and Tourism, 100 Cambridge Street, 13th Floor, Boston, MA 02202; (617) 727–3201 or (800) 447–MASS.

MASSACHUSETTS

Boston

With or Without a Car

EXPLORING THE HUB

---

2 NIGHTS

Museums • Restaurants • Colonial history
Universities • Performing arts

A college crew team muscling up the Charles. A mime surrounded by a crowd of eager viewers at Faneuil Hall Marketplace. A fragrant basement bakery on Beacon Hill. Like any major city, Boston has its share of famous historical and architectural attractions, but the little things give it its rich flavor. These are the things that will come to mind years later when you think of Boston.

You'll find history with just about every step you take, and you'll be taking many. Boston is very manageable on foot, so we've designed this itinerary predominantly as a walking tour. To reach the different neighborhoods, you can hop on the "T," the city's subway.

Three days is just enough time to sample the city's pleasures as well as make a quick visit to next-door Cambridge.

DAY 1

Morning

To reach Boston from New York, you can take Amtrak (800–872–7245) directly from Penn Station to South Station in about five hours. If you're driving, you can cruise up to Boston in less than four hours from Manhattan.

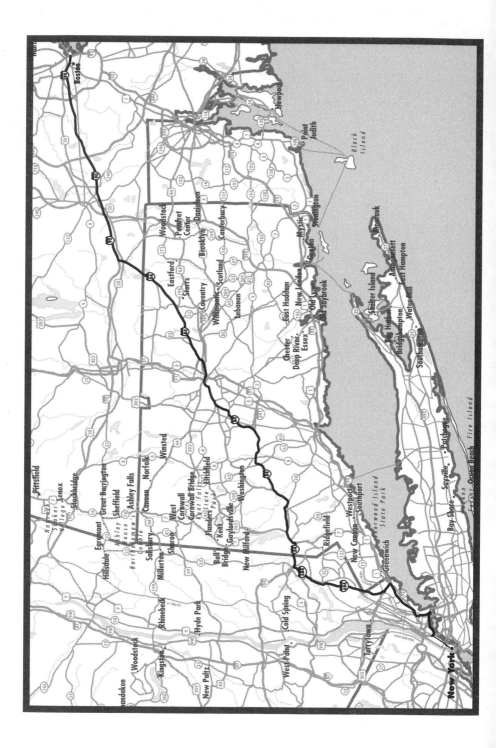

Take Route 684 north to Route 84 east. Then take Route 90 ("The Mass Pike") east and get off at the Prudential Center exit, which will get you right into the midtown area, near your hotel. Your best bet is to "pak the caah" in the garage of your hotel when you arrive. Be sure to wear reliable walking shoes.

Start by strolling through the **Boston Common** (take the Red or the Green Line to Park Street), which used to be the colonial town's common pastureland and is now the city's most popular park. Make your way up the slope to **Beacon Hill,** where you'll find the **Massachusetts State House** (you can't miss it; it's topped by a golden dome). This building was designed by Charles Bulfinch and was built in the late 1700s.

To the rear of the State House, you'll find **Mount Vernon Street,** which is lined with meticulously maintained brick Federal-style houses. Follow Mt. Vernon Street to **Louisburg Square,** which was laid out in the 1840s. The centerpiece of this incredibly beautiful square is an oval park. By now you're probably starved, and the timing for lunch couldn't be better.

LUNCH: A couple steps away from the State House is **The Black Goose** (21 Beacon Street; 617–720–4500), which specializes in provincial Italian cuisine.

Afternoon

One block over from Louisburg Square is **Acorn Street,** the street every Boston resident brings out-of-town visitors to when they want to show off. It, too, is lined with brick Federal-style row houses.

From Acorn Street wander back to Park Street, taking Chestnut (yet another picturesque street) to Walnut Street and then Beacon Street alongside the Common. Continue on to Park and turn right, following Park briefly to Tremont. On the corner of Park and Tremont stands **Park Street Church,** a major Boston landmark that was built in 1809. When you leave the church, turn left and walk along Tremont Street to the **Old Granary Burying Ground.** Some major American Revolution figures were buried here including Samuel Adams, John Hancock, and Paul Revere.

Continue northeast on Tremont to School Street, where you'll see **King's Chapel,** which dates back to 1754. John Winthrop was buried in the **Burying Ground,** right next to the chapel. A little farther along School Street is a **Statue of Benjamin Franklin** (though he made his fame and fortune in Philadelphia, Franklin was born in Boston). Keep going on School Street and you'll come to the **Old Corner Bookstore,** which was a gathering place for American authors in the nineteenth century. Turn right and walk a block to the **Old South Meeting House,** 310 Washington Street, at the corner of Milk Street (617–482–6439). It was from here that a group of Colonials set out to throw the Boston Tea Party back in 1773. The house is now a museum, open April through October daily from 9:30 A.M. to 5:00 P.M. and November through March from 10:00 A.M. to 4:00 P.M. Monday through Friday and from 10:00 A.M. to 5:00 P.M. Saturday and Sunday. Just around the corner on Milk Street is **Benjamin Franklin's Birthplace,** which is marked by a plaque on the side of a high-rise.

Backtrack on Washington, past the Old Corner Bookstore, to reach **The Old State House,** 206 Washington Street, which dates from 1713. The Declaration of Independence was read to Bostonians from its balcony in 1776. Follow Court Street and State Street to Congress Street, to the **Boston Massacre Site.** About half a mile away is **Faneuil Hall,** which was originally erected in 1742 as a public meeting hall and marketplace. It's now one of Boston's most popular attractions and is crammed with snack shops, chowder houses, cafes, bakeries, restaurants, and all sorts of boutiques.

DINNER: Legal Seafoods, 35 Columbus Avenue (617–426–4444), is an absolute must. A Boston institution, it's famed for its decently priced, spanking-fresh seafood. Expect to wait for a table. One restaurant is located in the Boston Park Plaza Hotel (though there are other locations); to reach it, take the Green Line to Arlington.

LODGING: Like any big city, Boston has several major downtown hotels. If you want to stay in a grand old Boston hotel (and feel like splurging), choose the **Copley Plaza Hotel,** Copley Square (617–267–5300), right in the heart of the city, facing Copley Square.

If you want to see a show while in town, arrange for theater tickets in advance or keep your fingers crossed and call Bostix (617–723–5181).

DAY 2

Morning

BREAKFAST: Rather than spend a wad on breakfast at your hotel, consider heading over to one of the coffee shops along Boylston Street.

Then wander around midtown, checking out **Trinity Church,** 206 Clarendon Street (617–536–0944), a hauntingly beautiful French-Romanesque building; the **Boston Public Library,** 666 Boylston Street (617–536–5400); and the **John Hancock Observatory** at the top of the John Hancock Tower, 200 Clarendon Street (617–572–6429), from which you can get a wraparound view of the whole city. The observatory is open Monday through Saturday from 9:00 A.M. to 10:00 P.M. and on Sunday from 10:00 A.M. to 10:00 P.M.

From the observatory head over to **Newbury Street** if you want to do some shopping, or hop on the "T" (take the Green Line's E trolley outbound and get off at Ruggles/Museum) to go to the **Museum of Fine Arts,** 465 Huntington Avenue (617–267–9300). The museum specializes in Impressionists, Egyptian artifacts, and Asian art. Visiting hours are from 10:00 A.M. to 4:45 P.M. Tuesday through Sunday (on Wednesdays it stays open until 9:45 P.M.).

LUNCH: There's a pleasant cafe at the Museum of Fine Arts.

Afternoon

If you're up for some more walking, consider taking the Green Line up to Government Center (this will get you back to the Faneuil Hall Marketplace) and explore the streets of Boston's **North End.** Among the attractions here are **Paul Revere's House,** 19 North Square (617–523–2338), which is open from 9:30 A.M. to 4:15 P.M.; **Old North Church,** 193 Salem Street (617 523 6676), in which the code "one if by land, two if by sea" was created; and **Bunker Hill,** which marks the spot where the Battle of Bunker Hill took place on June 17, 1775.

DINNER: Another Boston institution is **Durgin-Park,** North Market Building, 340 Faneuil Hall Marketplace (617–227–2038), where dining is communal. There are seafood and steak dishes.

DAY 3

Morning

If you're driving, take the "Mass Ave" bridge over the Charles River to Cambridge and head right to Harvard Square. Pull into any of the parking garages you see or park on a back street and walk a few blocks—or take the subway right to Harvard Square.

BREAKFAST: Starbuck's, right near Harvard Square, 36 John F. Kennedy Street, Cambridge (617–492–4881), serves *the* best coffee you'll find in these parts. You can also get a light breakfast here (croissants, muffins).

After breakfast get in on one of the free student-led tours around Harvard. Tours leave from the **Harvard University Information Center** (617–495–1573) at 10:00 A.M. and 2:00 P.M., Monday through Friday, and on Saturdays at 2:00 P.M. In an hour's time you'll see the Yard and the exterior of the university's magnificent buildings and surrounding museums. Afterward spend some time in the museums (the Busch-Reisinger, the Fogg Art Museum, the Sackler, and the Harvard University Natural History Museums are the biggies) or the **Harvard Coop,** 1400 Massachusetts Avenue, where you can buy anything from underwear to Frisbees, all emblazoned with the Harvard logo. There are many other shops to explore in Cambridge. You'll be tempted to extend your stay.

LUNCH: The **Blacksmith House Bakery and Cafe,** 56 Brattle Street, Cambridge (617–354–3036), is about a block and a half away from Harvard Square and has a wonderful outdoor terrace, where you can feast on internationally inspired dishes.

Afternoon

Head back to New York via Amtrak or the Massachusetts Pike, Route 84, and Route 684, or take I–95 down the coast.

THERE'S MORE

Harbor sightseeing. Several companies offer Boston harbor sightseeing cruises including Bay State Cruise Company (56 Long Wharf, 617–723–7800), Boston By Sail (66 Long Wharf, 617–742–3313), and Boston Harbor Cruises (On Long Wharf; 617-247-4320). The *Spirit of Boston* (60 Rowes Wharf, 617–569–6867) has lunch cruises and dinner/ dance cruises.

Concerts by the Boston Pops are held in the Hatch Memorial Shell.

Jogging. Jogging is one of the most popular pastimes in Boston. Running paths line both banks of the Charles River. For information on races contact the Boston Athletic Association (617–236–1652).

Trolley tours. If you're not up for sightseeing on foot, consider climbing into a trolley for a Boston tour. Boston Trolley Tours (617–427–8687) is one of several companies that offer trolley tours. They have a large fleet of hand-crafted trolleys that run year-round. There are well over a dozen boarding stops scattered around the city. The narrated tour lasts about one hundred minutes (though you can get on and off at any boarding stop).

Walking tours. In addition to the Freedom Trail, there are a variety of walking tours in Boston.

The Black Heritage Trail (617–742–5415) is a ninety-minute walk taking you to the city's nineteenth-century black community landmarks. You can opt for a guided tour or pick up a map and brochure and follow it on your own. Boston by Foot (617–367–2345 or 617–367–3766 for recorded information) has a variety of guided walks from May through October.

The Victorian Society in America (617–267–6338) takes you to the city's Victorian sights.

The Women's Heritage Trail (617–731–5597) focuses on the lives of twenty women who made significant contributions to the city.

Whale watches. The A.C. Cruise Company (617–426–8419), Bay State Cruise Company (617–723–7800), Boston Harbor Cruises (617–227–4320 or 617–227–4321), and The New England Aquarium (617–973–5277) offer whale-watching cruises.

SPECIAL EVENTS

April. Boston Marathon. Takes place on the third Monday every April. Runners run from Hopkinton to the Prudential Center.

July. Esplanade Concerts. Musical programs by the Boston Pops in the Hatch Shell on the Esplanade.

July 4th weekend. Harborfest. A seaside celebration with fireworks, chowder contests, boat races, historical reenactments, and a performance by the Boston Pops Orchestra.

October. Charles River Regatta. One of the rowing world's biggest races is held the third Sunday in October every year.

December. First Night Celebration. Boston Common on New Year's Eve.

OTHER RECOMMENDED RESTAURANTS AND LODGINGS

Boston

As with all major cities, there are dozens of hotels and restaurants to choose from in Boston. Here is a handful of some of the city's finest:

Boston Harbor Hotel, 70 Rowes Wharf; (617) 439–7000 or (800) 752–7077. A beautiful harbor hotel with a European accent.

Four Seasons Boston, 200 Boylston Street; (617) 338–4400 or (800) 332–3442. Overlooking Boston Common and the Public Garden, this hotel is wonderful in every way.

The Ritz-Carlton Boston, 15 Arlington Street; (617) 536–5700 or (800) 241–3333. If you're in the mood for all-out luxury, you'll love it here.

For a complete list of hotels, contact the tourism office listed below in "For More Information."

If you're interested in staying in a bed and breakfast, there are several booking agencies in town including Bed & Breakfast Associates Bay Colony Ltd. (800–347–5088 or 617–449–5302), Greater Boston Hospitality (617–277–5430), and Host Homes of Boston (617–244–1308).

Cambridge

The Charles Hotel at Harvard Square, One Bennett Street; (617) 864–1200. A full-service luxury hotel with an attached health spa.

The Inn at Harvard, 1201 Massachusetts Avenue; (617) 491–2222. Cambridge's newest hotel is adjacent to Harvard Yard.

FOR MORE INFORMATION

Greater Boston Convention & Visitors Bureau, Prudential Tower, Suite 400, Box 490, Boston, MA 02199; (800) 888–5515 or (617) 536–4100.

Massachusetts Office of Travel and Tourism, 100 Cambridge Street, 13th Floor, Boston, MA 02202; (617) 727–3201 or (800) 447–MASS.

NORTHERN
NEW ENGLAND
ESCAPES

Vermont's Northeast Kingdom

SCENERY AND THEN SOME

3 NIGHTS

Mountain scenery • Picture-perfect villages
Boutiques and antiques shops • Ben & Jerry's ice-cream factory
Distinguished inns • Autumn-leaf viewing • Winter sports

Nearly every inch of Vermont is New England just as you pictured it—covered bridges, immaculate dairy farms, steepled villages, and sagging old farmhouses where big-pawed golden retrievers sleep on front porches. Add to that the fact that every season has its own appeals, and choosing exactly when to go and just where to go can be a happy dilemma.

Fortunately, you can't go wrong in Vermont. In the fall the Crayola colors are everywhere (especially early to mid-October). At that time of year, the weather is often phenomenally beautiful, with flawless blue skies and plenty of sunshine. During winter the hills are alive with skiers and snowshoers. When the snows thaw, the landscape awakens into an extravaganza of blossoms and green. There's green everywhere, getting greener and greener each day as the state warms into summer.

Northern Vermont is perhaps the state's most sensationally scenic area (though many may argue that). There are miles and miles of cattle-dotted farmlands, silent lakes cupped in the hills as if precious jewels, and streams that really do sparkle. Add to that the backdrop of looming mountains, and you're looking at not just the state's, but some of our country's, most beautiful scenery.

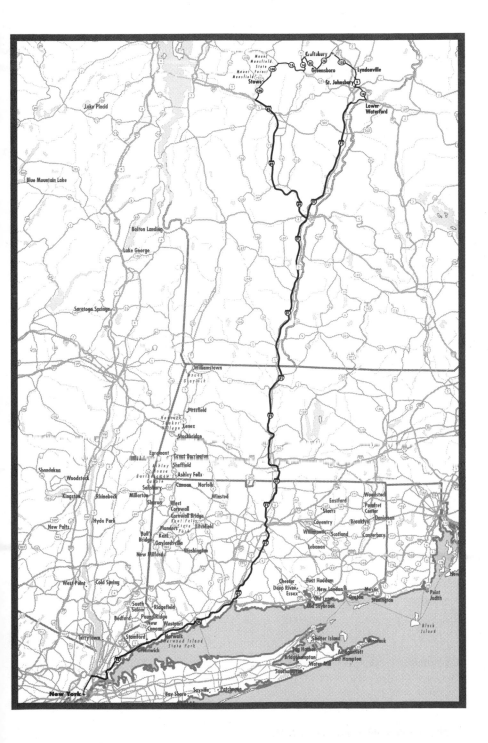

DAY 1

Morning

One of our longest escapes, this drive focuses on the northern woods and mountains of Vermont. Do yourselves a favor: Head out early in the day so that you can take some time to relax once you get up there. It can take about six hours to get to Stowe, which is your first stop. From New York City head east, picking up I–95. Take that to I–91 north and stay on that until you reach I–89 north. Stowe is only ten minutes from I–89. Get off at exit 10 and follow Route 100 10 miles into town.

LUNCH: Chances are you'll be starved well before you reach the Stowe area, so your best bet is to either pack picnic lunches or pull off to a roadside eatery.

On Route 100, you'll pass right through **Waterbury,** where you'll find the legendary **Ben & Jerry's** ice-cream factory. It's close enough to Stowe, so if you're too tired to visit now, keep in mind that you can stop by later during your stay. There are tours, exhibits, a gift shop, and an all-around air of carnival. Across the street is the **Cold Hollow Cider Mill,** where you can watch cider being pressed and see films on how cider and maple sugar are made.

Afternoon

Carry on a short distance and you'll come to **Stowe,** where you can settle in and take an afternoon hike (or go skiing, if it's winter) and follow it up with a great dinner. In winter this beautiful town is a mecca for skiers, with its daredevil trails, its exuberant after-ski life, and its lodges that look like Austria. Stowe is dominated by **Mount Mansfield,** Vermont's highest mountain (4,393 feet). But when the lifts are closed, Stowe is just as appealing. In town there are all sorts of wonderful little emporiums that sell everything from Christmas ornaments to handmade sweaters that look too pretty to wear. There are also several antiques shops to poke around.

DINNER: Depending on what you're in the mood for, Stowe has many dining options. A special treat, however, is dinner at **Edson Hill Manor** (1500 Edson Hill Road; 802–253–7371), which offers fine regional American cuisine.

LODGING: Trapp Family Lodge (42 Trapp Hill Road; 800–826–7000 or 802–253–8511) is an Austrian-style lodge propped up on a hilltop with far-reaching views. It's set on 2,000 acres and has hiking and cross-country skiing trails, an indoor/outdoor pool, and a fitness center.

DAY 2

Morning

BREAKFAST: A full hearty breakfast is served in the dining room at the Trapp Family Lodge.

Stowe's natural beauty is its strongest appeal. Give yourself the entire day to dip into its treasures. Though you can drive around and see plenty (in fact, you can drive to the top of Mansfield), consider taking time out to explore by foot. Much of the landscape is part of **Vermont's Mount Mansfield State Forest.** There are many hiking trails, camping areas, and picnic spots. Another way to enjoy the area's scenery (in warm weather months as well as winter) is to ride the gondola to the top of Mount Mansfield. For the ultimate view, climb into a glider at **Stowe Aviation.** For twenty minutes—or more, depending on which flight you opt for—you'll soar over the peaks and valleys like weightless birds. You can easily fill two days exploring Stowe, so allow enough time.

LUNCH: If the weather's nice, consider stopping by the **Harvest Market** (1031 Market Road; 802–253–3800) where you can get a gourmet lunch to-go for a picnic. Or choose one of the small eateries or bistros in town.

Afternoon

Spend the afternoon doing the things you weren't able to squeeze into the morning.

DINNER: For a French meal try the **Isle de France** (Mountain Road; 802–253–7751). Another option is the **Cliff House Restaurant,** which is located atop Mount Mansfield (802–253–3665) and is reached by gondola.

DAY 3

Morning

BREAKFAST: Breakfast at the lodge.

Before setting out consider stopping in town to get picnic lunches. Then head north on Route 100 and then turn right onto Route 15 in **Morrisville.** The landscape here is densely scenic. You'll pass huge red barns with silver silos, old farmhouses settled into the contour of the land, and fields full of cows and sturdy ponies with tangled manes. You'll see fishermen wading in rivers and thousands of white birch trees that look like fish bones against dark pine forests.

In **Hardwick** take Route 14 up to **Craftsbury** (you'll see signs), a Grandma Moses kind of village with crisp, clean white buildings, a billiard-green square, and flawless white fences all around.

LUNCH: If you're ready to dig into that picnic lunch, this is a good place to park yourselves.

Afterwards, consider stopping in at **Craftsbury Center** (follow the signs on the dirt roads), a camp—for both kids and adults—that is devoted to the graceful sport of sculling. In winter it turns into a cross-country ski center.

Afternoon

From Craftsbury follow the road to **Greensboro** (it's southeast of Craftsbury), which is home to Willey's General Store, an attraction in itself. Here you'll find everything from parts for balsa-wood planes to farm equipment. Then carry on to **Lyndonville,** where there are five covered bridges (one dating back to 1795) within the town's limits. Follow Route 16 north and then make a sharp right onto Route 122.

From Lyndonville head south on Route 5 to **St. Johnsbury,** which has some beautiful Victorian buildings along with an art gallery and a museum where you can learn all about the production of maple syrup. About fifteen minutes away is **Lower Waterford,** where you can settle in for dinner and the night (head east out of St. Johnsbury on Route 2, then south on Route 18).

DINNER: The French/American meals at **Rabbit Hill Inn** (Route 18 and Pucker Street, Lower Waterford; 802–748–5168 or 800–76–BUNNY) are candlelit and gourmet.

LODGING: Rabbit Hill Inn (Route 18 and Pucker Street, Lower Waterford) is a white Federal-style house full of romantic details and a rabbit theme throughout. Some of the rooms have fireplaces, some have Jacuzzis.

DAY 4

Morning

BREAKFAST: At the inn.

After breakfast and maybe a brisk walk, make your way back to New York City, following I–91 south and retrace your steps.

THERE'S MORE

City exploring. Vermont's largest city, **Burlington,** is situated on the shores of Lake Champlain, not far from the Stowe area. Consider spending some time exploring downtown, a small enough area to negotiate on foot. It's centerpieced by the Church Street Marketplace, a 4-block stretch of Church Street closed to traffic, with sidewalk cafes, benches, and all sorts of street performers.

Winter sports. There's no end to the amount of winter sports you'll find in this part of the world, including alpine and cross-country skiing, snowmo-biling, snowboarding, skating, and sleigh riding.

SPECIAL EVENTS

January–February. Stowe Winter Carnival, throughout Stowe; (802) 253–2329. Gala parties, ice sculptures, snowshoe races, fireworks, and more.

February. Snowflake Festival, Lyndonville; (802) 626–5475. Torchlight ski parade, pancake breakfasts, all sorts of family events.

March. Cirque Eloize, Burlington; (802) 863–5966. Gravity-defying balancing, energetic jugglers, clowns—all sorts of circus acts for all ages to enjoy.

May. Annual Basketry Festival, Stowe; (802) 253–7223. Seven days of basketmaking workshops.

Annual Spring Bird Walks, St. Johnsbury; (802) 748–2372. A series of bird walks, starting at the Fairbanks Museum.

June. Green Mountain Regatta, Stowe; (802) 253–7131. Remote-controlled model sailboat racing.

September. Annual British Invasion of Stowe, Stowe; (802) 253–7558. British car show, specialty foods, awards and more.

For Art's Sake/A Taste of Stowe, Stowe; (802) 253–8358. More than eighty artists display their works, which are for sale.

Intervale Organic Food Festival: Celebrating the Garden!, Stowe; (802) 660–3500. Hayrides, children's events, garden tours, music, and more.

Northeast Kingdom Annual Fall Foliage Festival—Marshfield, Walden, Cabot, Plainfield, Peacham, Barnet, Groton, St. Johnsbury; (802) 563–2472.

OTHER RECOMMENDED RESTAURANTS AND LODGINGS

Craftsbury Center

Inn on the Common, Craftsbury Common; (802) 586–9619. Sixteen antique-furnished bedrooms located in three buildings. Dinner and breakfast are served for guests (outside guests with reservations only).

Stowe

Topnotch at Stowe Resort & Spa, 4000 Mountain Road; (800) 451–8686 or (802) 253–8585. In addition to accommodations and fine dining, Topnotch has a complete spa and more than a dozen tennis courts.

Small, distinguished inns can be found all over Vermont—tucked away in forests, set on farmlands, prominently situated in villages, you name it. A complete list of inns (and many bed and breakfasts) is published by the Vermont Chamber of Commerce. For a copy write to them at P.O. Box 37, Montpelier, VT 05601 or call (802) 223–3443. Vermont also has a reservation service for bed and breakfasts. Write or call: Vermont Bed & Breakfast, Box 1, East Fairfield, VT 05448; (802) 827–3827.

FOR MORE INFORMATION

Stowe Area Association, Inc., P.O. Box 1320, Stowe, VT 05672; (800) 247–8693 or (802) 253–7321.

Vermont Department of Travel & Tourism, 134 State Street, Montpelier, VT 05602; (802) 828–3236.

Vermont Ski Areas Association, P.O. Box 368, Montpelier, VT 05601; (802) 223–2439.

The Coast of Maine

THE COAST WITH THE MOST

3 NIGHTS

Atlantic Ocean scenery • Seafood • Inns
Galleries • Antiques shops • Museums • Sailing
Boating • Hiking • Sports

For more than one hundred years, Maine's coast has been a popular summer vacation area. It's made up of a series of deeply cut coves and narrow peninsulas and has countless offshore islands. Along the way there are dozens of little fishing villages bursting with character. For this particular escape we take you up the Maine coast, from Kennebunkport to Bar Harbor. Keep in mind that many hotels, restaurants, and attractions close during the winter months (sometimes as early as October).

DAY 1

Morning

To reach **Kennebunkport** take I–95 north of New York City and follow it right up to Maine. In Maine take exit 3 and head east on 9A to Kennebunkport. You'll see signs for Kennebunk as well—that's the commercial center, whereas Kennebunkport is the port town. The latter is where you'll find most of the tourist activity. Kennebunkport is still known as Bush Country, nicknamed for former President Bush, whose summer home, Walker's Point, is located here. Since you will have spent the better part of the day traveling, your best bet is to grab lunch at a roadside eatery en route whenever hunger strikes. When you

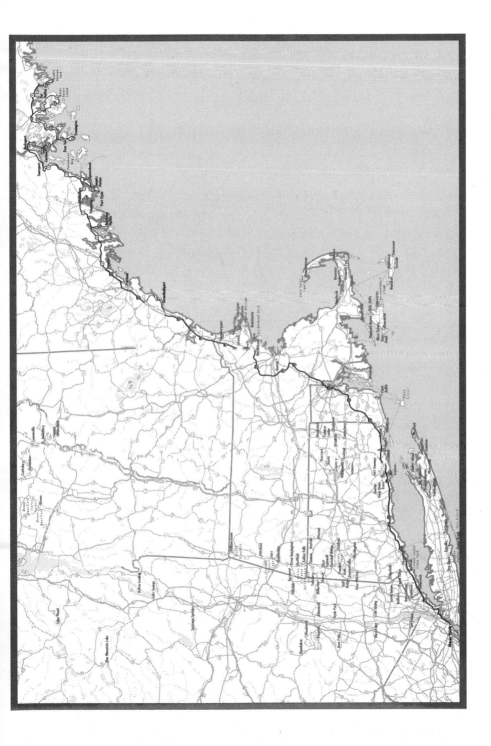

reach Kennebunkport, check into your hotel and rest a bit before going out to have a lobster dinner.

DINNER: The **White Barn Inn** (Beach Street; 207–967–2321) serves impeccably prepared contemporary American cuisine, with a concentration of New England flavors and fresh Maine seafood. A Relais & Château property, it's also wonderful for staying. On top of that it's New England's only five-star restaurant.

LODGING: The **Captain Lord Mansion,** Kennebunkport; (207) 967–3141. Designed by Captain Lord, a wealthy merchant and shipbuilder, this is a three-story Federal-style building that dates back to 1812. All sixteen rooms are beautifully decorated with period-reproduction wallpapers, exquisite antiques, and four-poster beds.

DAY 2

Morning

BREAKFAST: Breakfast at The Captain Lord Mansion. After breakfast take time to see the sites in and around Kennebunkport including **Nott House,** a stately Greek Revival house that dates back to 1853 (Maine Street; 207–967–2513—closed in winter), mansion-dotted **Ocean Avenue,** and the **Seashore Trolley Museum** (Log Cabin Road; 207–967–2712), located 3⁷⁄₁₀ miles up North Street from Kennebunkport. From there drive inland and take an architectural walking tour of **Kennebunk's National Register District** (very noteworthy is **The Brick Store Museum** at 117 Main Street; 207–985–4802). On Summer Street (Route 35), take a look at the **Wedding Cake House,** an 1826 house covered with white wooden latticework.

Then head up to **Portland,** where you can easily occupy yourselves for hours. Tops on our list of sightseeing attractions in Portland is the **Portland Museum of Art,** which is housed in a striking post-modern building that was designed by Henry N. Cobb of I. M. Pei. It contains extensive collections of Maine-based artists such as Andrew Wyeth, Edward Hopper, and Winslow Homer. Other Portland attractions include the Wadsworth-Longfellow House, where the poet spent his childhood, and the Old Port Exchange, a very attractive part of town lined with restaurants, taverns, and shops that occupy former warehouses and other nineteenth-century buildings.

The Captain Lord mansion is a beautifully decorated house that dates back to 1812.

LUNCH: David's Restaurant at the Oyster Club (164 Middle Street; 207–773–4340) has a raw bar upstairs, which is always abuzz with its regular clientele. Consider following up lunch with a cup of coffee at **Green Mountain Coffee Roasters** (15 Temple Street; 207–773–4475), where you can take your pick of blends.

Afternoon

About 20 miles north of Portland, on Route 1 is **Freeport,** home of L.L. Bean and several brand-name factory outlets (Polo–Ralph Lauren, Calvin Klein, Laura Ashley, etc.) where you can spend as much or as little time as you please.

Continue up the coast on Route 1 and then take Route 27 to **Boothbay Harbor.** This town started life as a tiny lobstering and fishing community and grew into a tourist mecca of sorts. It's a great place to go with young children.

As you carry on up the coast, you can stop and visit whichever towns appeal, keeping in mind your destination for the night: Castine.

The little village of **Waldoboro** is one of the next towns you'll come to as you continue up Route 1. It has several old homes and a Lutheran church that dates back to 1771. Farther out on that peninsula (following Route 220) is **Friendship,** a picturesque lobstering port. You have to go around the inlet and then out to the tip of St. George Peninsula to get to **Port Clyde,** where the mailboat for Monhegan Island runs year-round. You can head out to Monhegan Island from here or take a boat from Boothbay Harbor. On your way back to Route 1, take time out to visit the picture-perfect waterfront towns of **Tenants Harbor** and **Sprucehead.**

Around this point of the coast—at **Penobscot Bay**—you start to see the Maine coast everyone has always raved about. Startlingly beautiful islands rise abruptly out of the choppy waters. Sparkling sailboats gracefully skim about. Most beautiful, though, are the tall-masted windjammers that are famous in this area. You can spend a week on one eating hearty home-cooked meals and flitting about from one drop-dead gorgeous island to another. The main departure points are in the Rockland, Rockport, and Camden areas.

As you continue up the coast, you'll come to **Searsport,** an old shipping port with stately old sea-captain homes and a multitude of antiques shops. **Bucksport** is next, which is home to the **Fort Knox State Park,** a very impressively constructed fort that was manned during both the Civil and Spanish-American Wars.

Castine is the last stop for the day. The town itself is the attraction: A community of eighteenth- and nineteenth-century Georgian and Federal houses standing in impeccable condition. Most of these houses were originally erected in the mid-nineteenth century when Castine was a prosperous shipbuilding town. Many of them have since been restored by people "from away" (in other words, big-city folks with money to invest).

DINNER: Dennett's Wharf (Sea Street; 207–326–9045) is a net-hung, bustling fish house looking out over the harbor.

LODGING: The Castine Inn (Main Street; 207–326–4365) is a bed and breakfast in town with twenty antiques-furnished guest rooms.

DAY 3

Morning

BREAKFAST: At The Castine Inn.

From Castine it's a short, steadily scenic drive over to the village of **Blue Hill,** which is home to seventy-five buildings that are listed on the National Register of Historic Places. Take time out to walk around and poke in the pottery and crafts shops, for which Blue Hill is well known.

Head southwest of Blue Hill and you'll eventually cut through a corner of Little Deer Isle and then climb an arching suspension bridge that takes you over to **Deer Isle,** a wonderful little island almost too beautiful to promote. Don't miss the sweet little town of **Stonington** at the southern tip.

Ever since the mid-nineteenth century, **Mt. Desert Island** has been one of Maine's most popular destinations. Once you cross the bridge connecting it to the mainland, it's easy to see why. The island is home to **Cadillac Mountain,** which, at 1,530 feet, seems to scrape the sky. Looming all around are sixteen other mountains that drop right down into the sea. Fortunately, most of the island (35,000 acres) is under the protection of **Acadia National Park,** which is threaded with miles of hiking, driving, and biking trails. The Park Loop Road takes in the major sights of the park.

The island's main town is **Bar Harbor,** which, back in the late 1800s, was a thriving resort community for very wealthy and powerful American families. At present, it's quite a busy tourist hub, with lots of shops, motels, and restaurants.

LUNCH: If you want a quick lunch on the go, you'll find several casual eateries right in Bar Harbor. Consider, too, shopping for picnic items and taking a lunch hiking in the national park.

Afternoon

Divide your day between the natural treasures of the national park with the man-made attractions of Bar Harbor.

DINNER: Jordan Pond House, Park Loop Road (207–276–3316), has wonderful specialties such as lobster stew and baked haddock. It also offers a lovely mountain view.

LODGING: Clefstone Manor, 92 Eden Street; (207) 288–4951. This is a huge mansion that was built back in 1894 as a summer home for James Blair, secretary of the navy under President Lincoln.

DAY 4

Morning

BREAKFAST: At the manor or in town.

Take your time leisurely working your way back down the coast before picking up I–95 to return to New York.

THERE'S MORE

Beaches. The whole coast of Maine is dotted with beaches, most open to the public. Some names to know: Ogunquit Beach, Wells Beach, Gouche's Beach (near Kennebunkport), Colony Beach (Kennebunkport), Ferry Beach State Park (between Camp Ellis and Old Orchard Beach), Crescent Beach State Park (south of Portland), and more.

Gallery hopping. All along the coast of Maine, you'll find galleries displaying works of local painters and sculptors. On Deer Isle you can visit Haystack Mountain School of Crafts (Route 15; 207–348–2306) which attracts artists from around the world who work in metal, textiles, wood, glass, pottery, and paper.

Hiking. In addition to Acadia National Park, the southern coast of Maine has several state parks laced with hiking trails. These include Crescent Beach State Park, Wolf's Neck State Park, Popham Beach State Park, Reid State Park, and Camden Hills State Park, just to name a few.

Island excursion. Consider taking time out to visit Monhegan Island, just off the southern coast of Maine. A mere smidgen on the map (less than 2 miles long and 1 mile wide), it has been known as a popular artists' and writers' retreat for years. The scenery is arrestingly beautiful: steep cliffs, powerful surf, rich, green pine forests, and golden meadows. There's also a lighthouse that dates back to 1824. To reach it you can take a boat from either Port Clyde or Boothbay Harbor.

SPECIAL EVENTS

January. Winter Carnival, Bangor; (207) 945–9469. Family fun.

June. Annual Windjammer Days, Boothbay Harbor; (207) 633–2353. Windjammer and antique boat parade, concerts, and exhibits.

July. Native American Festival, Bar Harbor; (207) 288–3519. Celebration of Maliseet, Micmac, Passamaquoddy, and Penobscot People of Maine with food, crafts, dancing.

Bangor State Fair, Bangor; (207) 942–9000. A real old-fashioned fair.

Celebration of the Arts, Kennebunkport; (207) 967–5355. Demonstrations and musical performances.

August. Annual MS Regatta, Portland; (207) 761–5815. Sailing fund-raiser.

October. Fall Foliage Festival, Boothbay; (207) 633–4727. Craft fair, food, entertainment.

OTHER RECOMMENDED RESTAURANTS AND LODGINGS

Cape Neddick

The Cape Neddick House Bed & Breakfast, 1300 Route 1; (207) 363–2500. A beautifully restored Victorian inn.

Deer Isle

Goose Cove Lodge, Deer Isle, Sunset; (207) 348–2508. A very special inn with cottages and suites for staying. It's set on seventy acres.

East Boothbay

Five Gables Inn, Murray Hill Road; (207) 633–4551 or (800) 451–5048. A beautifully restored, 125-year-old inn overlooking Linekin Bay.

Isle au Haut

The Keeper's House, Lighthouse Point; (207) 469–3720. Listed on the National Register of Historic Places, this small inn has no electricity, telephones, roads or crowds! A true escape.

FOR MORE INFORMATION

The Maine Publicity Bureau, Inc., P.O. Box 2300, Hallowell, ME 04347-2300; (800) 533–9595 or (800) 323–6330 (from within Maine).

MID-ATLANTIC
ESCAPES

MID-ATLANTIC

Spring Lake

A SMALL SHORE TOWN

1 NIGHT

*Beaches • Nineteenth-century architecture
Seafood • Boardwalk*

About equidistant from Philadelphia and New York City, you'll find Spring Lake, one of the most pleasant towns on the Jersey shore. Since the early part of this century, it has been a vacation spot for travelers wanting to get away from both cities. Back then they came by carriage and stayed in what was the grandest hotel (but no longer exists)—the Monmouth House. There are several buildings that do live on from that era, however, including an impressive collection of Victorian "cottages."

For this trip we suggest driving down in the morning (the drive takes not much more than an hour), spending the day and night enjoying the simple pleasures of Spring Lake, and then slowly meandering back to the city, stopping in Red Bank en route.

DAY 1

Morning

Take exit 98 off the Garden State Parkway to Route 34 south. Go 1½ miles to the traffic circle and turn left onto Route 524. Follow Route 524 for about 3 miles, and it'll take you right into town.

One of the best ways to enjoy Spring Lake is to just stroll leisurely. A good starting place is the boardwalk, which stretches 2 miles along the ocean and is

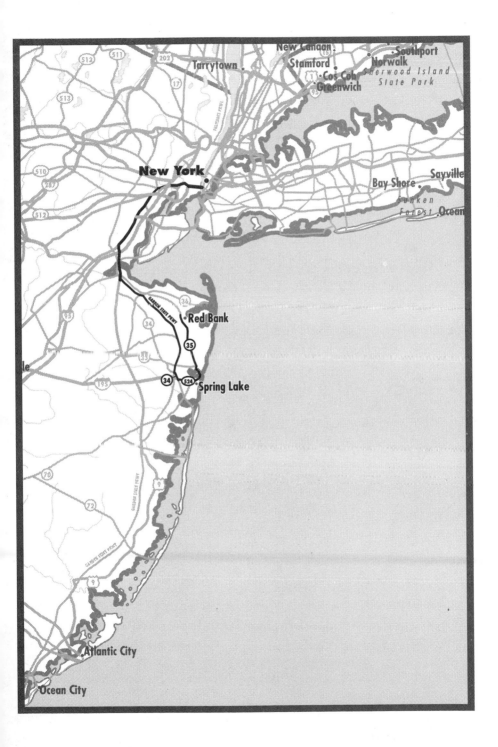

not colonized by arcades and the other amusements found at so many other boardwalks.

LUNCH: Right across from the boardwalk is the **Warren Hotel,** 901 Ocean Avenue (732–449–8800), where you can have a light lunch (a sandwich, a burger, maybe a salad) in the Peacock Cafe.

Afternoon

From the Warren Hotel you can wander through the wide, tree-lined streets of town admiring one beautiful turn-of-the-century house after another. The lake for which the town is named is right in the center of town, surrounded by a park.

Spend whatever time is left on the beach, which is half a block from your hotel. If you have a craving for ice cream, head for **The Sundae Times,** Atlantic Avenue (732–974–1236).

DINNER: The **Old Mill Inn,** Old Mill Road, Spring Lake Heights (732–449–1800), serves unfailingly good seafood and other American dishes. Many consider it a New Jersey institution.

LODGING: Sea Crest by the Sea, 19 Tuttle Avenue (732–449–9031), is an eleven-room Victorian guest house just half a block from the beach. All rooms are handsomely decorated with French and English furnishings from the 1880s.

DAY 2

Morning

If you're a jogger, consider lacing up and following the paths around the lake or run along the boardwalk, breathing in the invigorating ocean air.

BREAKFAST: Continental breakfast is included in the room price.

After a leisurely breakfast and some more time spent relaxing on the beach or playing croquet at Sea Crest, head north back toward Manhattan, taking time out to explore **Red Bank.** Poised on the shores of the Navesink River, Red Bank is a historic community with lots of shops. If you're interested in antiques, it's home to a major **Antiques Center,** along West Front Street and Shrewsbury Avenue.

Spring Lake, New Jersey, has long been a popular shore vacation spot.

From there you can easily pick up the Garden State Parkway north to return to Manhattan.

THERE'S MORE

Horse country. Slightly inland and just to the north of the Spring Lake area is a little chunk of horse country. The farms are in full view from the road and are concentrated in a little triangle of towns: Holmdel, Freehold, and Colt's Neck. Many of the farms can be seen along routes 537, 79, 520, and 34.

SPECIAL EVENTS

Summer months. Throughout the summer months, there are model-boat regattas on the lake on Sundays, croquet at Green Gables on Thursdays, and weekly concerts in Potter Park. Check the *Shore Holiday News* for listings.

OTHER RECOMMENDED RESTAURANTS AND LODGINGS

Rumson

Fromagerie, 26 Ridge Road; (732) 842–8088. This is one of the Jersey Shore's most outstanding restaurants. The food is French, the service very gracious, and the atmosphere elegant. Rumson is a short drive east of Red Bank.

Spring Lake

The Château, 500 Warren Avenue; (732) 974–2000. A renovated Victorian hotel with forty rooms. The beach is 4 blocks away.

FOR MORE INFORMATION

Red Bank Chamber of Commerce, Broad and Leroy Streets, Red Bank, NJ 07701; (732) 741–0055.

New Jersey Division of Travel and Tourism, C.N. 826, Trenton, NJ 08625; (609) 292–2470 or (800) JERSEY–7.

MID-ATLANTIC

The Jersey Cape
A SHORE THING

---

2 NIGHTS

*Shore scenery • Beaches • Seafood • Casinos • Fishing
Golfing • Boardwalk amusements • Victorian buildings
Biking • Bird-watching • Deep-sea fishing*

Mention New Jersey and lots of people automatically think of Atlantic City. Indeed, this casino hub has earned its place on the map, but casinos are just part of the picture in this part of the world.

Back in the late 1800s, the Atlantic seashore that runs roughly from just below Atlantic City to Cape May Point was a very popular place to vacation, so much so that after a while, it became too popular and ultimately drove away many vacationers. Attempting to bring back visitors, many towns introduced other activities such as amusement parks and convention facilities. The result, unfortunately, is that many of the lovely shore towns now stand behind boardwalks that are lined with amusement arcades, bowling alleys, pool halls, and fast-food restaurants. On the plus side, the beaches are still there, and the activity makes for good times round the year. The final destination for this escape—Cape May—is a lovely Victorian town where you can settle in for a couple of days.

For this escape we suggest making your first stop Atlantic City, then following Ocean Drive (a series of bridges connecting a series of narrow islands that run parallel to the mainland) down the coast to Cape May, making stops along the way.

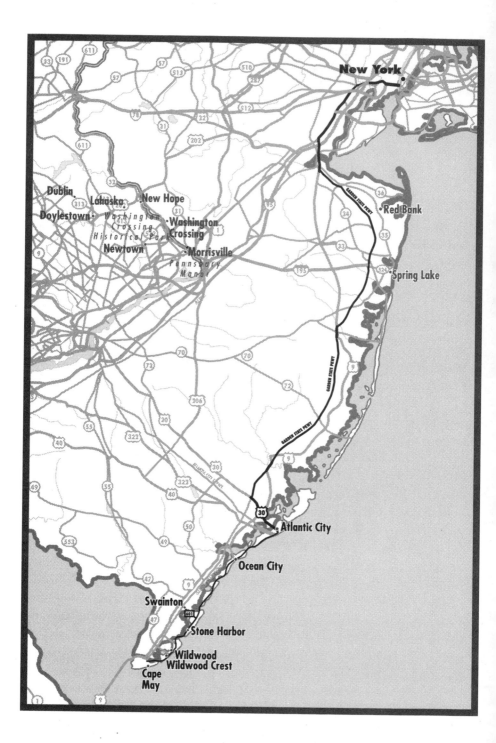

DAY 1

Morning

Set out early from Manhattan, keeping in mind that you can't do everything we suggest and still make it to Cape May in one day. Pick and choose as you go along and what you miss on the way down, pick up on the way back. To reach Atlantic City take the Garden State Parkway all the way south to the Atlantic City Expressway east.

Atlantic City, which was made famous by the board game Monopoly, continues to get national attention every fall when the Miss America Pageant takes place in town. On top of that, Atlantic City is a gambling hub, with thirteen major casinos including Bally's, Caesars, The Grand, Merv Griffin's, and the Trump casinos. These casinos are also famous for their big-name entertainment, world-championship sports, glittery shows and gourmet restaurants. Atlantic City is also home to a 60-foot-wide boardwalk extending along five miles of beaches lined with shops, amusement centers, and food stands. There is also a three-deck shopping complex—The Shops on Ocean One (1 Atlantic Ocean; 609–347–8082)—built to resemble an ocean liner.

LUNCH: While in Atlantic City, you can lunch at one of the casino restaurants (there are dozens) including **Planet Hollywood** at Caesars (609–347–7827).

Afternoon

From Atlantic City head south on Ocean Drive, making your next stop at **Ocean City,** which calls itself "America's Greatest Family Resort." Indeed, there is plenty to do for families on its 2-mile-long boardwalk and 8 miles of beaches. Ocean City prides itself on its wacky and inventive summertime festivals and contests. Every August, for example, there's a Hermit Crab Race and a Miss Crustacean Contest.

If you prefer natural over man-made diversions, continue down the coast to the **Stone Harbor** area, where you'll find **Leaming's Run Gardens** (1845 Route 9, Swainton; 609–465–5871), one of the finest gardens on the East Coast and the Wetlands Institute (1075 Stone Harbor Boulevard, Stone Harbor; 609–368–1211), an environmental center focusing on coastal ecology. At the latter there's an observation tower, a marsh trail, and an aquarium.

Cape May's Victorian heritage is preserved in its graceful old buildings.

Next on the itinerary are the **Wildwoods,** a quartet of shore towns. West Wildwood is a residential area, whereas the other three—North Wildwood, Wildwood, and Wildwood Crest—are lined with oceanfront hotels and motels. On Wildwood's beachfront you'll find the biggest concentration of amusements including six amusement piers with carnival-like rides.

Less than 10 miles away is **Cape May** (continue down the coast on Ocean Drive), which has been a popular beach resort since the days of the Revolution and, in fact, is the oldest seashore resort in the country that has very successfully preserved its Victorian heritage.

Once you arrive, settle into your hotel (some of the rooms at the Mainstay have parking spots; if yours doesn't, grab the first one you see on the street) for what's left of the afternoon.

DINNER: The **Washington Inn,** 801 Washington Street (609–884–5697), a former plantation house dating back to 1848, is a great spot for seafood and other continental dishes.

LODGING: The **Mainstay Inn,** 635 Columbus Avenue (609–884–8690), is an Italianate villa with a wraparound veranda. Inside are all sorts of Victorian details. Guests can stay in the main inn or in the more modernized adjacent cottage.

DAY 2

Morning

BREAKFAST: During the summer a light breakfast is served at the Mainstay. The rest of the year, it's a full breakfast.

The heart of town is the Washington Street Victorian Mall, which is a 3-block-long stretch closed to automobiles and lined with shops and restaurants. The real focus in Cape May, however, is the promenade, which runs along the Atlantic and offers a whole host of diversions.

To see the town's historic sites, consider joining a guided Historic District Walking Tour. These tours—which last about an hour and a half—are full of historical insights. Of course, you can also take yourself on a self-guided tour. The Welcome Center, at 405 Lafayette Street, can point you in the right direction and provide you with brochures. Most of the most beautiful Victorian buildings are now inns lined up majestically between the Welcome Center and the beach. These include The Abbey, a Gothic Revival house at Columbia Avenue and Gurney Street; Captain Mey's Inn, at 202 Ocean Street; The Mainstay Inn, at 635 Columbia Avenue; and the Angel of the Sea, at 5 Trenton Avenue.

LUNCH: For lunch consider grabbing something light (like a slab of pizza) at the mall or on the promenade.

Afternoon

Once you've had lunch and perhaps a short snooze on the beach, take a drive out to Cape May State Park (follow Sunset Boulevard) for a beautiful walk through one of Cape May's best birding areas. There are 3 miles of trails and a boardwalk that take you over ponds and through wooded areas and marsh-lands. Then climb the 218 steps to the top of the Cape May Lighthouse. Stick around for the sunset, which is astonishingly beautiful from Cape May Point.

DINNER: 410 Bank Street, at 410 Bank Street; (609) 884–2127. The menu here is Louisiana French. You can sit on the porch or in the garden.

DAY 3

Morning

BREAKFAST: At the inn.

After breakfast visit the shops in the mall area and near the beach or head back to the beach. The "Cape May diamonds," which you will inevitably see in shops all over town, are actually quartz, rounded by the waves.

Then meander your way back up the New Jersey coast, stopping at those attractions you might have missed on the way down.

THERE'S MORE

Bicycling. You can rent bikes right in town at The Village Bicycle Shop (at Ocean Street and the beginning of the mall); (609) 884–8500.

Bird-watching. Every fall thousands of migratory birds (including every-thing from small songbirds to falcons and eagles) stop here on their way south. The best viewing areas are Cape May State Park, the Cape May Migratory Bird Refuge, and Higbee's Beach.

Carriage rides. Carriages leave from Ocean Street and Washington Street Mall for half-hour historic district tours. Call (609) 884–4466 for more information.

Fishing. There are several great fishing areas around Cape May including the Second Avenue jetty and the World War II bunker by the lighthouse at Cape May Point.

Trolley tours. If you're not up for walking, you can take trolley tours around town. For information contact the Mid-Atlantic Center for the Arts (609–884–5404).

SPECIAL EVENTS

March. Atlantic City Antique and Collectibles Show, Atlantic City; (800) 526–2724.

April. Tulip Festival, Cape May; (609) 884–9562.

May. Crafts at Memorial Day, Cape May; (609) 884–2300.

May–June. Cape May Music Festival, Cape May; (609) 884–2736.

June. Beach Fest, Atlantic City; (609) 641–7811.

N.J. Fresh Seafood Festival, Atlantic City; (609) 344–1943.

Victorian Fair, Cape May; (609) 884–5404.

September. Miss America Pageant, Atlantic City; (609) 345–7571.

Super Fifties Weekend, Ocean City; (800) BEACH–NJ.

Wings' Water Festival, The Wetlands Institute, Stone Harbor; (609) 368 1211.

October. Victoria Week, Cape May; (609) 884–5404.

December. Christmas Candlelight Tour, Cape May; (609) 884–5404.

OTHER RECOMMENDED RESTAURANTS AND LODGINGS

Cape May

There are many guest houses and inns in Cape May. Here are just a few:

The Abbey, 34 Gurney Street, at Columbia Avenue; (609) 884–4506. A lovely Gothic-style inn.

Captain Mey's Inn, 202 Ocean Street; (609) 884–7793. A nine-room inn decorated with Victorian furnishings.

North Wildwood Candlelight Inn, 2310 Central Avenue. (609) 522–6200. An inn in a restored Queen Anne/Victorian-style house.

Ocean City

Serendipity Bed & Brunch, 712 Ninth Street, Ocean City; (609) 399–1554. A six-room inn, originally built in 1912.

FOR MORE INFORMATION

Atlantic City Convention & Visitors Authority, 2314 Pacific Avenue, Atlantic City, NJ 08401; (609) 348–7100.

Cape May Chamber of Commerce, P.O. Box 556, Cape May, NJ 08204; (609) 884–5508.

Cape May Welcome Center, 405 Lafayette Street, Cape May, NJ 08204; (609) 884–9562.

New Jersey Division of Travel and Tourism, C.N. 826, Trenton, NJ 08625; (609) 292–2470 or (800) JERSEY–7.

Bucks County

A LITTLE BIT OF HISTORY

2 NIGHTS

Revolutionary landmarks • Antiques • Inns
Natural beauty • Farm country • Galleries • Fine dining
Early Pennsylvania architecture • Covered bridges

In the southeast corner of Pennsylvania, Bucks County, which is bounded by Philadelphia County on the southwest and separated from New Jersey by the Delaware River to the east, offers just the right balance between sightseeing and relaxing. The area was first known to the Lenni-Lenape Indians and later settled by Dutch explorers, followed by Swedes, English Quakers, and Germans.

Today's visitor can dip into a little history, find dozens of antiques shops, sample local cuisine, and stay overnight in historic inns. The centerpiece of the county is New Hope, which has more than 200 properties older than a century and listed on the National Register of Historic Places.

There's a lot to do in Bucks County. This itinerary takes you to just some of the highlights.

DAY 1

Morning

Most of the county's attractions are centered in New Hope, which for years has been a magnet for artists and writers. To reach it take the New Jersey Turnpike to exit 10. Then follow Route 287 north to Route 22 west, to Route

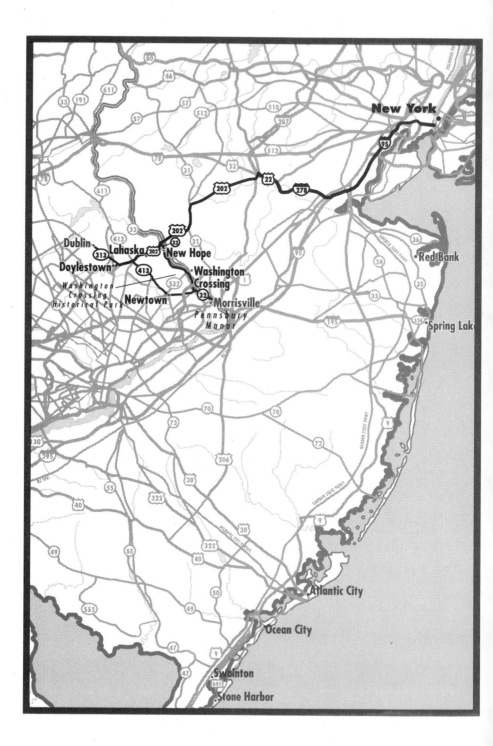

202 south. Follow Route 202 over the Delaware River Bridge and then get on Route 32 south. This will lead you right into town.

If you show up on a weekend, year-round, be prepared for a crowd scene. New Hope gets a lot of day-trippers from Philadelphia, New York, and New Jersey. Its streets are lined with boutiques selling everything from New Age crystals to antique paintings. Your best bet for parking is to drive west of Route 32 and then walk back.

Start by getting yourself a copy of the booklet *The Walking Tour of Historic New Hope*, at New Hope's information center, One West Mechanic Street.

From there walk along Main Street, which has the Delaware Canal on one side and the river on the other, and pop into any shops or galleries that appeal to you. The canal was opened in 1831 to carry whiskey and raw materials between different local towns as well as Philadelphia, Pittsburgh, and Lake Erie. Alongside the canal is a towpath, which is used for walking, cycling, and jogging.

One of the highlights of any visit to New Hope is a ride on a **Mule Barge** As you slide along the Delaware Canal on a flower-festooned barge, mules pulling alongside, a tour guide fills you in on New Hope's history. New Hope Mule Barge Co. rides start on New Street at the southern end of town at 11:30 A.M., 1:00, 2:00, 3:00, 4:30, and 6:00 P.M. April through November 15. You can also take a ride on the **New Hope & Ivyland Rail Road** (station on West Bridge Street; 215–862–2332), a restored stream train, though it's an awful lot to cram into the day. The train runs daily April through November and on weekends only from January through March.

If you're interested in antiques, don't miss the **Three Cranes Gallery** (18–22 Mechanic Street).

LUNCH: Directly across the street from the Three Cranes Gallery, you'll find **Karla's,** 5 West Mechanic Street (215–862–2612), a very informal place where you can grab a sandwich or a pasta dish.

Afternoon

After lunch wander over to **Parry Mansion,** 45 South Main Street (215–862–5652). Built by Benjamin Parry in 1784, it now is a museum of decorative arts. Each room is furnished to reflect a different period from Colonial to American Federal. The museum is open from May 1 to mid-December, Fridays, Saturdays, and Sundays from 1:00 to 5:00 P.M.

Consider returning to Main Street to sample some internationally flavored ice creams (Israel's milk and honey, Ukrainian rose petal, American pumpkin) at **Gerenser's Exotic Ice Cream,** 22 South Main Street (215–862–2050). Afterward you can burn the calories off by poking around some other shops.

Before the day is over, consider taking a horse and buggy ride at Bucks County Carriages, 2586 North River Road (215–862–3582), over to **Phillips Mill,** a gristmill complex built in 1765 by Aaron Phillips. For years it was a political forum and social center for local farm families.

DINNER: La Bonne Auberge, Village 2, off Mechanic Street; (215) 862–2462. French cuisine served in a historic stone farmhouse.

After dinner consider taking in a show at the legendary **Bucks County Playhouse,** 70 South Main Street; (215) 862–2041. Set on the banks of the Delaware, it used to be a mill but was converted into a theater in 1939.

LODGING: In New Hope, and all over Bucks County, there are many bed and breakfasts. For reservations contact **Plain & Fancy Bed and Breakfast Reservation Service,** 1905 Breckinridge Place, Tom's River, NJ 08755; (800) 374–STAY. Otherwise you can take your pick of many inns and hotels. An especially elegant inn is the **Whitehall Inn,** 1370 Pineville Road (215–598–7945), which is about five or six minutes outside of town.

DAY 2

Morning

BREAKFAST: An elaborate four-course breakfast is included in the room rate at the Whitehall Inn.

After breakfast follow the River Road (Route 32) south to **Washington Crossing Historical Park,** routes 32 and 532 (215–493–4076). This is one of Bucks County's many beautiful drives, taking you past magnificent homes and river views. The park is divided into two sections. The northern section of the park is dominated by **Bowman's Hill,** which is crowned by a tower commemorating a Revolutionary War lookout point. It's also a **Wildflower Preserve** (devoted entirely to Pennsylvania plants), the only wildflower preserve in North America to be accredited by the American Association of Museums. The lower part, which is 7 miles south of New Hope, is where George Washington and 2,400 soldiers in his Continental Army crossed the

Historic sites such as Pennsbury Manor abound in Bucks County.

Delaware on Christmas night in 1776 to make a surprise attack against the Crown's Hessian mercenaries in Trenton. There are picnic grounds, historic structures (including the old Patriot general store and post office), and the Washington Crossing Memorial building.

Continue down River Road until you reach Morrisville, where you'll turn left and follow signs for **Pennsbury Manor,** 400 Pennsbury Memorial Road, near Tullytown (215–946–0400), which was William Penn's summer mansion built on a bend of the Delaware. Penn's Georgian brick house stands on a multiacre plot of land (originally, it was an 8,400-acre plantation; now it's scaled down quite a bit) overlooking the river where he would travel by barge to and from Philadelphia. It and its many outbuildings (bake and brew house, blacksmith's and joiner's shops) have been totally reconstructed by the Pennsylvania Historical Commission. Costumed guides take visitors through the compound on one-and-a-half-hour tours. Call ahead; tour hours vary.

From Pennsbury follow the country roads north to **Newtown** (about a twenty-minute drive), the core of which is made up of eighteenth- and early-nineteenth-century houses that were laid out in a plan approved by Penn. More than 225 properties are listed on the National Register of Historic Places. Begin by stopping for lunch and then take your time looking at the different buildings.

LUNCH: Ye Olde Temperance House, 5–11 South State Street, Newton (215–860–0474), has an excellent Sunday jazz brunch with a live Dixieland band and a menu featuring jambalaya, Cajun blackened fish, and smoked-salmon omelets. Lunch is served every day of the week.

Afternoon

From Newtown follow Route 413 north to Route 202 over to **Doylestown,** your destination for the night.

DINNER: Doylestown Inn, 18 West State Street; (215) 345–6610. Here you can have a hearty basic dinner. Nothing special, but good.

LODGING: Pine Tree Farm, 2155 Lower State Road, Doylestown (215–348–0632), is one of several very welcoming bed and breakfasts in Doylestown. It's a four-room antiques-furnished stone farmhouse dating back to 1730.

DAY 3

Morning

BREAKFAST: Wonderful breakfasts are included in the room rate at Pine Tree Farm.

There's enough to keep you pretty busy all morning in Doylestown. It's home to two castles made of concrete as well as the Moravian Pottery & Tile Works. All three, which are designated as "Mercer Mile," were built between 1908 and 1916 by Henry Chapman Mercer, a local eccentric. **Fonthill,** a fanciful building with turrets, secret rooms, and unexpected stairways, Mercer built as a residence for himself. It's located on East Curt Street (215–348–9461). The hours are Monday through Saturday from 10:00 A.M. to 5:00 P.M. and Sunday from noon to 5:00 P.M. A short walk through the park will bring you to the **Moravian Pottery & Tile Works,** 130 Swamp Road

(215–345–6722), where you can watch tiles being made the same way they were made about ninety years ago. It's open seven days a week from 10:00 A.M. to 4:45 P.M.; the last tour begins at 4:00 P.M. The other castle, **Mercer Museum,** is on Pine and East Ashland Streets, less than a mile away. Mercer used the latter to house an enormous collection of tools and farm implements that were used by tradesmen in the nineteenth century. It's open Monday through Saturday from 10:00 A.M. to 5:00 P.M. and on Sunday from noon to 5:00 P.M.; also open on Tuesday evenings until 9:00 P.M.

Adjacent to the Mercer Museum is the **James A. Michener Arts Museum,** 138 South Pine Street (215–340–9800), which was named in honor of the Doylestown native. In addition to gallery space (which includes a permanent exhibition celebrating Michener's career as a writer, public servant, art collector, and philanthropist), it has a museum shop and a tea room. Other permanent exhibits include "Nakashima Reading Room," which is filled with furnishings by Bucks County's internationally known woodworker George Nakashima, and "Visual Heritage of Bucks County," which traces the art of the region from colonial times to the present. There are also changing exhibits. Hours are Tuesday through Friday from 10:00 A.M. to 4:30 P.M. and Saturday and Sunday from 10:00 A.M. to 5:00 P.M.; closed Mondays.

LUNCH: Cafe Airelle, 100 Main Street, Doylestown (215–345–5930), is a French bistro right on Main Street.

Afternoon

A few miles north of Doylestown at 520 Dublin Road (off Route 313, 1 mile southwest of Dublin), you'll find **Green Hills Farm** (800–220–BUCK or 215–249–0100), which was Pearl S. Buck's estate. Visitors can tour the 1835 stone house where the author lived when she returned to America (after growing up in China with missionary parents) from the age of thirty-two on. When the Nobel and Pulitzer prize–winning author died in 1973, she was buried on the premises. The house is open between March and December. Tours are given at 10:30 A.M., 1:30 P.M., and 2:30 P.M. Tuesday through Saturday and at 1:30 P.M. and 2:30 P.M. on Sundays.

Return to Doylestown and head east on Route 202 and you'll come to the town of **Lahaska.** On what was the old coach road that connected Philadelphia with New York, this town used to be home to several chicken farms. In 1962 the farms were transformed into **Peddler's Village,** which began as a collection of shops in reconstructed chicken coops but grew, very tastefully, as shops and restaurants were added. Today there are more than seventy shops (purveying antiques, art, crafts, and other collectibles), several restaurants, and a carousel museum.

From Lahaska return to New Hope and then retrace your steps back to New York.

THERE'S MORE

Ghost tours. In New Hope tours meet at the cannon on Main Street every Saturday night at 8:00 P.M. from June through November. During October and early November, tours run every Friday and Saturday night at 8:00 P.M.

Outlet shopping. Just over the Bucks County border toward Philadelphia is the Franklin Mills Mall (off I–95, exit 22/Woodhaven Road) with about 200 outlets.

Polo. Matches are played from spring through fall at the Bucks County Horse Park on Route 611, between Revere and Ferndale.

Sesame Place. If you're traveling with children, don't miss this stellar attraction. It's located at 100 Sesame Road in Langhorne; (215) 752–7070.

Wineries. There are several wineries in the area including the Buckingham Valley Vineyards in Buckingham (215–794–7188), Peace Valley Winery in Chalfont (215–249–9058), Rushland Ridge Vineyards & Winery in Rushland (215–598–0251), and Sand Castle Winery in Erwinna (800–PA2–WINE).

SPECIAL EVENTS

Mid-May. Mercer Folk Festival, Mercer Museum, Doylestown.

Early June. Bucks County Antiques Dealers Association Show. More than forty dealers show their collections at Delaware Valley College, at Route 202 and New Britain Road in Doylestown.

Bucks County Balloon and Vineyard Festival, Quakertown Airport, 2425 Milford Square Pike, Quakertown. Hot-air balloons, aircraft, wine tasting, food booths, arts and crafts, and entertainment.

September. State Craft Festival, at Tyler State Park, Route 332, Newtown.

October. Bucks County Artists' Show, Green Hills Farm (Pearl S. Buck's estate).

Late November. Bucks County Antiques Dealers Association Show, held on Thanksgiving Day weekend at Delaware Valley College, Route 202 and New Britain Road, Doylestown.

December 25. Reenactment of Washington crossing the Delaware. Every Christmas the successful maneuver by George Washington and the Continental Army, which led to a decisive victory for the colonies, is reenacted at Washington Crossing Historical Park, 7 miles south of New Hope. For more information call (215) 493–4076.

OTHER RECOMMENDED RESTAURANTS AND LODGINGS

Doylestown

Highland Farms, 70 East Road; (215) 340–1354. This stone country house used to be the estate of lyricist Oscar Hammerstein II. It's listed on the National Register of Historic Places.

Inn at Fordhook Farm, 105 New Britain Road; (215) 345–1766. An eighteenth-century house on the National Register of Historic Places.

Lahaska

Golden Plough Inn of Peddler's Village, Route 202 and Street Road; (215) 794–4004. A lovely country inn.

Lumberville

Black Bass Hotel, Route 32; (215) 297–5815. An antiques-furnished inn on the Delaware River.

Cuttalossa Inn, River Road; (215) 297–5082. American cuisine in a very romantic setting.

Newtown

Jean Pierre's, 101 South State Street; (215) 968–6201. An exceptionally good French restaurant.

FOR MORE INFORMATION

Bucks County Tourist Commission, Inc., 152 Swamp Road, Doylestown, PA 18901. In Pennsylvania call (800) 836–BUCKS; elsewhere, (215) 345–4552.

Pennsylvania Tourism (800–VISIT–PA) provides a booklet for the state.

MID-ATLANTIC

Lancaster County

PENNSYLVANIA DUTCH COUNTRY

2 NIGHTS

Farms • Plain People communities
Farmers' markets • Traditional home cooking • Auctions
Waterwheels and windmills • Handicrafts

You don't have to go far from New York to feel as if you're in a foreign country. In Lancaster county, which is less than three hours away, you'll see horse-drawn buggies used as a mode of transportation and farms being worked with horse or mule teams.

Lancaster County is the heart of Pennsylvania Dutch Country, which is home to a large population of "Plain People" (Amish, Brethren, and Mennonite). Most of them carry on their lives as they did in the seventeenth century, shunning anything modern such as automobiles, electricity, and chemical fertilizers.

In addition to the steadily scenic Amish farmlands for which the area is so well known, there are a whole host of historical attractions including the National Clock and Watch Museum, the Landis Valley Museum, Robert Fulton's birthplace, Wright's Ferry Mansion, and more. There are a number of interesting towns including Lititz, Strasburg (a must for railroad buffs), and the town of Lancaster itself, which contains President James Buchanan's home and other historic buildings.

From the eastern edge of Lancaster County to the Susquehanna River on the west, the distance is a mere 45 miles; nevertheless, the area should be explored slowly. Take time to wander down any road that looks interesting. Though all tourist maps will direct you to follow Route 30 in order to see

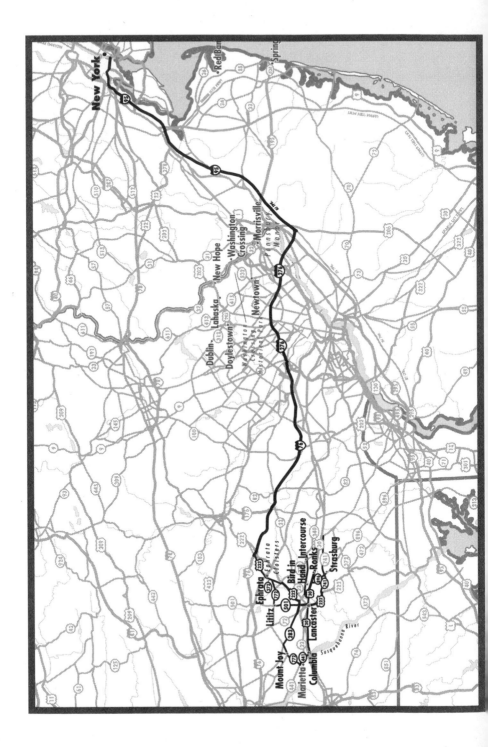

the Amish farms, you'll quickly find that this thoroughfare is painfully over-commercialized and usually a traffic nightmare. Routes 340 and 772 are better bets. As you explore, enjoy the names of some of the towns—Bird-in-Hand, Blue Ball, Fertility, Paradise, Intercourse.

If you're traveling during a weekend, keep in mind that many of the family-owned Amish shops and services are closed on Sundays. This partic-ular itinerary is set up so that you leave early Friday morning, stay over Fri-day and Saturday nights, and return on Sunday. Even though the area is so dense with attractions that you could use one inn as your base, we've selected two so that you can have a fuller experience.

A word about when to go: During summer weekends the throngs of tourists in Lancaster can be overwhelming. The best time to go is during the week in spring or fall.

DAY 1

Morning

Driving to Pennsylvania Dutch country from New York is a breeze. You take the New Jersey Turnpike to the Pennsylvania Turnpike west. Then get off at exit 21 and head south on Route 222. About 5 miles south of Lancaster, make your first stop at the **Hans Herr House,** 1849 Hans Herr Drive, Lancaster (717–464–4438). This is the county's oldest structure and the oldest Mennon-ite meetinghouse. Back in 1710 a collective of eight Mennonite families bought ten thousand acres of land (for a whopping 25 cents an acre); nine years later the Herr family built their house on the land. Open to visitors from April 1 to December 31 (daily, except Sundays), the house is a beautiful exam-ple of steep-roofed medieval German architecture. Guided tours help give you an understanding of how our forefathers lived.

From the Hans Herr House, head east on Route 741 to **Strasburg,** where you can pause for lunch and have a look around the historic railroad and its museum.

LUNCH: Though more popular for its homemade ice cream (in handmade cones and mixed with M&Ms, Reese's Pieces, and other favorites), the **Stras-burg Country Store & Creamery,** One West Main Street (717–687–0766), serves a great "loaf of soup" for lunch—a small, round loaf of bread that is scooped out and filled with the soup of the day.

Horse-drawn carriages are a common sight on Lancaster County roads

Afternoon

Strasburg is home to **The Railroad Museum of Pennsylvania,** Route 741 (717–687–8628), and **The Strasburg Rail Road.** The latter offers forty-five-minute round-trip rides between Strasburg and nearby Paradise on wooden coaches pulled by steam locomotives.

From Strasburg it's a short ride up to Route 30 (take Route 896) and **The Amish Farm and House** (717–394–6185), which all the tourist brochures, and most guidebooks, will tell you is a perfect introduction to Amish lifestyles. Indeed it is, with its nineteenth-century buildings furnished and decorated as old-order Amish households, waterwheels, windmills, carriages, and sleighs. Conscientious guides take you through the main house, which has been faithfully restored to look as it did in the early 1800s.

From there it's a short drive to the town of **Intercourse,** where you'll find many tourist traps as well as some worthwhile shops and attractions. The name Intercourse is derived from the fact that Route 772 intersects Route 340 in the village (back in the 1700s and early 1800s, these roads were major commerce routes). If you're interested in learning more about the local quilts (made by the women at quilting bees), don't miss **The People's Place Quilt Museum,** upstairs from the Old Country Store on Route 340 in the center of town (717–768–7171). Quilts are for sale in the Old Country Store itself.

DINNER: Miller's Smorgasbord, 2811 Lincoln Highway East, Ronks (717–687–6621), offers a Pennsylvania Dutch smorgasbord. It's very casual and hearty and down-home priced.

LODGING: The **Dingeldein House,** 1105 East King Street in Lancaster (717–293–1723), is a small (four guest rooms) B&B within easy reach of Lancaster's attractions.

DAY 2

Morning

BREAKFAST: A full breakfast, complete with home-baked breads and delicious pancakes, is included in the price of a room at The Dingeldein House.

After breakfast drive into town (about a mile away), where you'll find plenty of parking in lots and garages at a cost of about 70 cents an hour, which, by New York standards, is a real bargain. One of the best ways to see the town is to take the ninety-minute **Lancaster Historic Walking Tour,** which departs from the Southern Market at 10:00 A.M. and 1:30 P.M., Monday through Saturday, and at 1:30 P.M. only on Sundays, April through October.

Lancaster is the county seat, and, back in 1777, for one full day it was home to the Continental Congress when Philadelphia was captured by the British. Its cobbled streets are rich in American history, stories of which are well told by knowledgeable guides.

Lancaster's many attractions include **Wheatland,** the last home of President James Buchanan, 1120 Marietta Avenue (open April 1–November 30); the **Fulton Opera House,** 12 North Prince Street (717–397–7425), one of the oldest American theaters; and the **Heritage Center of Lancaster**

County, Penn Square (717–299–6440), which contains examples of early Lancaster arts and crafts and home furnishings. Lancaster is also home to several Georgian churches, Federal-style buildings, and the nation's oldest publicly owned farmers' market, the Central Market on Penn Square. The latter is a huge gabled brick structure filled with produce, crafts, and flower stands.

From Lancaster make your way west to **Mount Joy.** Take Route 283 west; then turn left onto Route 230.

LUNCH: Groff's Farm Restaurant, 650 Pinkerton Road, Mount Joy; (717) 653–2048. Situated in a family-owned farmhouse that was built in 1756, Groff's is widely respected for its "light" Pennsylvania Dutch cooking. The owner, Betty Groff, is the author of several cookbooks.

Afternoon

After lunch follow Route 772 to Marietta and turn left onto Route 441. This will take you along the banks of the Susquehanna River to **Wright's Ferry Mansion,** Second and Cherry Streets in Columbia (717–684–4325). In 1738 this was the site of an important river crossing for early settlers on land owned by Susanna Wright, an English Quaker. The house, a magnificent example of an early English Georgian Pennsylvania country mansion, is filled with eighteenth-century furnishings. It's open from May through October on Tuesdays, Wednesdays, Fridays, and Saturdays. Also in Columbia is **The Watch and Clock Museum,** 514 Poplar Street (717–684–8261), with more than eight thousand time-related pieces. Between May and September the museum is open Tuesday through Saturday and Sunday afternoons; the rest of the year, just Tuesday through Saturday.

From Wright's Ferry Mansion take Route 30 to Route 272, which will get you to the **Landis Valley Museum,** 2451 Kissel Road, Lancaster (717–569–0401), a complex of nearly two dozen original buildings dating back to the mid-1800s. Open from May through October, the museum has a restaurant and a gift shop that specializes in local crafts and furnishings.

Make sure you save enough time to visit **Lititz,** a beautiful town first settled by Moravians. Lititz is home to a tree-lined main street, well-preserved eighteenth-century houses, a church built in 1787, and the oldest girls' boarding school in the country, Linden Hall. For many, however, Lititz's biggest attraction is the **Sturgis Pretzel House,** 219 East Main Street (717–626–4354), which was the first U.S. commercial pretzel bakery (1861).

Visitors can learn all about the pretzel-making process and try their hand at twisting some. Open daily except Sunday.

Carry on to **Ephrata** (Route 772 east to Route 272 north), your home for the night.

DINNER: Doneckers, 318–324 North State Street, Ephrata; (717) 738–9502. This elegant, supremely sophisticated French restaurant is highly respected by gourmets.

LODGING: 1777 House, 301 West Main Street, Ephrata; (717) 738–9502. A beautifully restored clockmaker's house filled with antiques and hand-cut stenciling.

DAY 3

Morning

BREAKFAST: A continental breakfast is included in the room rate at the 1777 House.

Start the day by going to the **Ephrata Cloister,** 632 West Main Street (717–733–6600). Here you'll find a collection of half-timbered and stone buildings, with steep Germanic roofs, which were originally erected in 1732 in a religious experiment by Conrad Beissel, a German Seventh Day Adventist. Living as a recluse, he started a community of recluses, and by 1750 there were 300 members. Many of them died from typhus, which they contracted while nursing the sick and wounded after the Battle of Brandywine. The rest died off because celibacy was a requirement of their order.

After a serene saunter around the Cloister, consider heading back to Lancaster, where you can outlet-mall hop (Rockvale Square and Millstream are the biggies). They're open daily from 9:30 A.M. to 5:00 P.M. and on Sundays from noon to 5:00 P.M. If you prefer, you can retrace your steps back to New York City.

THERE'S MORE

Antiques. Throughout the year the Adamstown Antique Market takes place every Sunday from 8:00 A.M. to 5:00 P.M.

Markets. You'll find farmers' markets at various locations on Tuesdays, Fridays, and Saturdays throughout the year.

Roots Country Market takes place Tuesdays on Graystone Road near the intersection of Route 72 near Manheim.

In Lancaster the farmers' market takes place at Central Market (Queen and King Streets) on Tuesdays and Fridays and on Saturday mornings.

Green Dragon Farmers' Market and Auction starts at 10:00 A.M. and goes to 10:00 P.M. every Friday on Green Spot Road, north of Ephrata off Route 272.

SPECIAL EVENTS

Early March. Gordonville Fire Co. Auction. A huge auction featuring quilts, farm equipment, and animals.

Mid-May. Carriage and Sleigh Auction. This annual event takes place at Martin's Sales Pavilion in the town of Intercourse.

Late May. Spring Craft Show. An annual Lancaster event.

Early June. Craft days at Landis Museum Valley in Lancaster. Crafts, crafts, and more crafts in Lancaster.

Early July. All-American Ragtime Festival and Contest. Strasburg.

July 4. Fourth of July celebration in Lititz. Thousands of candles are lit and reflected in the narrow waterways in Lititz Springs Park.

July–Labor Day. *Vorspiel* performances at Ephrata Cloister in Ephrata. Every Saturday night, a musical drama about life at the cloister takes place. For information call (717) 733–6600.

Mid–September. Annual Strasburg Heritage Day Antique & Craft Show. Held at the Strasburg Playground. More than fifty antiques dealers and dozens of craftspeople.

Late September. Street Fair in Ephrata. One of Pennsylvania's biggest street fairs.

Annual Harvest Festival. Held at Kitchen Kettle Village on Route 340 in Intercourse. A celebration of the fall harvest season including strolling musicians, baked goods, and regional foods.

Early October. Harvest Days at Landis Valley Museum, 2451 Kissel Hill Road, Lancaster. Food booths, craft demonstrations, harvest activities.

Second week of December. Christmas at the Cloister. An annual concert that takes place at the Ephrata Cloister. For information call (717) 733–6600.

Late December. Christmas Candlelight Tours. At the Ephrata Cloister; (717) 733–6600.

OTHER RECOMMENDED RESTAURANTS AND LODGINGS

Lancaster

Windows on Steinman Park, 16–18 West King Street (adjoining Steinman Park); (717) 295–1316. French cuisine amid lovely flowers, glassware, and fine china.

Lititz

General Sutter Inn, 14 East Main Street; (717) 626–2115. A landmark inn with twelve rooms decorated with antique country and Victorian furniture.

Mount Joy

Cameron Estate Inn, 1895 Donegal Springs Road; (717) 653–1773. A full-service country hotel with many antiques and Oriental rugs.

FOR MORE INFORMATION

Pennyslvania Dutch Convention and Visitors Bureau, 501 Greenfield Road, Lancaster, PA 17601; (717) 299–8901.

For statewide information call (800) VISIT–PA.

MID-ATLANTIC

Capitalizing
on the Capital Area
HISTORY AND HERITAGE

2 NIGHTS (OR MORE)

Hunt Country • Civil War sites • Mountain scenery • Hiking

This escape takes you to the countryside west of Washington, D.C., taking in some of the highlights of Virginia, West Virginia, Maryland, and Pennsylvania, all in a matter of a couple of days. Consider combining a visit to the capital itself, visiting some of the museums and attractions.

DAY 1

Morning

Best way to reach this area from New York is to take I–95 down the coast. When you get to the D.C. area, head southwest on I–495 and take Exit 13 for Route 193 west. Follow that for about 4 miles and then turn onto Route 738 to **Great Falls Park,** which is a great place to have a picnic lunch. Here you can hike up to 15 miles of trails (from easy terrain to somewhat rugged) and see the swirling Great Falls of the Potomac River.

Afternoon

From Great Falls Park go through the town of Great Falls and then get on Route 7 north at Dranesville. Follow that to **Leesburg,** which is in the heart of Virginia's Hunt Country. For a bit of history on the area, have a look around

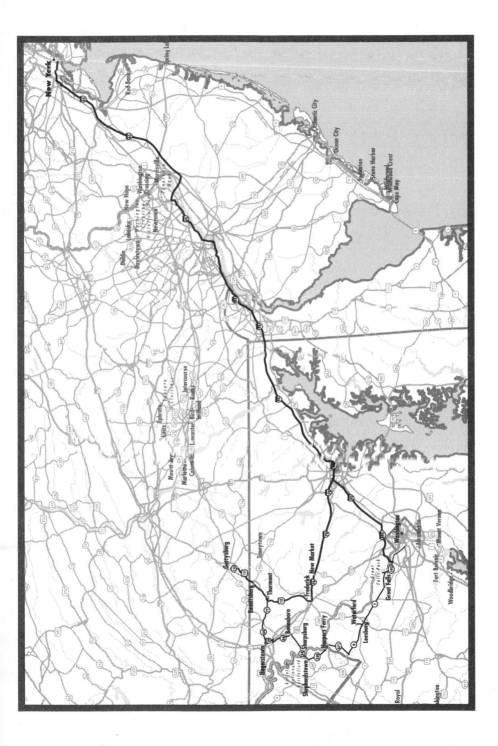

the **Loudoun Museum** (16 Loudoun Street SW) and take a walk around the historic district. Also worthwhile (especially for the horsey set) is the **Museum of Hounds and Hunting** and the **Morven Park International Equestrian Institute in Morven Park** about a mile north of town. Morven Park (which sprawls over 1,500 acres) also includes a twenty-eight room mansion, a carriage museum with more than one hundred horse-drawn vehicles, and boxwood gardens.

DINNER: Green Tree (15 South King Street; 703–777–7246) prides itself on its authentic eighteenth-century recipes.

LODGING: Norris House (108 Loudoun Street SW; 800–644–1806) is a six-room inn that was built in 1760. It has a lovely veranda overlooking the gardens and tasteful antique furnishings.

DAY 2

Morning

BREAKFAST: At the inn.

The countryside surrounding Leesburg is beautiful in every direction with rolling hills, thoroughbred horse farms, and beautiful rural villages. To the north (Route 662) is **Waterford,** an eighteenth-century Quaker village, designated a National Historic Landmark. Six miles south of town (on Route 15) is **Oatlands,** a 261-acre estate that used to be the center of a 5,000-acre plantation. Spend the morning exploring.

Then carry on, making your next stop **Harpers Ferry,** West Virginia. Because of its strategic location, it was a town that changed hands many times during the Civil War. It was also the site of the U.S. arsenal captured by abolitionist John Brown in 1859. To reach it, take Route 9 from Leesburg to Route 671. You're now at the junction of the Shenandoah and Potomac rivers, where West Virginia, Virginia, and Maryland meet. The whole area (covering more than 2,200 acres) is a National Historical Park. There is a Visitor Center, just off of Route 340, where tours begin. From Harpers Ferry go west on Route 340 for about 2 miles then turn right onto Route 230 towards Shepherdstown. Cross the Potomac River into Maryland and follow Route 34 to **Sharpsburg.** Just north of town you'll find **Antietam National Battlefield,** where one of the bloodiest battles of the Civil War took place on September 17, 1862. At this site more than 23,000 men were killed or wounded when Union forces blocked the first Confederate invasion of the North. There's a self-guided auto tour of the major landmarks.

Afternoon

Emmitsburg (which is just south of the Pennsylvania line) is your next destination. The drive—through Maryland's Blue Ridge region—is lovely. You pass through mountain scenery (the Appalachian Trail cuts through this area). Take Route 34 from Sharpsburg to Boonsboro. Then follow Route 66 north to Wagners Crossroads and continue north on Route 40 to Hagerstown. From there head east on Route 64 and then 77 to Thurmont (consider pausing for a picnic at Cunningham Falls State Park or in Catoctin Mountain Park just before reaching Thurmont). Then turn left onto Route 15 and follow it for about 9 miles to **Emmitsburg.**

As you approach Emmitsburg, you'll come to two of the area's most famous attractions. First, the National Shrine Grotto of Lourdes, which is a replica of the French shrine (one third the size of the original) and then the Shrine of St. Elizabeth Ann Seton, the first American-born saint. Emmitsburg itself is listed on the National Register of Historic Towns. If you're in the market for antiques, check out the Emmitsburg Antique Mall (One Chesapeake Avenue) which has more than 120 dealers displaying their collections.

Your hotel (and restaurant) for the night is actually 10 miles east of Emmitsburg, on Route 140 in Taneytown.

DINNER: Antrim 1844, 30 Trevanion Road, Taneytown, (410) 756-6812. Here the menu offers both French and American specialties.

LODGING: Antrim 1844, 30 Trevanion Road, Taneytown; (410) 756-6812. An antebellum plantation house (1844) on twenty-five acres with fourteen antiques-furnished rooms, some with balconies.

DAY 3

Morning

BREAKFAST: At the inn.

From the hotel backtrack to Emmitsburg via Route 140 and then head north on Route 15 to Route 134 across the Mason-Dixon Line into **Gettysburg,** where the Civil War's most decisive battle was fought between July

1 and 3, 1863. The park has more than 35 miles of roads through 5,700 acres of battlefield area. You can tour the sites with a **Battlefield Guide,** licensed by the National Park Service, or venture out on your own.

Afternoon

Retrace your steps back to Thurmont on Route 15 and then continue south on Route 15 toward **Frederick.** Founded in 1745, this lovely Colonial town is famous for its numerous eighteenth- and nineteenth-century houses along tree-lined streets. It's a town rich with history, having been the home of Francis Scott Key, author of "The Star Spangled Banner," and Chief Justice Roger Brooke Taney (who issued the famous Dred Scott decision), and Barbara Fritchie, the ardent Unionist immortalized by Whittier's poem. Several historic buildings are open for touring including the Barbara Fritchie House (154 West Patrick Street); Schifferstadt (Rosemont Avenue and Second Street), a farmhouse built in 1756; and the Roger Brooke Taney and Francis Scott Key Museum (121 South Bentz Street). Also worthwhile: Trinity Chapel (where Francis Scott Key was baptized), the Mt. Olivet Cemetery (monuments mark the graves of Francis Scott Key and Barbara Fritchie), the Historical Society of Frederick County Museum, and Monocacy Battlefield (3 miles south of town on Route 355).

About 7 miles east of Frederick (take I–70) you'll find the town of **New Market,** which is rife with antiques shops. From there, continue east on I–70 toward Baltimore and then head north on I–95 back to the New York area.

THERE'S MORE

Outdoor Sports. There are all sorts of outdoor activities you can do in this part of the world including fishing, boating, and—come winter—cross-country skiing.

SPECIAL EVENTS

January. Hunt Country Antiques Fair, Leesburg, Virginia; (703) 777–3174.

April. Leesburg Flower and Garden Show, Leesburg, Virginia; (703) 777–1262.

May. Annual Crafts Fair, Frederick, Maryland, (301) 663–8687.

December. Old Tyme Christmas, Harpers Ferry, West Virginia, (304) 725–8019.

FOR MORE INFORMATION

Maryland Office of Tourism Development, 217 East Redwood Street, Baltimore, MD 21202; (800) 543–1036 or (410) 333–6611.

Pennsylania Travel Council, 902 North Second Street, Harrisburg, PA 17102; (800) 847–4872 or (717) 232–8880.

Virginia Division of Tourism, 901 East Byrd Street, Richmond, VA 23219; (804) 786–4484.

West Virginia Division of Tourism & Parks, Capital Complex, Building 17, 2101 Washington Street East, Charleston, WV 25305; (800) CALL–WVA or (304) 558–2766.

Northern Virginia

PAST AND PRESENT

3 NIGHTS

Civil War battlesites
George Washington's home and other historic buildings
Shenandoah National Park • Underground caverns • Wildlife
Hiking and other outdoor activities

Be prepared to soak up lots of American history in a short time when visiting this part of the country. Though not a large area, it's densely historic. Within the span of two days, you can visit several major Civil War sites and tour many historically significant buildings including George Washington's house. The area is also naturally beautiful, holding one of the country's national parks, Shenandoah, which is an Indian word meaning "daughter of the stars."

Like Mid-Atlantic Escape Five, this trip can be combined with a visit to our nation's capital or taken as a trip of its own.

DAY 1

Morning

Set out early from New York, taking I–95 down the coast to the D.C. area. Pick up I–495 heading southwest and then get on I–66 heading west. Best bet is to stop for lunch somewhere along the way, breaking up the trip.

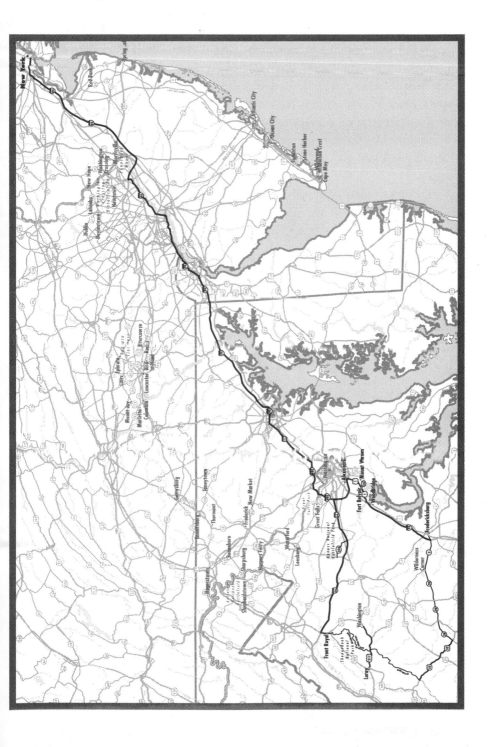

Make your first stop **Manassas National Battlefield Park.** The scene of two major Civil War battles, this 5,000-acre park has several sites to see including **Bull Run,** the creek along which the battles were fought. Stop by the Visitor Center (on Henry Hill, just north of I–66 on Route 234), where you can pick up information on self-guided tours (you can take a walking tour and a driving tour of the various areas). Be sure to walk to the top of Henry Hill, which was a key spot in both battles; from there you can see the entire battle area.

From Manassas National Battlefield Park, continue west on I–66 to the town of Front Royal, where you can check into your hotel for the night.

DINNER: Four & Twenty Blackbirds (US 522 and Virginia 647, Flint Hill; 540–675–1111) prides itself on its regional specialties. It's ten miles south of Front Royal on US 522.

LODGING: Chester House (43 Chester Street, Front Royal; 540–635–3937) is a small (six-room) inn.

DAY 2

Morning

BREAKFAST: A full breakfast is included in the price of the room at Chester House.

Before leaving town, stop at **J's** on Royal Avenue and pick up a gourmet picnic lunch to take along with you.

Just south of Front Royal, you'll find the start of the **Skyline Drive,** a two-lane scenic highway that runs the length of the **Shenandoah National Park** on the crest of the Blue Ridge. The park, which is 80 miles long and from 2 to 13 miles wide, encompasses some 300 square miles of the Blue Ridge. Along the way, there are about seventy scenic overlooks with outstanding views of the **Shenandoah Valley** below. Most of the area is wooded, with more than 100 species of hardwood trees that are in full glory during the autumn months. The park is also a wildlife sanctuary with deer, bear, fox, and bobcat plus more than 200 varieties of birds.

LUNCH: You'll find plenty of wonderful places to spread out your picnic.

Afternoon

One especially worthwhile detour off the Skyline Drive is the short drive west (turn right onto Route 211 at Thornton Gap) to Luray Caverns. Here you can go underground to see rock formations and hear the sounds of a "stalacpipe."

Plan to spend the day enjoying the numerous outdoor activities in the park. You can hike, fish, horseback ride, bicycle, bird-watch, picnic, and camp overnight. There are also ranger-led nature walks. At the entrance station pick up a copy of the *Shenandoah Overlook,* a free newspaper that lists daily activities.

To reach your hotel for the night, take Route 211 east to the little town of Washington.

DINNER: The **Inn at Little Washington** (Middle and Main Streets, Washington, VA 22747; 540–675–3800) offers one of the best dining experiences in the state.

LODGING. The **Inn at Little Washington,** Middle and Main Streets, Washington, VA 22747; (540) 675–3800. A true find, this Relais & Château inn has just a dozen rooms (some of them are suites), all individually and exquisitely decorated.

DAY 3

Morning

BREAKFAST: At the inn.

After breakfast continue south on Skyline Drive and then exit onto Route 33, heading east to Barboursville. From there take Route 20 north through Orange to Wilderness Corner, where you'll turn onto Route 3, which will take you to Chancellorsville and then on to **Fredericksburg.** Four major Civil War battles were fought between December 1862 and May 1864 in this general area. You can tour the sites by car or foot. They include **Wilderness National Military Park, Chancellorsville National Military Site, Fredericksburg** and **Spotsylvania County battlefields Memorial National Military Park,** and **Fredericksburg National Military Park.**

The gardens of Mount Vernon are a great escape.

Plan to spend some time looking around Fredericksburg, which is where George Washington went to school and where his mother and sister lived. Though the city was ravaged during the Civil War, many buildings dating before 1775 still stand and are well preserved. Start by stopping at the Visitor Center (706 Caroline Street), where you can watch an orientation film and then set about on a walking tour. Some of the tour's highlights include the **Hugh Mercer Apothecary Shop,** an eighteenth-century doctor's office and pharmacy; a tavern that was not only a stagecoach stop but an important social and political center built by Washington's brother, Charles; the Masonic Lodge where Washington was initiated in 1752; and the house he bought for his mother. There are also historic churches, cemeteries, and museums.

Afternoon

LUNCH: The Ristorante Renato (422 William Street, Fredericksburg; 540–371–8228) serves Northern Italian specialties.

From Fredericksburg head north on I–95. Get off at Route 1, which is just after Woodbridge. Follow signs to Fort Belvoir. Go past Fort Belvoir and then turn right onto Route 235 and follow signs to Mount Vernon, the home of George and Martha Washington. You can tour the house and grounds and see George and Martha's tomb.

Alexandria, which was a prosperous tobacco port back in the 1740s, is the last official stop for this escape. There are guided walking tours of the cobbled streets of Old Town taking in **Robert E. Lee's boyhood home,** the **Stabler-Leadbeater Apothecary Museum** (the largest collection of apothecary glass in its original setting in the nation), and other historically significant buildings dating back to the late 1700s.

DINNER: If you're in the mood for a wonderful French meal, try **La Bergerie** (218 North Lee Street, second floor of Crilley Warehouse, in Old Town Alexandria; 703–683–1007) or **Le Galois** (1106 King Street in Old Town Alexandria; 703–739–9494).

LODGING: Morrison House (116 South Alfred Street, Alexandria; 703–838–8000) is an elegant red-brick building furnished completely in the Federal style.

DAY 4

Morning

BREAKFAST: Breakfast at your hotel.

If you're eager to get back to New York, get on I–495/95 and head north, or drive into D.C. which is just 7 miles away.

THERE'S MORE

Carillon concerts. On Saturday nights all summer long, there are free carillon recitals at the Netherlands Carillon on the grounds of the Iwo Jima Memorial in Arlington, Virginia, from 6:00 to 8:00 P.M. For more information, call 202–619–7222.

SPECIAL EVENTS

January. Lee Birthday Celebrations, Alexandria; (703) 548–1789.

March. Fine Arts Exhibit, Fredericksburg; (540) 372–1086.

June. Alexandria Red Cross Waterfront Festival, Alexandria; (703) 838–5005.
Annual Fredericksburg Arts Festival, Fredericksburg; (540) 372–1086.
Fredericksburg Festival of the Arts, Fredericksburg; (800) 678–4748.
Martha Washington's Birthday, Mount Vernon; (703) 780–2000.

July. Annual Scottish Games, Alexandria; (703) 838–5005.

October. Alexandria Wine and Arts Festival, Alexandria; (703) 787–0380.
Outdoor Antiques Fair, Fredericksburg; (540) 371–4504.

November. Annual Crafts Show, Fredericksburg; (540) 372–1086.

December. Anniversary of the Battle of Fredericksburg, Fredericksburg; (800) 678–4748.
Annual Scottish Christmas Walk, Alexandria; (703) 838–5005.
A Victorian Christmas, Fredericksburg; (800) 678–4748.
Christmas Candlelight Tour, Fredericksburg; (540) 371–4504.
Christmas Parade, Fredericksburg; (800) 678–4748.
Mount Vernon by Moonlight, Mount Vernon; (703) 780–2000.
Old Town Christmas Candlelight Tour, Alexandria; (703) 838–4200.

OTHER RECOMMENDED RESTAURANTS AND LODGINGS

Alexandria

Geranio (722 King Street, in Old Town Alexandria; 703–548–0088) is an Italian restaurant specializing in veal, seafood, and pasta.

Union Street Public House (121 South Union Street, between King and Prince Streets, in Old Town Alexandria; 703–548–1785) serves up apple–smoked barbecue pork ribs, linguine with lobster and smoked scallops, and delicious grilled seafood.

Villa D'Este (18 North St. Asaph Street; 703–549–9477) serves Northern Italian specialties.

Stanley (near Luray)

Jordan Hollow Farm Inn (Route 2, Stanley; 540–778–2285) is a converted forty-five-acre horse farm with twenty-one guest rooms. To reach it head south on Route 340 from Luray, then east on Virginia 624, north on Virginia 689, and then east on Virginia 626.

FOR MORE INFORMATION

Virginia Division of Tourism, 901 East Byrd Street, Richmond, VA 23219; (800) 932–5827 or (804) 786–4484.

Cape May

With or Without a Car

VICTORIAN HERITAGE

---

2 NIGHTS

Victorian buildings • *Beach*
Boardwalk amusements • *Bicycling* • *Bird-watching*

Off in a little world of its own, Cape May is sensationally situated on the southernmost tip of New Jersey, with the Atlantic Ocean on one side and Delaware Bay on the other.

Cape May has been a popular beach resort since the days of the American Revolution and, in fact, is the oldest seashore resort in the country. Several U.S. presidents visited here including Lincoln, Grant, Pierce, Buchanan, and Harrison plus other name-names such as Horace Greeley and John Wanamaker.

Home to more than 600 Victorian buildings (many of which have been faithfully restored), Cape May is one of four U.S. seaports that has very successfully preserved its Victorian heritage (Mendocino, California; Galveston, Texas; and Port Townsend, Washington, are the others). In fact the entire town has been proclaimed a National Historic Landmark, and for the most part, can be seen on foot.

The heart of town is the Washington Street Victorian Mall, which is a 3-block-long stretch closed to automobiles and lined with shops and restaurants. The real focus here, however, is the promenade which runs along the Atlantic and offers a host of diversions.

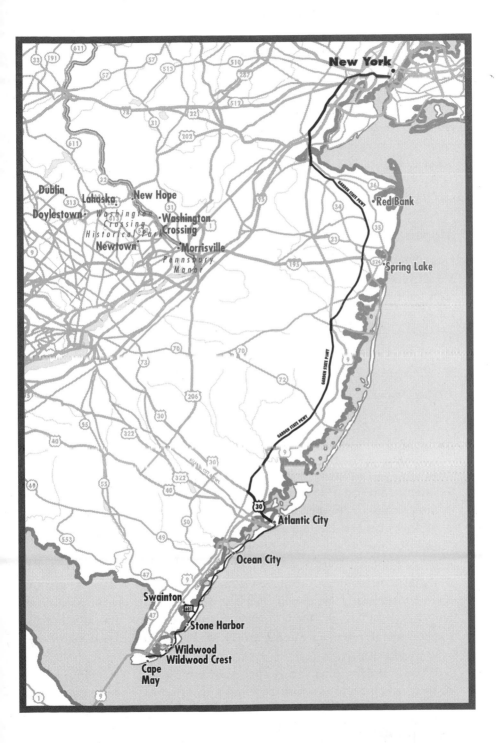

A couple of days here can be easily divided between a little sightseeing and some all-out relaxing. In between there are a handful of exceptionally good seafood restaurants to sample and many shops to browse through.

Keep in mind that some places close during winter in Cape May. In spring, summer, and fall, many of the guest houses require a two- to three-night minimum stay on weekends and holidays. If you want to avoid the crowds, go before Memorial Day or after Labor Day.

DAY 1

Morning

From New York City's Port Authority you can take a bus directly to Cape May. It's about a five to five-and-a-half hour trip and gets you right into the heart of town. For more information call New Jersey Transit at (201) 762–5100. If you prefer to drive, follow the Garden State Parkway south as far as it will go. Then follow Lafayette Street right into Cape May. The drive takes about three and a half hours, so if you set out early, you'll arrive just in time for lunch.

LUNCH: Water's Edge, Beach and Pittsburgh Avenue (609–884–1717), right across the street from the beach, is a good choice for seafood.

Afternoon

Right after lunch plan to take a tour of the **Emlen Physick Estate,** 1048 Washington Street (609–884–5404), which is a fully restored eighteen-room Victorian mansion designed by Frank Furness and an excellent introduction to the Victorian era. The estate is also headquarters for the **Mid-Atlantic Center for the Arts,** which organizes several walking tours around town including a historic-district walking tour, a tour of Cape May's beaches, and a stained-glass walking tour. We suggest taking the historic-district walking tour tomorrow morning, but double-check to make sure it's scheduled (hours vary). The estate is open daily from May through December, Tuesday through Thursday and Saturday and Sunday during March and April, and weekends in January and February.

If you're driving, after lunch ditch your car (some of the rooms at the Mainstay have parking spots; otherwise grab the first spot you see on the street nearby) and check in. You'll be given a beach pass, which provides free admission to the beaches.

Spend the afternoon on the beach (it's about a block and half from the hotel) watching the huge waves roll in, or people-watch on the promenade.

DINNER: The **Washington Inn,** 801 Washington Street (609–884–5697), a former plantation house dating back to 1848, is a great spot for seafood and other continental dishes.

LODGING: The **Mainstay Inn,** 635 Columbus Avenue (609–884–8690) is an Italianate villa with a wraparound veranda. Inside are all sorts of Victorian details. Guests can stay in the main inn or in the more modernized adjacent cottage.

DAY 2

Morning

BREAKFAST: During summer a light breakfast is served at the Mainstay. The rest of the year, it's a full breakfast.

After breakfast head over to the information booth on the corner of Ocean Street and the Mall to get in on a **Historic District Walking Tour.** The tour, which lasts about an hour and a half, is full of historical insights.

Of course you can also take yourself on a self-guided tour. The **Welcome Center** at 405 Lafayette Street can point you in the right direction and provide you with brochures. Most of the most beautiful Victorian buildings are now inns, lined up majestically between the Welcome Center and the beach. These include The Abbey, a Gothic Revival house at Columbia Avenue and Gurney Street, Captain Mey's Inn at 202 Ocean Street, The Mainstay (your hotel) at 635 Columbia Avenue, and the Angel of the Sea, at 5 Trenton Avenue.

LUNCH: For lunch consider grabbing something light (like a slab of pizza) at the mall or on the promenade.

Afternoon

After lunch walk or bike out to **Cape May State Park** (follow Sunset Boulevard) for a beautiful walk through one of Cape May's best birding areas. There

Fishing off Cape May is just one of this coastal town's many diversions.

are 3 miles of trails and a boardwalk taking you over ponds and through wooded areas and marshlands. Then climb the 218 steps to the top of **Cape May Lighthouse.** It's open daily in summer from 9:00 A.M. to 8:00 P.M.; shorter hours rest of the year. Call (609) 884–5404 for information.

Stick around for the sunset, which is astonishingly beautiful from **Cape May Point.**

DINNER: 410 Bank Street, 410 Bank Street; (609) 884–2127. The menu here is Louisiana French. You can sit on the porch or in the garden.

DAY 3

Morning

BREAKFAST: At the inn.

After breakfast visit the shops in the mall area and near the beach or head back to the beach. The "Cape May diamonds," which you will inevitably see in shops all over town, are actually quartz, rounded by the waves.

When you're ready, board a bus back to New York or return to the Garden State Parkway and head north to New York City in your car.

THERE'S MORE

Bicycling. You can rent bikes right in town at The Village Bicycle Shop, at Ocean Street and the beginning of the mall; (609) 884–8500.

Bird-watching. Every fall thousands of migratory birds (including everything from small songbirds to falcons and eagles) stop here on their way south. The best viewing areas are Cape May State Park, the Cape May Migratory Bird Refuge, and Higbee's Beach.

Carriage rides. Carriages leave from Ocean Street and Washington Street Mall for half-hour historic district tours. Call (609) 884–4466 for more information.

Fishing. There are several great fishing areas around Cape May including the Second Avenue jetty and the World War II bunker by the lighthouse at Cape May Point.

Trolley tours. If you're not up for walking, you can take trolley tours around town. For information contact the Mid-Atlantic Center for the Arts (609–884–5404).

SPECIAL EVENTS

May. Tulip Festival.

July. Promenade Art Exhibit.

September. Fish Festival. Celebrates Cape May's role as a major fishing port. Exhibits, seafood, and other activities.

Mid-October. Victorian Week. House tours; crafts shows and period fashion shows at the Mid-Atlantic Center for the Arts.

December. Christmas celebrations, including house tours and concerts, take place throughout the month of December.

OTHER RECOMMENDED RESTAURANTS AND LODGINGS

There are many guest houses and inns in Cape May. Here are just a few favorites.

The Abbey, 34 Gurney Street, at Columbia Avenue; (609) 884–4506. A lovely Gothic-style inn.

Captain Mey's Inn, 202 Ocean Street; (609) 884–7793. A nine-room inn decorated with Victorian furnishings.

FOR MORE INFORMATION

Cape May Chamber of Commerce, P.O. Box 556, Cape May, NJ 08204; (609) 884–5508.

Cape May Welcome Center, 405 Lafayette Street, Cape May, NJ 08204; (609) 884–9562.

New Jersey Division of Travel and Tourism, C.N. 826, Trenton, NJ 08625; (609) 292–2470 or (800) JERSEY–7.

INDEX

Bedford Village, 30, 36
Bee and Thistle Inn, 97
Beechtree House, The, 53
Beechwood, 172
Beekman 1766 Tavern, 7
Belle Crest House, 52
Ben & Jerry's, 204
Berskhire Museum, 149
Berkshires, The, 144–53
Bertrand, 81
Bidwell Tavern, 109
Bird & Bottle Inn, 14
Bird Watcher's General Store, 168
Bishopsgate Inn, 98
Bistro Twenty-Two, 36
Black Bass Hotel, 24
Black Dog Tavern, 180
Black Goose, The, 193
Black Pearl, The, 130
Blacksmith House Bakery and
 Cafe, 196
Blantyre, 153
Block Island, 134–42
Blue Dolphin Diner, 36
Blue Hill, 215
Blue Mountain Lake, 59
Boarding House, The, 188
Bolton Landing, 57
Boothbay Harbor, 214
Boscobel, 13
Boston, 191–99
Boston Common, 193
Boston Harbor Hotel, 199
Boston Massacre Site, 194
Boston Public Library, 195

Boulders Inn, 122, 123
Brass Key Guesthouse, The, 170
Brayton Grist Mill and Marcy
 Blacksmith Museum, 111
Breakers, The, 109
Breakfast at Saratoga, 57
Brewster, 167, 172
Brick School House, 109
Brick Stone Museum, The, 212
Bridge Cafe, 78
Bridgehampton, 42, 45
Bridgehampton Motel, 45
Brookfield Craft Center, 89
Brookfield/SoNo Craft Center, 77
Brooklyn, 111
Bruce Museum, 76
Bucks County, 233–42
Bucks County Playhouse, 236
Bucksport, 214
Buell's Greenhouses, 112
Bull's Bridge, 117
Bull's Head Diner, 76
Bunker Hill, 195
Bush-Holley House, 76
Butler-Meyer Sanctuary, 35

C

Cadillac Mountain, 215
Cafe Airelle, 239
Cafe Blase, 169
Cafe Christina, 79
Cameron Estate Inn, 251
Campbell Falls, 119–20
Canaan, 118
Cannery Cafe, The, 120

Green Tree, 254
Greenwich, 74
Greenwood's Gate, 120
Griswold Inn, 94, 98
Groff's Farm Restaurant, 248
Groton, 102
Guild Hall Museum, 42
Gurleyville Grist Mill, 112
Gurney's Inn Resort & Spa, 44, 45

H

Hadwen House, 187
Haight Vineyard and Winery, 121
Halibut Point State Park, 161
Halle Ravine, 35
Hammersmith Farm, 130
Hammertown Barn, 8
Hammond Castle Museum, 158
Hammond Museum and Japanese
    Stroll Garden, 33
Hamptons, The, 38–47
Hancock Shaker Village, 149
Hans Herr House, 245
Harbor Light Inn, 157
Harborside Inn, 138
Harbor Sweets, 157
Harbor View Resort, 182
Hardwick, 206
Harpers Ferry, 254
Harrald's, 17
Harvard Coop, 196
Harvard University Information
    Center, 196
Harvest Market, The, 205
Harvest on Fort Pond, The, 47

Hawthorne Hotel, 163
Hay Day Cafe, 87
Hemlock Hall, 60
Heritage Center of Lancaster
    County, 247–48
Heritage Plantation, 166
Herring Cove, 169
Highland Farms, 241
Historic Congress Park, 56
Historic Mulford Farm, 42
Hitchcock Museum, 120
Homestead, 74
"Home Sweet Home" House, 42
Honest Diner, 43
Hopkins Vineyard, 122
Hotel Manisses, The, 136, 139
Hotel Montauket, 46
Housatonic Railroad, 118
House of the Seven Gables,
    Nantucket, Mass., 185
House of the Seven Gables,
    Salem, Mass., 157
Hudson, 6
Hudson House, 14
Hudson River Maritime Museum
    and Rondout Lighthouse, 22
Hudson River Museum, 16
Hunter House, 127
Hyannis, 173
Hyde Park, 7

I

Impudent Oyster, 170
Inn at Castle Hill, The, 130, 133
Inn at Fordhook Farm, 241

ABOUT THE AUTHOR

Susan Farewell first started exploring the areas around New York City as a child growing up in South Salem, New York. Back then she traveled with her family, notebook always in hand. She later went on to study at Boston University and then became a travel editor at The Condé Nast Publications. She now writes for dozens of magazines and newspapers around the world, frequently covering the New York and New England areas. She lives in Westport, Connecticut.